D0620901

NATIONAL UNIVERSITY
LIBRARY

Children's Learning
and Attention Problems

Children's Learning and Attention Problems

Marcel Kinsbourne, D.M., M.R.C.P. (Lond.)

Professor, Department of Pediatrics,
University of Toronto Faculty of Medicine;
Professor, Department of Psychology,
University of Toronto; Senior Staff Physician,
The Hospital for Sick Children,
Toronto, Ontario

Paula J. Caplan, Ph.D.

Lecturer, Department of Psychiatry,
University of Toronto; Psychologist,
Family Court Clinic, Clarke Institute
of Psychiatry, Toronto, Ontario

Little, Brown and Company   Boston

Copyright © 1979 by Little, Brown and
Company (Inc.)

First Edition

All rights reserved. No part of this book may
be reproduced in any form or by any
electronic or mechanical means, including
information storage and retrieval systems,
without permission in writing from the
publisher, except by a reviewer who may
quote brief passages in a review.

Library of Congress Catalog Card
No. 78-73080

ISBN 0-316-49395-3

Printed in the United States of America

To our children Emily, Jeremy, Daniel, and David

Preface

We have written this book for physicians and other professionals concerned with the assessment and management of children with problems of learning and attention. Intended as a practical guide to that subject, it emphasizes specifics of how to question, test, prescribe for, and interpret to those children and how to interpret to parents, educators, and other concerned individuals. We address theoretical issues only to the extent necessary to provide proper explanations when questions about them are raised by parents, teachers, and others. As we intend this book to be intelligible to practitioners across a wide range of disciplines, and also to the interested layperson, we have kept technical jargon to a minimum.

Our main concern is to outline the practical steps one takes to find out how children with learning and attention problems may best be helped. The individual approach described arose from our cumulative experience with children who had school problems in North Carolina and in Ontario. It is idealized in the sense that it calls for a certain organization and certain resources that we regard as optimal. It does not represent in complete detail the actual current practice of any particular clinic dealing with those problems.

With respect to learning disabilities, our experience derives largely from individual efforts. In the area of hyperactivity, however, we have been fortunate in profiting from the total experience of an extensive program of applied research directed by one of us (M. K.) in collaboration with Dr. James Swanson. Such merit as that approach has must be credited to a major degree to Dr. Swanson's skill and vision, as well as to insights offered by both the research findings and the clinical observations of our colleagues in this work: Andrew Barlow, Ph.D., Barbara Bell, M.A., Bruce Caplan, Ph.D., Thomas Dalby, M.A., Julian Fisher, M.D., Margaret Flintoff, B.A., Richard Freeman, M.A., Merrill Hiscock, Ph.D., Thomas Humphries, Ph.D., Gary Kapelus, B.A., Laura Kurland, B.A., Karen Mock, Ph.D., Wendy Roberts, M.D., Gordon Serfontein, M.D., Daniel Stone, B.A., Lynda Thompson, M.A., and Catherine Thurston, M.A.

M. K.
P. J. C.

Contents

I. Overview

1. Introduction

The purpose of this book is to outline the possibilities and the limitations involved in helping a child who is having school trouble or failing in school. We shall be discussing children of at least average intelligence and motivation who are offered a traditionally adequate educational experience, but who nevertheless fail to learn at the expected level in one or more subjects.

Failure to achieve in school results from an unsuccessful interaction between the school system and the child. The unsuccessful school-child interactions addressed here are those that result from a misfit between the learning requirements determined by the child's own constitution and the learning experience that the school offers. Because of variations in brain development, the children dealt with in this book—as compared to their peers—fall short in attention skills, cognitive readiness, or a combination of the two.

BRIEF DEFINITIONS

Human behavior is divisible into selection and processing activities. "Selection" means choosing what to do, what to think about, which problem to solve, where to direct attention. Selecting what to attend to and maintaining concentration on that thing, rather than on irrelevancies, is one part of adaptive behavior. The other part is processing—actually using the information one attends to for the intended purpose. Having chosen to attend to a person who is speaking, and attending selectively to what that speaker is saying, one still has to process the information received in order to understand the message.

The learning failures of the children discussed here can occur because of maladaptive selection, inadequate processing, or both. There are two basic types of attention (selection) disorders. Some children fail because they are overly impulsive, not maintaining their focus of attention long enough to learn the material. Although their thinking equipment is adequate, they leave a task before the concept involved is fully grasped. They have the necessary processing potential for grade-school readiness, but they are immature with respect to the intensity and duration of their concentration, their ability to maintain a focus of attention on the task at hand. Other children fail because they are overly compulsive, concentrating so long on one bit of work that they do not learn enough overall. We shall use the term *cognitive style disorders* (or *attention disorders*) to refer to both overly impulsive and overly compulsive behavior. Extreme impulsiveness is also sometimes called *hyperactivity* or *underfocused attention*. Extreme compulsiveness may also be called *overfocused attention*.

Other children, although perfectly able to concentrate appropriately on the task at hand, experience an unusual amount of difficulty in grasping certain concepts or remembering certain types of information that they are supposed to learn in grade-school. This is not because they are retarded, but rather because in general children's mental development, like their physical development, is uneven, and the cognitive development of these children includes some low points that are more dramatic than most. We shall use the term *cognitive power disorders* to refer to this kind of problem. We shall also use the term *learning disabilities* to refer to cognitive power disorders—because it is a commonly used phrase, does not imply particular etiologies, and when used in the plural form, suggests the wide variety of difficulties encompassed. Table 1 lists some of the labels that have been applied to children with cognitive style and cognitive power disorders.

An essential reason for interviewing, examining, and testing children who have failed in school is to make the distinction between cognitive style and cognitive power disorders. (Some children will have disorders of both types, but that too can be brought out by the initial investigations.) Once we know which category of disorders is involved, we know what further investigations are necessary, and we have some basic information about how to begin treatment.

This book describes the diagnosis and treatment of cognitive style and cognitive power disorders and examines the emotional effects these problems are likely to have upon the family. Part II will deal primarily with cognitive power disorders and Part III with cognitive style disorders, although much of the Part II material on interviewing and interpreting to parents (Chaps. 4 and 5) will be applicable to both.

COGNITIVE POWER DISORDERS

It is important to distinguish between *learning disabilities* or *cognitive power disorders* and other causes of school failure. If one blurs distinctions between learning disabled children and the larger pool of children who have various other kinds of school trouble, then one cannot prescribe specifically enough to help an individual child.

Learning disabled children differ from culturally deprived children who underachieve; their limitations are intrinsic (i.e., brain-based) rather than imposed upon them by an adverse environment (e.g., one that is impoverished, culturally alienated, or inadequate with respect to quality or quantity of schooling). Further, their

Table 1. Alternative Labels for Cognitive Power and Style Disorders

Cognitive Power Disorders

Congenital	Dyslexia	Disability
Constitutional	Dyscalculia	Disorder
Developmental	Word Blindness	Handicap
Pure	Arithmetic	Problem
Selective	Learning	
Specific	Perceptual	
	Reading	
	Writing	

Minimal
Brain } { Damage
Cerebral } { Dysfunction

Constitutional
Developmental
Organic

Cognitive Style Disorders

Underfocusing	Overfocusing
Hyperactivity	Anxiety
Hyperactive Impulse Disorder	Autistoid behavior
Hyperkinesis	Compulsive behavior
Overactivity	

brain-based limitations are cognitive rather than emotional. There-fore, their problems should also be distinguished from the primar-ily emotional causes of inadequate school achievement. (Emotional problems that commonly implicate school progress include anxiety states, school phobias, psychoses, and a variety of conditions in-duced in the child by adverse family dynamics.)

Children with learning disabilities differ from those children who are slow with regard to most cognitive abilities. Children who are slow in all mental processes and uniformly unready in their ability to focus concentration on a task are mentally retarded ("slow learners"). Learning disabled children have *selective* cogni-tive difficulties. They are neither bright nor dull throughout; they are both bright and dull, in different respects. But not all selective cognitive deficits qualify as *learning* disability. Learning disability implies a selective weakness that impinges on *academic* perfor-mance.

We all have strengths and weaknesses. None of us has a totally uniform level of abilities across all aspects of intelligence. Most of us conceal deficits inside our heads. Many people are totally un-able to croak out a musical tune. This, of course, would lay them open to the charge of brain damage with respect to musical abili-ties. Such people protect themselves from this accusation by not singing. Fortunately, society does not require everyone to sing, but instead relies on those without that kind of brain dysfunction to do the singing for the rest. It would be convenient if, in a similar way, those who had deficits relating to school subjects could let the rest of us write and calculate for them. They could be the exec-utives, and we could be their secretaries. That would be just as ra-tional as accusing them of being brain-damaged. But the learning disabled child has the misfortune of doing badly at one of the few things that society asks of children and in fact insists upon — per-formance at school.

One can hardly overestimate the impact that social expectations have upon the child and the ways these expectations distort our approaches and our theorizing. A disturbing consequence of social pressure is that children with selective school-related cognitive deficits are constantly stuck with labels like "brain damage" or "minimal cerebral dysfunction," whereas tone-deaf people are not. Although the reading disabled have a dysfunction in one brain area, the amusics have just as real a dysfunction in another. In dealing with learning disabilities we are not discussing the full range of children with selective immaturities or weaknesses in cognition but only those whose deficits obstruct traditional school learning. The learning problem generates a social problem — a dis-crepancy between social expectations and what the child can com-

fortably produce. So the intellectual lacunae that give rise to a
learning problem are compounded in their ill effect by the fact that
they impinge on an area about which society is sensitive.

The typical feeling that parents of a learning disabled child report is surprise: This child seemed normal during the first five
years of life, so why is there a learning problem now? This distinguishes learning disability from mental retardation, where one
usually knows from the beginning that the child is slow. It also
distinguishes it from the emotional and environmental causes of
school failure, which are all too obvious and not in the least surprising. That feeling of surprise ("As Hilary has been so smart all
along, why is Hilary dumb now? ") is really based on an unjustified expectation that human beings will be uniform in their development. They often are not. Many children who have unexpected
difficulty in mastering material upon entering first grade are having temporary lags in mental development. That situation could
not have been predicted, nor will it necessarily endure.

There are many combinations of learning skills that can cause a
child trouble, because any small part or combination of parts of
the brain can be slow to mature. Thus, for example, one child will
have trouble only with keeping letters and numbers in the proper
order. Another child able to do that will be unable to break a word
down into the simple sounds of which it is composed. A third
child will have both of these problems. The ability to read has
many components, among which are differentiating and remembering letters, shapes, orientations, sequences, and sounds. A child
may have trouble with any one or any combination of these; or a
child may read well and only have trouble with one or more components of arithmetic. Moreover, in any given family it is possible
for more than one person or member of a generation to have such
a lag, or it is possible for only one child to have it. When other
family members have had learning problems, the patterns of difficulty sometimes resemble each other and sometimes do not.

The lack of uniformity in school-relevant abilities of these children renders them unsuited to conventional group instruction. But
while these children would not succeed and do not succeed with
traditional instruction, they are equally unsuited to special education classes. These are children whose learning needs and learning
requirements can only be met by individualized programs. It is
the task of the clinician who is consulted to set into motion efforts
to organize an individualized program of this kind.

Cognitive power disorders are best viewed as resulting from selective developmental lag. This implies that the orderly schedule
for acquiring increasing mental skills with increasing age is disturbed, not by a generally slower across-the-board rate of acquir-

ing all skills (as in mental retardation) but by a selective delay in mastering some subset of mental skills. The potential for any form of developing mental activity is primarily determined by sufficient maturation of the part of the brain that normally comes to control that activity. Thus, the presumption made by the developmental lag or delay model is that the relevant brain area was unduly slow to mature, leaving the child "unready" to perform the behavior in question. This is not to imply that brain maturation is all that is needed for cognitive development. Such maturation is necessary but not necessarily sufficient; unless the environment affords the child a normal range of opportunities to model and exercise the skills involved, the potential provided by brain maturation may remain unrealized. Thus, the ultimate outcomes of brain-based developmental lag and of environmental deprivation may be the same: a child who is unacquainted with certain age-appropriate mental operations. However, in the case of the deprived child the difficulty can be overcome by supplying the deficient experience. This will work if the child is still motivated or can be motivated to take advantage of it. In this way the child's potential is realized. In the case of the learning disabled child, however, such intervention is not effective. Children who are mentally unready will not benefit from the provision of a normal environment (which in most cases they never lacked anyway), and no amount of motivating will do the trick. Instead, they will have to be taught the material in a way that takes account of their selective mental immaturity. That is, they will need to be taught the particular material as one would teach it to a younger normal child who is as yet unready to learn this sort of thing. This is accomplished by providing them with a cognitive structure that is normally unnecessary at their age, because normally children of that age provide it for themselves. Some general guidelines for doing this are offered in Chapter 7.

What are the origins of developmental lag? Because of the tremendous variation in kinds and combinations of lag, no satisfactory investigation of their etiology has been done. In many studies, attempts have been made to find common birth or childhood factors in children presenting problems with different patterns. But to seek a common etiology in such a miscellaneous group of patients just because each has some cognitive problem is as fruitless as seeking a common etiology for aphasics, amnesics, demented patients, and paralyzed patients just because all have suffered some kind of damage at some place in the same organ, the brain. We know in principle that a lag in cognitive development can derive either from an individual variation in genetic programming or from early damage to an area of the brain destined subsequently to control the behavior in question. In an individual case, we sometimes have enough information to estimate the probability that one of these two general mechanisms is at work, but we have no available procedures that can incriminate either one with certainty. However, from the prognostic point of view this is immaterial, since there is no general rule that invests either genetic or structural flaws with the greater capability for delaying development. From the therapeutic point of view the distinction is equally academic, since knowledge of antecedents does not help select more effectively from the range of therapeutic options.

What will happen in the future to the lagging part of the brain and to the related performance difficulties is no more precisely predictable for slow learners than is growth outcome for children of short stature. The affected children will probably grow progressively better able to perform the problem tasks as time passes, just as short 6-year-old children usually continue to gain in height. But whether a disabled learner will ever catch up is no more predictable than whether the short child will ever be as tall as the average adult. Recalling our use of the word "lag" for these children, we note that the word includes all of the possibilities one sees in such children; that is, the lag may disappear or lessen; and if it lessens, it may do so to any degree. Referring to the difficulty as "developmental lag" also keeps the child's problem in the correct perspective. For compared to other children, the patient has only a lag in development, *not* any development of a strange or different kind.

Adults differ from each other with respect to many physical and mental attributes; but children differ from each other even more, because they differ in an additional way. Adults have reached a plateau of development, so if they differ from each other in some way today, that difference will probably be about the same five years hence. With children there is also a changing *pattern* over time. At any one time different normal children have different patterns of ability, and these patterns themselves are subject to change within each child over time. Mental development is not linear; children do not develop at a steady rate but rather in fits and starts, just as they grow in height. A child's current abilities do not very reliably predict future abilities. That is particularly true in the first three years of life. For instance, the age at which a child first learns to walk is a topic of great concern. Parents whose children walk at 9 months are proud, and parents whose children walk at 18 months are ashamed; but at five years these children are all walking, and it makes no difference at what age they first learned. Nor does that age predict anything else. The early walker is not necessarily going to be the person who walks through high-school examinations without trouble. There is no harm in parents comparing notes about motor milestones, but they should not think that differences within the normal range mean anything. This is almost as true of language development. For groups of thousands of children, some of whom developed language early and some of whom developed it late, there will be group differences twenty years later; but for the individual this timing predicts very little. That is something to keep in mind when one talks about early identification and early action, subjects that will be discussed in Chapter 6.

Cognitive Style Disorders

There are two basic categories of cognitive style disorders: (1) the overfocused or compulsive and (2) the underfocused or impulsive-distractible.

Overfocused children are those who maintain their attention too long on one thing before moving to the next. There may be some genetically based physiological predisposition to this style, and it is certain that anxiety can also have such an effect. This is especially true if the child is anxious about the schoolwork itself. Fear of not having learned one bit of material well enough may make such a child inordinately hesitant to move to the next bit. Or, anxiety about something unrelated to school may occupy so much of the child's attention that it leaves little attention available for schoolwork, and the child's hesitation about moving through the material may be justified; that is, the child may be so upset that it will take much longer than normal to register and remember the lessons. If this condition persists, the child comes to have a school problem because of not having learned enough.

Less is known about the etiology, treatment, and development of the overfocused child than about the underfocused. The main point to take note of at this stage of our discussion is the primary symptom: the child's extreme slowness in shifting attention from one thing to the next.

Underfocused children shift attention too quickly from one thing to the next. Some of the causes are primarily emotional; for example, the child hates school, is terrified of failing, is too worried about making friends to concentrate on schoolwork, etc. For children with these emotional problems psychotherapy is often the best course of action. But some children with rapidly shifting attention clearly have a disorder that is primarily brain-based, one that usually follows a recognizable pattern of development and presenting symptoms. These children have often been called *hyperactive.* Their failure to keep their attention on the assigned task leads them to move when they should be still and concentrating. Because the word *hyperactive* has for so long been associated with this disorder, and because other suggested names are cumbersome, vague, or even more misleading, we shall refer to this type of brain-based underfocusing disorder as *hyperactivity*. In Part III we will describe the typical case history of a hyperactive child; here we will merely outline the primary symptom, the underfocusing itself, since it seems to give rise to many of the secondary consequences associated with the disorder.

Among children who do not pay attention to an assigned task, one may distinguish two general types. One type behaves in a concentrated, goal-directed way, sustaining attention well; but the object attended to is not the one that the teacher, parent, or other child wishes. Children whose school troubles are psychogenic are sometimes misclassified as distractible or hyperactive, whereas in fact they are concentrating quite well on getting back home to mother and father, on the frightening consequences of failing in school, or on the intricacies of an escapist fantasy life. The other type of child behaves in an impulsive, distractible way characterized by fragmentary and unpredictable activities. It is the latter child who exhibits the underfocused, hyperactive behavior.

What does it mean in practice for a child to be underfocused? Before taking any action, an animal or person considers information relevant to that action. For example, "I see a thing over there. Shall I move toward it, move away, or not move at all? In order to decide, I need to recall what I know about that thing. Is it friendly or hostile? What will it do if I move closer, stay here, or move away?" etc. The organism reviews information and then makes a decision about whether to act and how to act. One can make such a decision without knowing anything at all, or after reviewing either a little or a lot of the relevant information. The typical hyperactive child makes decisions too soon, before obtaining or reviewing enough of the information needed to make a decision that is likely to produce successful (or at any rate not harmful) results. It is understandable why such children often experience school failure: They stop listening to the teacher before they have heard the directions. Likewise, when answering questions they may start to answer before they finish hearing or reading the question. And even if they understand the question, they impulsively choose an answer that is often wrong, either because they did not consider all the relevant aspects (and thus produced a close but incorrect answer) or did not consider any relevant aspects (and thus produced a wildly incorrect answer). For similar reasons, these children are often hard to discipline, making decisions about how to behave before fully considering, first, what the teacher or parent wants, and second, what are the alternative ways in which they can behave. The same underprocessing of information often results in poor peer relationships. Hyperactive children tend to inadequately consider what they can do to get along with other children; and so they rush around, producing rapid bursts of ill-considered behavior, without stopping to reflect that other children exclude them because of such behavior.

LOGICAL, PRAGMATIC, AND NORMATIVE APPROACH
Our approach to the general matter of children's learning and attention problems is aimed at finding out what one can do to help a child who is failing or having difficulty in school. For those school problems that are not caused purely by emotional factors, the most practical and helpful thing to do is first to pinpoint and understand in specific detail the nature of the symptoms and then to prescribe treatment based on that understanding.

THE LOGICAL (NONTECHNOLOGICAL) APPROACH
The area of school problems is beset by a bewildering variety of opinions that leave both parents and various specialists confused. The confusion is not due to any inherently excessive complexities in the area; it is due to the premature introduction of a technological approach. In medicine we customarily adopt what is called a medical model: We make a diagnosis and, based on this, we unroll our technology of treatment. But usually the use of this model depends on our understanding of the disorder's etiology. Typically we prefer to treat the cause, not the symptom. Unfortunately, very little is known about the causes of learning problems, and certainly no way has been discovered to dispose of school problems by directly modifying the brain or body. This technology is not yet available.

Nevertheless, in our technological society we tend to focus on gimmicks and techniques in the hope that they will help. We commonly insist, in fact, on technologies that may be glittering and complex but that are not rational. These must be rejected. In the case of most children with learning disabilities (cognitive power disorders) for example, the available special techniques have not been shown to work better than more mundane individualized teaching. Most children with learning disabilities do not have problems that are in principle hard to solve. Most children with learning disabilities do not need an approach that is highly technical or that deviates greatly from what an excellent tutor would intuitively do. Rather, many children have what might have been only transitory immaturities in their mental development; but those immaturities become translated into permanent performance deficits by the rigidity and ignorance that we as parents, teachers, and professionals exhibit in our responses to them.

THE PRAGMATIC (NONTHEORETICAL) APPROACH

Much theorizing has gone on about the nature of both learning disability and hyperactivity. This theorizing may yet prove to inspire important research that will transform our present level of ignorance into a level of understanding at which *valid* technological approaches become a possibility. Indeed, in the area of hyperactivity these technological beginnings are apparent and will be discussed. But in this book we concentrate on what we know today rather than what we may (or may not) discover tomorrow. Today our theories are out of touch with the children we are supposed to be helping. So our approach will be directed at choosing between available management options, rather than at documenting facts that do not suggest action or at validating theories whose validity, or lack of it, has no practical significance for the children involved.

THE NORMATIVE (NONPATHOLOGICAL) APPROACH

Disturbingly little is known about whatever neurochemical or neurophysiological mechanisms may cause the learning disabilities. When one understands little about etiology, and when—as is now the case with learning disabilities—treatment does not depend upon it, one can take either a pathological or a normative view. When a child with learning disability has trouble learning, what is the nature of that trouble? Is it different in kind from the trouble that normal children encounter (and surmount) in learning the material? Many people base their treatment on the assumption that it is different. For example, they say that a child has "perceptual" problems, doesn't see or hear things as we see and hear them, sees things backward, etc. We shall discuss this issue at length in Chapter 3, but it is important here to state our general approach. In brief, it is this: Virtually all of the learning disabilities (as distinct from cognitive style disorders) result from delay in some aspect of the normal development of mental abilities. They are identified as selective disabilities because they appear in children who are, in most or all other respects, developmentally on a par with their peers.

This normative approach (centered around normal development) provides a useful backdrop against which to view learning disabilities; and, more important, it provides a logical way to identify the exact nature of the disability in a given child. From there, it is a brief step to precise and practical treatment recommendations.

With respect to cognitive style disorders the normative approach is not as useful or productive. It does apply, nevertheless, in a different way to children with these disorders. Such children represent the extremes of normal variation with respect to the general population of children their own age. On the other hand, children with cognitive style disorders only superficially resemble younger normal children. If one were guided by activity levels, one might think they resembled younger normal children, for in general child activity levels decrease as children grow older. And, in a sense, a hyperactive child is as active as a younger normal child. But closer scrutiny reveals that the nature of the activity is different. The impulsive underfocused style of a group of hyperactive children—as well as the cautious *overfocused* style of a contrasting group of children with a cognitive style disorder for which there is no generally accepted name—does not recapitulate earlier developmental stages. But these two groups are not discontinuous from normality either; rather, they are extremes of normal variation. They are normal biologically, in that they are often though not always products of polygenic inheritance. But from the adaptive point of view they are not normal at all.

WHY INTERVENE?

Some children who have these immaturities continue to lag year after year and thus are behind, even to an alarming degree, with respect to mental functions needed to comprehend school material and to maintain appropriate attention. But most such children have only transitory problems when entering first grade and a little later are able to concentrate and to understand the concepts involved. Even so, for practical purposes a little later may be too late, because we may have made it too late for them. There are vicious cycles into which such a child can easily be thrown (see Fig. 1). For example, the child, although selectively unready, enters the regular first grade. This is the first mistake. A first-grade child who is not ready and nevertheless is taught in a routine rather than an individualized fashion will fail. The consequences of this failure are: for the child, a lower self-image; for the parents, disappointment; for the teacher, frustration; for the child's brothers and sisters, the feeling of being ignored in favor of the sibling with a problem; and for the child's peers in the classroom, the feeling of being ignored by the teacher in favor of the problem pupil. So this simple failure of one individual affects a whole group of related people, and it does so in a way that has further repercussions for the child. Not only does the child have to bear the burden of manifest failure day after day, not knowing the answers the other first-graders do; the child also becomes exquisitely aware of the parents' frustrated disappointment and the teachers' puzzled resentment (both of which are understandable human reactions). This is the problem of being different, of feeling different, and of being regarded as different by others—including other children who come to view the affected child both as an alien and as a threat detracting from the attention that they should get. All this generates either explicit or implicit classroom pressures on failing children to succeed, as well as a feeling that the other children resent them. And that in turn aggravates the lowering of the child's self-image and its consequences: fear of failure, reluctance to take the risk of trying again (for fear of failing again), and a feeling of helplessness and hopelessness that translates itself into under-motivated learning. So now we have a secondary complication. Not only do these children have the handicap of temporarily immature mental processes, which means that they must work harder than is usually necessary to cover the customary ground, but this is now aggravated by their withholding of mental effort. They become underachievers even with respect to their currently limited potential. Now there are two reasons for failure: primary developmental reasons and secondary emotional ones.

At about that point the educational system, regardless of whether the child has mastered the first-grade material, often insists on having the child enter the second grade. This is the monstrous act known as "social promotion," which does much to perpetuate children's learning failure. Of course, the arguments are familiar: "The child has made friends with the other children in the class." This is sometimes true, but not always. "It would be an admission of failure for the child to be held back." Well, yes, it would be upsetting; reality sometimes is. But not facing reality is worse ultimately than facing reality. The reason for social promotion (other than physical maturity) is not to let such children experience their failure; but they experience it every day anyway. One should not promote children who have failed a grade, because one thereby places them even more out of their depth; such children will lack the first-year foundations that would make the second year's curriculum intelligible. They have started with a lower than average learning *potential*. But they are not even allowed to learn at that lower level, because grade two instruction is not geared to the level of children who do not know grade one material. Such children naturally become passengers in grade two classes; depending upon their individual personalities, they will stay there briefly (if they have emotional outbursts) or longer (if they suffer in silence). Meanwhile they will fall more and more behind, but not necessarily because of their brain-based learning disability. It may even be that after the first year or 18 months their mental maturation has actually caught up. They may now in fact be ready to master the first-grade curriculum, but nobody is teaching them that. So their potential learning ability remains unused, and the time may come when they reject further education, even when the proper level of instruction is offered.

After a certain amount of such pressure, children become alien-

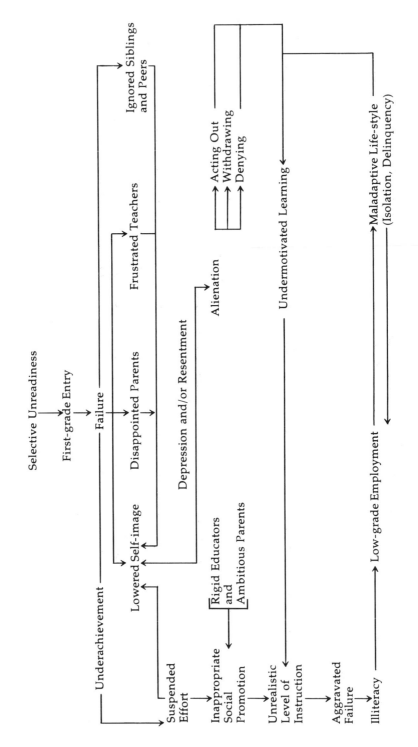

Figure 1. Vicious cycle of school failure.

ated. They then react in one of three basic ways, depending upon their personalities. Typically, when faced by a threat or disturbing experience that is not mastered, a person may move against it, move away from it, or move sideways and shift the ground of discourse. Thus, a child whose failures are painfully obvious may act out and move against the situation, may withdraw into isolation, or may pretend it is not happening by denying it. All three are protective mechanisms which safeguard the self temporarily. In so doing they have short-term usefulness; nevertheless, they are ultimately self-defeating, because they smother the potential for mental and intellectual growth. So, in an aggravated case, we end up with unsatisfying employment, poor financial circumstances, limited resources for living, and a maladaptive life-style that restricts the personality, limits the individual in contacts with others, or even pits the individual against others and against the social group. In some severe cases this would have happened no matter what one did; but ahead of time we cannot sort these cases out from the rest. Therefore, we should initially assume in every case that something can be done to prevent it.

What we fear is a widening spiral of difficulty. It begins with a limited deficit, a shortcoming that really has only an educational impact; but it then widens out into matters affecting the well-being — physical and mental — of the whole child. Once this has happened, we can no longer remedy the situation through the single-handed intervention of a professional. At this point, however, it is essential to avoid serial consultations with professionals, each of whom gives an opinion that may be correct as far as it goes but by itself makes no significant impact on the whole situation. To retrieve the situation, a number of disciplines have to intervene in concert.

WHO SHOULD INTERVENE?

Each profession has its own important perspective on learning disabilities. A teacher must directly and daily confront the child's failure to learn; a teacher or special educator is also the person most likely to have the specific skills needed to tutor the child once a detailed identification of the child's learning requirements has been made. A psychologist can administer some of the tests that are needed to diagnose and understand the child's problem. A clinical psychologist or a psychiatrist can identify and give psychotherapy for emotional disturbances that may accompany the failure to learn. A pediatrician or family physician may have advised the parents about various aspects of the child's life since its birth.

In principle, members of any of these disciplines can coordinate the services for one child. But because there has been an increasing tendency for children with learning problems to show up in physicians' offices, and because physicians in many ways have the least training to prepare them for such cases, we shall mention some of the strengths physicians have that are relevant to this field.

Through medical training, the pediatrician is in an ideal position to understand the nature of problems caused by slow maturation of one or more parts of the brain. First, the pediatrician knows that the different parts of the brain develop at different speeds and times, even in the normal child, and that this produces tremendous variation in the rates at which any given child acquires the abilities to talk, run, make fine finger movements, and grow tall. From this knowledge, it is but one step to understanding the great variations that differential brain growth can produce in a child's abilities to read, spell, write, calculate, think logically, or arrange things in sequence and in space. A child's general intelligence has usually been measured and defined in terms of these abilities and perhaps some others.

The pediatrician is also well placed to understand that, just as a normal adult may suffer a stroke in one small part of the brain and thereafter be perfectly normal except in the ability to speak clearly or to remember names of colors, so a child may, in general, have normal intelligence while being unable to read or do arithmetic. Knowing how many different functions are controlled by separate parts of the brain, the pediatrician will understand that the number of kinds and combinations of learning problems a child can have is limitless.

The physician can also understand a point that is crucial, both for the treatment of the child and for the setting of appropriate, realistic limits for parents' expectations about the child's progress. Destroyed brain cells cannot regenerate, and there is no way to make a slowly-maturing brain mature faster.

What should be the posture of the physician with respect to children's learning? There are five options. The simplest one is to refuse all such referrals because, after all, the physician probably did not learn in medical school how to handle them. When you are asked a question to which you cannot possibly know the answer, it is legitimate to refuse to answer the question. But that is not always easy, because society often makes physicians the "experts." So, you may feel called upon to summon skills that you do not possess. You can then adopt one of the other four postures, each of which has advantages and disadvantages.

The first is to be strictly a consultant and make a strictly medical evaluation. There are some rare causes of school failure that are very much within your province to investigate and handle. You can also check the child for treatable disease that might actually be unrelated to school failure, but that proper diagnostic procedures will discover. In most cases this approach will lead you to draw conclusions which, however valid, are irrelevant to the problem. This is a time-honored medical activity.

The second option is to carry out the medical exercises just outlined and also to attempt to determine whether there really is a learning disability. Does this child definitely have normal intelligence, so that it is reasonable to have expected normal school progress? Is the achievement age of the child really substantially behind reasonable expectations? Sometimes parents' and teachers' expectations are unreasonable, and you are being asked to deal with a problem of academic failure that does not exist. The child, in fact, may be achieving at the level of national norms or even above them, and the parents' and teachers' expectations may be overly ambitious. You will therefore see that the necessary tests are done before you refer the child for more specific educational testing and teaching; for without standard testing, you cannot be certain that the child is of normal intelligence or is truly failing (see Chap. 4). If you are prepared to assume long-term responsibility for the child, if necessary, you can also determine whether pharmacological intervention is needed. If it is, you can manage that yourself. The use of stimulant medications for some children will be discussed in detail in Part III.

The third option is, in addition, to be a member of a multidisciplinary team. You may even assume the responsibility of chairing a team of multiple specialists: psychologists, speech pathologists, educators, social workers, occupational therapists, physical therapists, and psychiatric colleagues. You may be designated to coordinate the information from those fields with your own and to communicate the decisions. Now for that, of course, you need some understanding of those other specialties (see Chap. 4), and that takes work.

The fourth option takes still more work. It is to combine within your own head enough of these multiple aspects of expertise to do most of the job yourself, or at least to coordinate it yourself. In effect, you have committee meetings in your own head, debate the various points of view with yourself, and come out with one voice, representing a personal consensus. You might wonder "How can I, even if I would wish to, assimilate the expertise of all these people? " The answer is, you do not have to. You do not have to know all of clinical psychology, or all of speech pathology, just those aspects most likely to be relevant to school problems. On an apprenticeship basis, devoting about a year to working in a properly pragmatic learning clinic, a person can make a good beginning.

In this latter case one individual—who can be based in any of a number of relevant professions—secures all the necessary cross-disciplinary consultations and exercises the decision-making functions. Such a person should be sufficiently acquainted with the principles of the other disciplines to be able to interpret findings and evaluate recommendations. That person must also be very familiar with the community resources or how to locate them and must be prepared to serve as a stable point of reference for the family for many years.

The advantage of individual management is clear-cut decision-making, which makes for consistency of management and is a comfort to the family. The drawback is the difficulty that one person might experience in mastering the many disciplines that are sources of relevant information.

In practice, such a person will specialize in school problems, or at least see a substantial and continuing flow of such children. It is not practical to assume this responsibility on an occasional basis.

So, these are the four roles from among which you can choose. Define your role for yourself, and keep within it. If you are a consultant, you cannot be possessive. If you are part of a multidisciplinary team, you must be democratic. If you conduct it all inside your head, you must have the courage of your convictions and not compromise.

In any case, the pediatrician, family physician, or other professional can use their social roles to good advantage for overseeing remedial treatment that may be prescribed for the child. As mentioned, many of the people whose services may be required to help the child use technical jargon that often confuses and repels. But there is no aspect of children's learning problems that cannot be explained clearly and easily to the parents or even to the child. The same is true for all productive means of remediation: They can be explained so that all concerned can understand how they work. As a professional and one who traditionally fills the role of a counselor with authority, the pediatrician is particularly well placed to insist on clear, nontechnical evaluations and plans for remediation from the personnel chosen to assess and help the child. This is important because it will increase the understanding of parent, child, and teacher about what the child's problem is, and thus it can: (1) focus everyone's attention on the child's trouble by giving them a common language, (2) maximize their cooperation with each other, and (3) remove the mystery and technical language from the scene so that the child is treated as a normal child who happens to have trouble, say, in reading, rather than as an alien specimen termed a *dyslexic* or *minimally brain-dysfunctional* child.

For further medical opinion, physicians most often refer cases of learning failure to the neurologist. Therefore, we now briefly review the possible forms of the neurologist's participation. (Neurologists, of course, may restrict their role to specialist-consultants, or may coordinate the overall investigation). As a *specialist*, a neurologist can:

1. Rule out alternative diagnoses (e.g., progressive cerebral degeneration, petit mal status)
2. Establish the need for ancillary investigation (e.g., audiometry)
3. Identify the cause of sensorimotor complaints relevant to school performance (e.g., clumsiness)
4. Determine whether the learning difficulty is associated with signs of disordered (hard signs) or delayed (soft signs) neurological development
5. Identify disorders of higher mental function that require medical management (e.g., hyperactivity) and supervise that management
6. Hypothesize the pathogenesis of the disability (e.g., genetic, perinatal trauma)
7. Explain to parents the irrelevance in practice of such hypotheses as those in item 6
8. Counteract pressures on parents to resort to crank remedial programs based on unsubstantiated neurological theories

As a *general coordinator,* a neurologist must be sufficiently conversant with psychometric and educational technicalities and resources to be able to make specific recommendations about educational placement and remedial methods.

THE FUNCTION OF A LEARNING CLINIC
How Should the Clinic Be Staffed?
The multidisciplinary approach
A group of professionals can constitute a multidisciplinary team that varies somewhat in composition but typically includes a pediatrician, a psychologist, a psychiatrist, an educator, a social worker, and perhaps a speech pathologist, physical therapist, and occupational therapist. Current trends indicate that a nutritionist may join many such teams. There is usually a chairperson, often a physician, but the chairing is usually relatively nondirective. Customarily all team members see each case, meet to discuss it, and then delegate a subset of this committee to interpret to the par-

ents. At best the report includes some effort to integrate the information, but it usually consists mainly of a series of specialists' reports.

One advantage of this organization is that it offers an in-depth investigation (which is particularly suitable for children who have already gone through assessments elsewhere without satisfaction). The organization is democratic, so that each discipline can be heard. The need for outside consultation is minimized, the various specialists communicating freely and being familiar with each others' terminology, orientation and personalities. Everyone's findings are open to debate by the group.

The drawbacks are lack of economy and lack of clear direction. It is thoroughly wasteful of expert time and effort to have each child seen by all or even most of the disciplines. But, unfortunately, a team ethic usually develops that regards it as prejudicial to a discipline to "leave it out." In some sense, all the professionals are defending the relevance and importance of their particular contributions. The result is often a disjointed miscellany of recommendations that cater more to professional pride and prejudice than to the child's interest. All of the specialists like to identify a problem in their own areas of expertise, so the child may come with a school problem but may leave with language delay, brain damage, motor deficit, psychosis, and a lisp. The recommendations that are made become similarly fragmented into a dash of speech therapy, a smattering of psychotherapy, and a little bit of remedial education. So, in practice, a multidisciplinary arrangement can deteriorate into a time and resource waster, and the attempt at a democratic process may deteriorate into anarchy. Also, there are too many affected children to have so many specialists involved with each child.

The nuclear group approach

Such is the pressure of work generated by the many children with school problems that the multidisciplinary team is an unaffordable luxury. Yet the individual practitioner is rarely completely qualified. We therefore advocate a nuclear group approach. Suppose the group consists of a physician and a psychologist. They should do their work first, share information, and interpret right away if the issues are already clear. If the issues are not clear, these two primary specialists decide who should be consulted, and those persons automatically join the decision-making team. One of the primary two is then responsible for an integrated final report.

The advantages of this organization are that many children who do not need the more elaborate workups are assessed with dispatch and after a minimal waiting period. It is possible to interpret on the spot, rather than have the parents come back another day. The time of other professionals is drawn upon only when this is clearly important, and then their input is given full weight. Relatively large numbers of patients can be seen efficiently as well as expeditiously.

The drawback of this arrangement is that it demands flexible scheduling, because it is not clear ahead of time how long each child will be seen. People with rigid, compulsive personalities would be uncomfortable in such a design. A variation on this design would incorporate an educator in the primary group. The triad that results should have the advantage of excellent communication with the school system. Other dyads and triads can also be used, depending on the local availability of interested and competent professionals.

SHOULD THE CLINIC BE LOCATED IN A HOSPITAL OR
MEDICAL BUILDING?
The advantages of a medical location are that a variety of ancillary services (electroencephalography, audiology, allergy testing, and pharmacy facilities) are close at hand. The drawback can be an unduly heavy medical emphasis and a labeling of the children, by themselves as well as by others, as medical cases. One convenient compromise is to have the clinic in a medical building but with a separate entrance free of medical insignia, paraphernalia, and smells.

WHO SHOULD BE ALLOWED TO REFER CHILDREN TO THE
CLINIC?
Typically, learning clinics in hospitals take referrals only from physicians. This offers the advantage that some continuity of care can be anticipated after the assessment. However, when parents and teachers agree that a referral is needed but the family physician is unwilling or uninterested, then the referral should be accepted from them instead; the physician should be notified and the physician's assistance sought. When we courteously inform local physicians that the parents of one of the children under their care have sought our advice, we receive full cooperation, and we are not regarded as having breached professional etiquette.

SHOULD A LEARNING CLINIC HAVE A REMEDIAL
TEACHING COMPONENT?
Long-term teaching is an inefficient way of using clinic resources, because it duplicates the efforts of school and remedial education centers. Usually only a limited number of children can be handled, and to teach small groups in this way is administratively ineffi-

cient. But short-term experimental teaching is a different matter. It is in the interest of learning clinic personnel to keep in touch with how children are taught by doing it themselves occasionally. It is also of benefit to students training in the clinic to do this under supervision. When a specific educational approach has been prescribed, it is salutary to devote half a dozen sessions in quick succession to trial teaching in the prescribed manner, then to report back to the team and, if the trial teaching seems to be working, to inform the school personnel.

SHOULD CLINIC PERSONNEL VISIT SCHOOLS?
The staff should be acquainted with local educational establishments. A visit will accomplish this and will also consolidate good personal relations. But routine visits to observe a particular child are time-wasters and are not recommended. The amount the visitor learns rarely justifies the time spent traveling, courtesy-visiting teachers, waiting for the child to return from the playground or toilet, and watching a classroom routine that only occasionally calls for action from the child in question. Relevant information can usually be obtained efficiently through telephone conversations with the classroom teacher. A followup consultation with the child's teacher in the school is useful in selected cases, but by and large the pressure of work must preclude traveling to schools.

WHOM TO BELIEVE
When a case of learning disability persists and resists remedial efforts, it is inevitable that parents, and often the physician who is managing the case as well, come up against contradictory appraisals and advice from various expert consultants. Since objective criteria for judging between expert opinions in learning disabilities do not exist, the physician is often left to make an arbitrary decision. One general guideline can be offered, however, to any professional or parent who faces this dilemma: Accept that counsel which makes the fewest untestable claims and the most sense.

Validated technologies do not exist. The onus is therefore on the proponent of any particular approach to justify it in a manner that is clear and intelligible to the informed nonexpert. In Chapter 7, we shall outline some applications of this commonsense approach, as a demonstration of how to decide whom to believe.

SUGGESTED READING
Kinsbourne, M.   School problems. *Pediatrics 52:* 697–710, 1973.

2. Incidence

Boys have more reported school problems than girls. This is the case with regard to both cognitive power disorders and hyperactivity. With respect to overfocusing, however, so little is known about it that no statement can be made as to its relative incidence. The reasons for this male predominance are not entirely understood, but we can review what is known about them and what is likely to be the case.

The ratio of boys to girls, in the case of cognitive power disorders or learning disability, has been estimated differently; but the males are always in the majority, the ratios ranging from 1.5:1 to as much as 10:1.

One of the reasons is that certain types of processing disorders seem to be genetically predetermined, or at least predisposed, in a sex-linked way that makes them more common in males. Insofar as male babies are subject to greater prenatal, perinatal, and postnatal traumata, damage suffered at those times probably further increases the preponderance of males with cognitive power problems. The lesser frequency of such traumata in female babies may be partly responsible for young girls' superior verbal abilities.

In addition, there appear to be innate sex differences in behavior that could be relevant. Inconsistent behavior over time among newborns has been found to indicate subsequent emotional disorder. Furthermore, such inconsistency is more frequently observed in male than in female babies. These facts could clearly be relevant to the male predominance in behavior disorders, including hyperactivity and impulse disorders. However, there is also a more general implication. For many physical parameters, male development exhibits greater irregularity than female development. Whether this is also true for cognitive antecedents of school readiness is unclear, but if so, this could have an important bearing on the greater frequency among males of relative reading disability. That is, a greater variation in readiness would imply that more males are relatively unready at school entry (and also that more males are ready earlier, though this is not relevant for us). As long as school entry is rigidly determined by chronological age, more males will be prematurely instructed, will fall behind, and, unless given individual attention, will risk long-term educational disability.

Besides these constitutional factors, there are aspects of societal expectations for the two sexes that probably contribute to this male predominance. First of all, adults seem to believe it is a more serious problem if a boy fails to learn to read than if a girl does so [3]. Boys' learning failures are thus more likely to be noticed and brought to the attention of parents and school authorities, and they are likely to produce greater pressure to take counter-measures.

Second, a child who fails may seek out other avenues by which to win approval. We already know that the failure may be regarded as more serious for a boy than for a girl, so a failing boy may experience greater pressure than a failing girl to find another type of unpunished behavior. But the alternatives for a boy are much more stringent than for a girl. When children were asked what kinds of school behavior were desirable, and then asked which of those were appropriate for a boy and which for a girl, the following results were obtained [4]: Children of both sexes felt that "to be nice" was the most desirable behavior. Much lower on the scale were "to be good at sports" and "to be a leader." They classified "being nice" as appropriate for girls and the other two alternatives as appropriate for boys. Now, all of the girls in the class can be nice, and they can be nice in the classroom and on the playground. But not all of the boys can be good at sports or be good leaders; furthermore, sports and leadership abilities are not as visible in the classroom as "being nice." A boy who is failing to learn in school, then, is less likely than a girl to find a sex-appropriate alternative to "being smart" that does not annoy the teacher or get him into trouble. Of course, he has the "male-appropriate" alternative of making noise in class and being generally disruptive or even combative. That is a mixed blessing, however, because even a teacher who tolerates such behavior as "just boyishness" will have trouble allowing it to go unpunished in the classroom. Therefore, a failing boy is far more likely than a failing girl to experience frustration above and beyond the frustration of failing to learn to read, write, or do mathematics. When we add to this problem the fact that boys tend to respond to frustration with antisocial aggression more than girls do, we can understand the self-reinforcing cycle that is set up: Boys fail to learn some skill, have trouble finding appropriate alternative ways to behave, experience still further frustration, handle all this frustration by behaving in antisocial ways, are punished for that, and become even less willing than before to try to learn at their own levels and to cooperate with their teachers and peers.

All of this means two things, both of which are important: (1) Boys' apparent learning failures are more likely to be recognized and even aggravated needlessly; and (2) girls' learning failures are likely to go unnoticed, because they compensate by seeking approval through "good" behavior, which is really unobtrusive and which leads to social promotions. (In one extreme case that we observed, a 10-year-old girl who was a developmental aphasic—i.e., had never spoken, read, written, or used anything but the most primitive symbolic communication—had been promoted on up to the fifth grade with her age-mates because she was so quiet and well-behaved.)

In the case of cognitive style disorders, the question of gender takes a slightly different twist. For some of the reasons discussed above, impulsive, distractible types of children are more likely to make their problems known than are overfocused, compulsive children who make little noise and move around the classroom less. There is a clear genetic predominance of boys over girls in the impulsive, distractible category. But this is complicated by two factors. First, girls' impulsiveness is more likely to shock and dismay parents than similar behavior by their brothers, so impulsive girls run up against far stronger efforts to squelch or hide such behavior than do impulsive boys, and these efforts often prove effective. Second, a little impulsiveness in a girl seems more noteworthy than the same amount of impulsiveness in a boy, so the former is more likely to be classified as a problem that needs treatment. An impulsive, distractible girl whose parents' efforts to squelch her are successful is likely to become depressed (so, for that matter, is a boy who receives similar treatment). She may not appear "hyperactive" to an onlooker, but her efforts to control her behavior have to be so strong in order to succeed that she becomes depressed. So a highly impulsive girl may appear to present a case of depression. On the other hand, a bit of impulsiveness, or even normal physical activity, in a girl may be misclassified as "hyperactivity" by parents who are nervous or who possess a rigid stereotyped concept of sex roles. For example, in one case the mother of a 5-year-old girl complained that her daughter was extremely active, never sat still, never stopped talking. During three hours of interviewing, testing, and playing with the child we saw no signs of such behavior. Then, as we accompanied the child and her mother up a flight of stairs toward the cafeteria, the girl took two steps at a time, and the mother gave us a significant look and said, "See what I mean?"

For the most part, the roles of the two parents of a child who fails in school should not differ from each other. Both should give the child good-quality attention, should be sensitive to the child's needs, and should show interest in aspects of the child other than school performance and achievement. As a general rule, neither parent need spend more time than the other with the child. There are only a couple of instances where this is not quite true. For boys who are impulsive and distractible, or whose frustration at failing in school has produced aggressive antisocial behavior, a special kind of role for the father becomes increasingly important. Because society delivers two conflicting messages to boys about antisocial behavior ("That's a typical boy for you," but also "You will be punished for behaving that way in class"), the father can model and support alternate kinds of behavior for his son. By being warm and supportive as well as active and strong, and by not behaving in the stereotyped aggressive "male" ways, the father of such a boy can demonstrate that he will respect his son for *not* behaving antisocially and for being a strong, warm, active person. In short, he can indicate that antisocial behavior is not the only fitting alternative for a boy.

What about girls who are failing to learn, but about whom no one is concerned because of their sex? The mothers of these girls can, of course, encourage them to try to learn up to their potential and can model achievement-oriented behavior for them, demonstrating that such behavior is appropriate for girls as well as for boys. Many girls in the primary grades work hard in school to win the teacher's approval, rather than for the sake of actual learning or achievement [1]. Mothers can try to correct this situation, and in so doing can help ensure that their failing daughters do not sweep their failure to learn under the rug of "good" classroom behavior.

In this context, it is interesting to note that although girls and boys may have learned the same amount of information in the classroom, the girls tend to receive higher grades than the boys. This is probably because the girls' classroom behavior is more helpful, quiet, and prosocial.

But, perhaps oddly, it has been shown that the attitudes and behavior of fathers has more of an effect on girls' achievement motivation than the attitudes and behaviors of mothers. This may be because society presents fathers as the representatives of the achievement ideal and mothers as the representatives of the nurturant ideal. So, until such time as this tendency may change, fathers should be made aware that they can do much to encourage and show approval of their daughters' efforts to learn for learning's sake, not for the approval of the teacher or parent.

In families that have problem children of any sort, the typical pattern is for the mother to bear the burden of dealing with the problem child. The fathers in these families often begin to spend more time at work than necessary in order to stay away from home until the "problem" has gone to sleep. The fathers then often blame the mother for the child's problem or for the problem's continuation, since "She is the one who's home with the child all day, so why doesn't she do something about it?"

For this reason, and because of the other gender-related patterns already noted, girls who fail tend to be ignored, and fathers who withdraw tend to be allowed to remain out of the picture. These tendencies are deeply woven into the fabric of social expectations, and they are so pervasive that the average person is very likely to associate (even unconsciously) "school problem child" with "boy" and "parent or teacher of such a child" with "woman."

AGE*

At what age is a child ready to learn to read? Different countries have by implication proposed different answers to this question, ranging from "age 5" to "age 7." In every case the answer is purely intuitive and is not based on systematic research. In fact, it is certain that systematic research would render the question meaningless. It would have to be rephrased in the following way: What is the age range within which most (e.g., 95 percent) of all children become ready to learn to read? and, What is the cost-efficiency (in terms of teacher hours and teacher-student ratios) of teaching children to read at each of the ages within that range? It is well known that a few children can be taught to read at ages as low as 4, and that some do not really make adequate progress until as late as age 10. However, those children who appear unready to learn to read at whatever age children start school in their area are not customarily described in terms of "normal biological variation," but rather in terms of "reading deficit" or "development lag." In a sense, these terms are justified. What constitutes a deficit depends on social expectations as well as upon the vagaries of biology. And, obviously, slow development lags behind fast development. However, these perspectives beg the central question: Is there any advantage in teaching children to read before they are ready, just because they have reached a certain age?

PREMATURE READING INSTRUCTION

Ultimately, the only possible justification for reading instruction is the utility of possessing reading skills. Because of these skills, important sources of information are open to individuals that will ultimately help them to function effectively within their social groups. But no one has shown that between, say, the ages of 4 and 10 children can better meet the responsibilities of childhood because they are able to read. Therefore, the pressure on children to learn to read does not relate to what is expected of them as children so much as to what is expected of them later on. So whether children

---

* This section discusses only the incidence of cognitive power disorders with respect to age. The incidence of hyperactivity and variation of its presenting symptoms with age are discussed in Chapter 9.

begin to read at age 4 or at age 10 makes no difference if they can read adequately at age 16. Thus, the pressures for learning to read early would only be justifiable if it were shown that earlier starting results in a higher ultimate level of skill. This has never been shown.

Another important consideration is the cost-efficiency of teaching individuals certain material at different ages. Being "ready" to learn to read sounds rather definite and absolute, but it is not. In fact, reading readiness should be considered in relative terms: What would it take in terms of teacher effort and the teacher-student ratio to teach a child to read at various ages? We learn from investigations of early reading programs that 4-year-olds who turn out to be amenable to reading instruction progress at a slower rate than beginning readers who are older. This is true despite the fact that early reading programs characteristically offer advantageous teacher-student ratios, often select children of above average intelligence who come from unusually literate and competitive home settings, and employ teachers of above average ability who are motivated by the unusual challenge. So even if we can teach a 4-year-old a vocabulary of thirty or fifty or seventy words, could we not teach the same child that material much more efficiently, and with less work on the part of all concerned, if we waited another year or two or three? Undoubtedly the answer is yes. In fact, this logic can be extended considerably. To take an extreme case, there is an argument about the best disposition of resources in developing countries that suggests the following course: If one is short of teachers and teaching materials, would it not be most reasonable to postpone all teaching until the individual has reached full mental maturity, at which time he will be in a position to learn most efficiently? By this logic it might be advantageous to postpone education in countries where the illiteracy rate is very high to, say until age 18, at which time a year or two of instruction might acquaint mature pupils with the full curriculum that is slowly and laboriously learned by children of more conventional "school age."

Applying this logic to developed countries one naturally comes up against the force of tradition, the ambitions of parents and therefore also the ambitions of children, and the additional socializing effects of schools—including their major though little-acknowledged function of taking children off their parents' hands and keeping them off the streets. However, the argument is still enlightening. In particular, it demonstrates forcefully that beginning reading instruction at any arbitrarily selected age will do injustice to many children. It will unduly hold up those who are ready early, and it will unduly accelerate those who are ready late.

Thus a reasonable goal for educational research, and ultimately educational policy, would be to find a way of determining each child's educational readiness longitudinally, so that instruction in a subject can begin at a time when the child's readiness makes instruction in that subject not only possible but cost-efficient. In fact, this approach is so obviously superior to the more rigid present one that persistence of the latter must be attributed to bureaucratic inflexibility combined with the administrative difficulty of individualizing instruction in this way.

It is clear, then, that one disadvantage of beginning reading instruction at too young an age is that some children will be subjected to unnecessary failure. In the long run, this could depress their motivation to achieve. A second drawback is that resources have to be squandered on smaller classes; and, if the practice continues, extensive provision must be made for remedial instruction. A third possible problem, of which people are generally unaware, is that if children learn material at a time when they are mentally unready, then they may not be learning it in the same way they would if they were taught it later. They may, indeed, be learning it in a manner capable of inculcating strategies that would ultimately stand in their way.

What would be likely to happen if one tries to teach reading to children who are perceptually immature in the manner described in Chapter 3? According to the approach to perceptual development outlined previously, one would expect these children to experience maximum difficulty in discriminating letter groupings (i.e., patterns) that are very similar to each other. On the other hand, they might find it quite possible to discriminate between words of totally dissimilar spelling. Assuming that their vocabularies are thereby limited to words that bear little resemblance to each other in print, they could then use the following strategy: They know by heart an inventory of words that they have learned to "read." Therefore, when asked to read a word, they assume it is one of those they have learned and test it for resemblance to the words in their inventory. They will then read the word correctly in most cases and will obtain credit on achievement tests that require the reading of word lists.

Nevertheless, there is a problem. If the children are shown a word not contained in their inventory, will they be able to recognize that fact? After all, there is limited advantage in being able to read certain words if one also misreads unknown words by mistaking them for those already learned. Such "false-positive" word recognition is not tested for by standard achievement tests and appears not to have been investigated by studies of early reading. However, our understanding of perceptual development suggests to us that children whose perceptual systems are immature would be prone to making approximate matches between letter groupings they see and the words they know they have "learned to read;" and this could lead them to make such a high proportion of false-positive identifications as to render them useless as readers in the practical sense.

When one looks at the curricula and achievements of early reading enterprises, one notes just those conditions that would justify the above suspicion. The children learn a limited vocabulary, usually 30 to 50 words and rarely more than 100. These are simple, familiar words that differ widely from each other in appearance. Therefore, when told that an early reading group has made a certain amount of progress in word recognition, it is logical to show some skepticism until it has been demonstrated that the sight vocabulary obtained is not vitiated by a correspondingly extensive tendency to misidentify other words as ones within the sight vocabulary. Rather than create this situation, it would be a sounder policy to wait until children have matured enough perceptually to master the same vocabulary—not only much more quickly in all probability, but also without a tendency to make false-positive recognition errors.

Incidentally, when children with selective reading disability are painstakingly taught word recognition, the same precaution should be taken as is advocated here for younger normal children upon whom early reading programs have been imposed.

Finally, a careful followup of early trainees is necessary. For how many grades do they maintain their advantage? Does their early start in any way reflect on the ultimate plateau of reading performance that they achieve?

With respect to arithmetic and drawing disabilities, society's notably lesser concern about these difficulties (compared to its concern about reading disability) has resulted in a paucity of information.

It is well recognized that children who become able to perform in particular ways early tend ultimately to perform better in those ways. In other words, individuals who ultimately turn out to have great aptitudes will be ones who, on the whole, also begin to manifest those aptitudes early. It is a seemingly democratic but mindless approach to try to override these individual differences, which are biological in nature, by forcing everyone into an early start. The generalization, after all, does not hold for that. When we say that someone who shows early aptitude will ultimately show better skill, that is not to say that someone who is forced to do something early will ultimately do it better. For that latter proposition there is no evidence whatsoever.

AGES OF LEARNING DISABLED CHILDREN
Insofar as the definition of learning disability incorporates the notion of school failure, the age range to which this label is applicable will roughly coincide with a school age of 6 to 18 years. If the term is strictly defined, a child might have to accumulate substantial failure before being labeled as learning disabled. For instance, many studies restrict themselves to children who have fallen behind at least two years in one or more basic academic subjects; this, of course, is impossible for children below 8 years of age. At the other end of the range, individuals who have abandoned schooling, particularly after reaching the age of 18, are not usually considered learning disabled, for the trivial reason that they have lost contact with the educational system. Within the school-age range, there is no clear information about the relationship between age and the incidence of learning disability. Some cases picked up early are resolved, while others are picked up relatively late. But we lack objective ways to determine, when a child improves, whether improvement was due to excellent teaching or to a change in brain physiology. Similarly, when a child fails to improve, we cannot tell whether it is because of persistent brain-based immaturity, or because of the emotional sequelae of protracted failure. Thus it is not possible to qualify the overall percentage of learning disabled children (about eight percent of the general population) in terms of age.

It would be most useful if one could directly measure the brain's degree of maturation in its relevant areas. The closest we can come to this, however, is not very close; we can only observe a prevalence of slower than normal electroencephalographic (EEG) rhythms over the posterior section of the scalp. Relationships between these EEG characteristics and learning disability — in terms of false-positive and false-negative identifications — are unknown.

RACE AND SOCIOECONOMIC STATUS
Any attempt to determine different frequencies of learning disability in different racial and ethnic groups is hopelessly confounded by cultural, social, and economic differences, and by different criteria for making the diagnosis. Learning disability used to be discussed most in England and the Scandinavian countries. Now, however, it receives wide public attention in North America. To a much lesser extent, news of the problem also comes from France, Germany, Italy, Spain, and Latin America. Assertions of freedom from learning disabilities come particularly from Japan [3].

In many countries, the possible role of learning disability as a cause of illiteracy is simply not considered. In others, poverty-stricken populations receive such unsteady and inefficient education that the children's learning potential is barely tapped—and barely relevant. Here motivational and environmental blocks to learning must be considered first; only then can learning disability be identified.

Even in prosperous countries, differences in diagnostic practices render incidence figures equivocal. It is certainly tempting to attribute a lower incidence of selective reading disability to the use of phonetic scripts, as in Germany, Italy, and Spain; and the Japanese dearth of such cases could have to do with the availability of nonalphabetical (syllabic and ideographic) scripts in that country. But no adequate evidence for this is available. Incidentally, a phonetic script in English, the ITA (initial teaching alphabet), has not fulfilled early expectations that it would provide an effective path to fluent reading for the learning disabled.

With respect to extremes of cognitive style, cultural differences and diagnostic biases are equally effective in obscuring true relative incidences. Differences in cultural norms and child-rearing practices profoundly affect both the public concept of what constitutes an abnormality and the public (parental and educator) response to it in terms of disciplinary and other measures. If hyperactivity is rarely recognized in certain countries, the reason could of course be genetic; but equally, a rigid culture (such as the traditional Chinese) might deny children the opportunity to act out impulses, whereas a slack culture (such as the Afro-American) might regard impulsive behavior as within the bounds of normality or might at least give messages of censure ("You're *bad!*") that are overlaid with implied approval. A culture prone to self-blame (such as the British) might sweepingly blame parents (notably mothers) for children's impulsive behavior, thus implicating family dynamics while ignoring the child's constitutional bent. On the other hand, a culture prone to blaming others (such as the North American) would tend to suspect such things as toxins lurking in food and the general environment and would tend to blame the "system" for children's difficulties.

Finally, a radical body of opinion that deals in the "myth of mental illness" would eagerly discern social oppression behind the label "hyperactivity" and would refuse to recognize the existence of any such condition on the grounds of political belief. This would result in an incidence estimate of zero for that disorder.

Some estimates of hyperactivity incidences are mentioned in Chapter 9. It is important, however, for physicians to divest themselves of any preconceptions about what percentage of schoolchildren "should" be so diagnosed and to treat individual children appropriately, without attempting to defend someone else's guess about how many comparable children exist.

SPECIAL POPULATIONS

LEFTHANDED AND CROSSED-DOMINANT CHILDREN

Many studies claim that there is an unusually high proportion of learning disabled children among the lefthanded, but many other studies disconfirm this. The same applies to crossed dominance. The present situation is best summarized as follows: Among otherwise normal healthy populations, anomalies of handedness and crossed dominance bear no relationship to cognitive deficit [5]. In damaged populations (retarded, cerebrally palsied, epileptic, premature, etc.) the incidence of nonrighthandedness (crossed dominance) may increase; but this fact is by no means a cause of the damage. Rather, the damaging agent will have caused the deficit independently and prompted the deviation from right-hand preference [6].

DELINQUENT CHILDREN

At age 13½ the typical contemporary juvenile delinquent has an estimated IQ of 95, is four times more likely to be male than female, and is three to five years behind academically, especially in reading and spelling. One-third of all delinquents with normal intelligence are said to meet the criteria for learning disability. Indeed, a history of school failure is the single most effective predictor of subsequent delinquency.

The relationships that link school failure to delinquency are complex. On the one hand, a delinquent child may lack the motivation needed or may be too preoccupied with other events to concentrate on schoolwork. But on the other hand, persistent school failure linked to some cognitive power deficit might orient the child toward alternative antisocial routes to success and peer approbation; or poverty and alienation at home might steer the child away from socially approved forms of expression toward socially disapproved ones; or an impulsive temperament might reduce the child's concentration on classroom activities and foster impulsive behavior heedless of long-term consequences. Until we are able to sort out these alternatives, it will remain impossible to achieve a more detailed understanding of the high rate of school failure among delinquents [8].

BILINGUAL CHILDREN

No figures are available on the incidence of learning disability among bilingual children, perhaps because the diagnosis is so difficult to make with confidence if a child is bilingual [7]. One has to document selective academic difficulties in both languages. Even if this proves practicable, one is left wondering whether it would have occurred had the child's mental resources not been divided between two languages. It is usually recommended that a bilingual child be taught and addressed as much as possible in one language, but outcome figures for this expedient are not on record. If they were, they might give some rough guide as to whether a learning disability will manifest itself in the same way regardless of whether a child is monolingual or bilingual.

LEARNING TO READ DIFFERENT LANGUAGES

Languages differ with respect to both the degree of phonetic correspondence between the spoken and written word and the nature of the writing system. Writing systems can be classified into (1) alphabetic systems, in which each character represents a phoneme, (2) syllabic systems, in which each character represents a syllable, and (3) logographic systems, in which each character stands for a morpheme (a unit of meaning).

Countries also differ with respect to the age at which reading instruction commences, the rate of student attrition in the higher grades, the general level of literacy, the excellence of the available teaching, and a variety of other relevant cultural and socioeconomic variables.

What do we know about the effects of these factors upon achievement of literacy by the population as a whole and upon the recognition and prevalence of reading disability within that population?

The traditional Chinese script is logographic, although a phonetic alphabetized script has recently been introduced. Literacy rates in China are relatively low; some have attributed this to the logographic nature of the script, claiming that it burdens the individual with an excessive load of different symbol classes to learn. However, logographs are by no means arbitrary, and related words are related with respect to the symbol's constituents. Interestingly enough, young children seem to find it relatively easy to learn logographic symbols. What is more, they find it easiest to learn the more complex ones. That is because the limitation on immature perceptual systems is the difficulty of discriminating between patterns that are highly similar. The more complex the logograph, the more likely it is to be easily discriminated from others.

Japan provides an interesting test case, in that it possesses logographic, syllabic, and alphabetic scripts. The literacy rate in Japan is very high, and it has been claimed that the incidence of reading disability among the whole population there is less than 0.01 percent. It has been argued that this is due to the syllabic scripts available to Japanese children. In terms of phonetic correspondence, these are relatively easy to learn [9]. (Incidentally, the Cherokee Indians also have a syllabic script, and this might be related to the high level of literacy among its users.) However, it is not possible to disassociate these considerations about writing methods from other cultural factors. For instance, it has been found that Japanese parents are particularly interested and well-informed regarding their children's educational progress, and this might well contribute to the progress made by beginning readers.

Alphabetic scripts vary widely with regard to the exactness of their phonetic correspondence. Some languages, such as Finnish, have virtually perfect phonetic scripts. Others, like English and Danish, have morphophonemic scripts which diverge greatly from exact phonetic correspondence. Possible variations are virtually endless. In Thai words are run together, and in Hebrew and Arabic the vowels are omitted.

The simple idea that the more exact the one-to-one symbol-to-sound correspondence, the easier it is to learn to read the language, is not borne out by literacy statistics. Literacy levels are high in Britain, where correspondence of the script is highly irregular. The use of the initial teaching alphabet, a recently designed script of 48 characters that enables the writer to use exact sound-symbol correspondence for the English language, has not produced any convincing advantage for beginning reading; and it has certainly not done so for more advanced reading, where the structural redundancies of English orthography and its morphophonemic nature appear to be quite useful to the reader.

Appraisal of the implications of literacy rates in different countries must of course be tempered by recognition that the level of teacher training in different countries varies widely. In particular, it has become apparent that teachers in countries that have been studied — countries such as Argentina and France as well as less developed countries — are relatively undertrained compared to teachers in the English-speaking and Scandinavian countries. Also, the level of public interest in and concern about children's reading achievement varies widely. In the Scandinavian countries the interest level is high, and remedial help is readily available. In Sweden and Britain the teaching methods are individualized as much as possible for children who are allowed to proceed at their own rate; while in North America the emphasis is on the curriculum, which is considered generally applicable to children at a given level.

The age of beginning reading varies widely. In Britain it is age five; in the United States, France, Germany, India, Israel, and Japan, age six; and in the Soviet Union, Denmark, Finland, Norway, and Sweden, age seven. Again, little relationship can be established between this variable and literacy rates. After all, these rates are relatively high, both in Britain (where reading instruction begins early) and in Scandinavia (where it begins late).

Large-scale studies of reading comprehension levels in different countries have made it clear that the writing system used is not a significant predictor of these levels. The major predictors are the socioeconomic level of the child's family and the availability in the home of books and other reading materials.

It is hard to derive reliable conclusions from these diverse findings, as the variables that distinguish one country from another are so many and complex. On the whole, one gains the impression that when the developed countries are considered, literacy rates have more to do with attitudes in the home and school—the amount of public attention paid to reading achievement and its remedial supports—than they do with more immediately manipulable factors such as the nature of the writing system (whether logographic, syllabic, or alphabetic), or the degree of sound-to-symbol correspondence within an alphabetic system. One conclusion seems certain: The adoption of a writing system with a strict one-to-one sound-symbol correspondence does not resolve the issue of selective reading disability.

PROFESSIONAL PERSPECTIVES ON LEARNING DISABILITY

Both the incidence of learning disability and the composition of the whole category of learning disabled children seem different to professionals from different relevant disciplines. This is true for both subjective and objective reasons. One's profession subtly attunes one's expectations, so that different professionals are differentially sensitive to different aspects of children's problems. Also, one's profession has a powerful biasing effect on the type of child one most commonly sees. Unless one is aware of these influences, one can become quite bewildered by the contrasting accounts of learning disability and hyperactivity prevailing in different professions.

PEDIATRICIANS AND FAMILY PHYSICIANS

The majority of children with school problems will experience moderately severe selective academic failure or impulsive cognitive style problems, usually before matters are severely complicated by emotional disorder. Most of these children will be within or close to the normal range of intelligence, and there will be a heavy emphasis on reading and writing problems. Examining physicians, except for cerebral palsy specialists, generally find the proportion of soft neurological signs to be moderate and that of hard signs to be low. Overall, physicians tend to gain an impression of disease entities discontinuous from the normal range and are somewhat impressed by concomitants suggestive of brain damage; therefore, they are moderately attracted to the seductive concept of "minimal brain dysfunction" (MBD).

CHILD NEUROLOGISTS

These subspecialists see a higher proportion of intractable cases, with a somewhat higher average age and a much higher incidence of neurologically abnormal signs. This is partly because child neurologists are more thorough in checking those signs and partly because children with such signs are preferentially channeled to child neurologists. Particularly if they read their own patients' EEGs, they will be impressed by the high incidence of nonspecific abnormality in the electroencephalographic tracings. They will tend to be more impressed by the frequency of hyperactivity and less by the frequency of selective learning disability than will the pediatric generalist.

CHILD PSYCHIATRISTS

These subspecialists see mostly children with severely complicating behavior disorders and disturbed family dynamics. In looking into personal and family histories, they will usually find it possible to uncover events that could have generated the learning problem as a secondary effect. They are particularly likely to see aggressive acting-out hyperactives; withdrawn, compulsive, and overactive borderline children who respond adversely to stimulants; and older children with selective academic failure who have become thoroughly dispirited and emotionally disturbed. Many of their patients will already have passed through the hands of pediatricians and neurologists, without apparent benefit.

CLINICAL PSYCHOLOGISTS

These professionals see children referred to them by physicians and others for mental and other testing. They will be impressed by the incidence of selective academic difficulty in normally intelligent children and by children whose inattentiveness is manifest during testing. They will be little impressed by the organic aspects of the cases, unless they go in for neuropsychological (Reitan) battery testing.

SCHOOL OR EDUCATIONAL PSYCHOLOGISTS AND SPECIAL EDUCATORS

These professionals do not think in terms of pathological entities, but rather in terms of extremes along a continuum of school performance and classroom behavior. To them, organic hypotheses will have low priority and social deprivation will frequently complicate the picture. They will be more aware than others that selective difficulties may be experienced in subjects other than reading and writing, and so will have little regard for the exclusivity of the "dyslexia" concept. There will be wide differences of opinion among them as to whether failing children should be kept within educational settings and protected from medical "interference" or whether most failing children should "have a neurological examination."

SPEECH PATHOLOGISTS
These professionals are impressed by the general language disability that is often in the background of reading and writing problems, and are apt to think in terms of both traditional speech therapy and language enrichment.

PHYSICAL AND OCCUPATIONAL THERAPISTS
These professionals see a very high proportion of children who have associated motor deficits or immaturities. This makes them susceptible to "neurologizing" hypotheses that confound motor and cognitive levels of organization. Like neurologists, they are often under the spell of "MBD."

CLASSROOM TEACHERS
Teachers often doubt the reality of learning disability and hyperactivity until clear-cut instances occur in their own classrooms. They then become quite open-minded on these issues.

OVERALL ESTIMATES
Subject to all the qualifications implicit in the discussions in this chapter, we can now quote some prevalent figures that have been offered. These tend to run at 15 percent of children in the schools [10] (representing some eight million children in the United States). Similar estimates apply to Canada, Denmark, France, and Great Britain.

REFERENCES
1. Caplan, P. J.   Beyond the box score. A boundary condition for sex differences in aggression and achievement striving. *Prog. Exp. Pers. Res.* In press, 1978.
2. Caplan, P. J.   Helping parents help their children. *Bull. Orton Soc.* 26:108–123, 1976.
3. Caplan, P. J.   Sex, age, behavior and school subjects as determinants of report of learning problems. *J. Learn. Disabil.* 10:314–316, 1977.
4. Caplan, P. J., and Kinsbourne, M.   Sex differences in response to school failure. *J. Learn. Disabil.* 7:232–235, 1974.
5. Hardyck, C., and Petrinovich, L. F.   Left-handedness. *Psychol. Bull.* 84: 385–404, 1977.

6. Hicks, R. E., and Kinsbourne, M.   Handedness Differences: Left Hand-edness. In M. Kinsbourne (Ed.), *The Asymmetrical Function of the Brain.* New York: Cambridge University Press, 1978.
7. McLaughlin, B.   Second-language learning in children. *Psychol. Bull.* 84:438–459, 1977.
8. Poremba, C. D. Learning Disabilities, Youth and Delinquency: Pro-grams for Intervention. In H. R. Myklebust (Ed.), *Progress in Learning Disabilities.* Vol. 3. New York: Grune & Stratton, 1975. Pp. 123–149.
9. Rozin, P., Poritsky, S., and Sotsky, P.   American children with reading problems can easily learn to read English represented by Chinese char-acters. *Science* 171:1264–1267, 1971.

SUGGESTED READING

Eisenberg, L.   The Epidemiology of Reading Retardation and a Program for Preventive Intervention. In J. Money (Ed.), *The Disabled Reader.* Baltimore: Johns Hopkins Press, 1966. Pp. 3–19.
Gibson, E. J. & Levin, H.   *The Psychology of Reading.* Cambridge, Mass.: M.I.T. Press, 1969.

II. Cognitive Power Disorders

3. Differential Diagnosis and Descriptions

COGNITIVE DISORDER OR UNDERACHIEVEMENT?

When normally intelligent children perform poorly in one or more school subjects, either they are not performing up to their potential (underachievement), or their potential for specific forms of learning is abnormally limited (cognitive disorder). Underachievement can have environmental or emotional causes (see Table 2). Cognitive disorder, as discussed in the section that follows, may relate to either cognitive power or cognitive style problems.

"Underachievement" is variously defined. We use this term to describe children's failure to work up to their intellectual potential (the potential that they would realize through full use of their brain-based cognitive powers). That this underachievement cannot be judged on the basis of age alone is shown by the phenomenon of mental retardation. Retarded children do not underachieve if they achieve at a level that approximately corresponds to their mental age. But because learning disabilities exist, this potential cannot simply be measured in accord with a child's chronological age—or even mental age, as indicated by performance on a standard intelligence test. Because of learning disability a child of superior intelligence may perform very poorly in academic subjects and yet not be underachieving. This is because a high level of general intelligence is not a sufficient foundation for scholastic success. Rather, the child needs the specific readiness functions called for by the instructional process. If the child does not have these available, then the failure cannot be regarded as underachievement, since the child was failing because of a limited potential, rather than because of nonrealization of a higher potential.

Putting it another way, underachieving children would achieve normally if they applied themselves to their work with customary diligence. The learning disabled child would not achieve normally under such circumstances; this child would have to try much harder and work longer hours to achieve comparable success. Underachieving children do not use their learning abilities to full advantage. This is because they are undermotivated, preoccupied, inadequately taught, or unable to communicate in the classroom (Table 2).

Children who come from foreign cultural backgrounds are apt to feel themselves in an unfamiliar situation in the classroom and to feel subjected to unintelligible demands. They may think, fatalis-

Table 2. Causes of Underachievement

Emotional		Environmental	
Preoccupation	Undermotivation	Inadequate Schooling	Poor Communication
Fear	Cultural alienation	Poor teaching	Poor socialization
Anxiety	Poverty	Crowded classroom	Foreign language
Depression	Debility	School absence	
Thought disorder		Frequent switching of schools	

tically, that the opportunities for which schooling is supposed to prepare children are foreclosed to them; so they may see little point in making an effort. Children from impoverished homes may also be pessimistic or cynical about their long-term outlook, regardless of school achievement. Culturally alienated and impoverished children may have anti-intellectual biases that tell them book-learning is at best irrelevant, at worst oppressive or demeaning. Poor children may be hungry, which naturally makes it hard to think about what is happening in the classroom. Children who have debilitating diseases, such as chronic anemia or worm infestations, may feel too tired to try hard. And children who are chronically anxious, continually sad and depressed, or preoccupied with psychotic thoughts, may have little attention to spare for schoolwork.

In addition, unskilled or listless teaching and crowded classrooms leave children uninstructed. The same is true if children are often absent on account of truancy or illness, or if their families relocate frequently (as often happens with poor, military, and executive families).

Moreover, children who are unsocialized because of poor parental guidance or neglect may lack the ability to adapt to classroom situations. And children from immigrant families may not know English well enough to understand what is said in class.

The first step in diagnosing a cognitive disorder is to exclude the various causes of underachievement. This is not always easy. Also, it is possible for a cognitive disorder and undermotivation to coexist. It can then be difficult to determine how much trouble is due to each. And sometimes one can only discover the existence of a cognitive disorder once the underachievement has been corrected.

The pediatric history and examination will screen for deafness, visual failure, motor deficits, and chronic debilitating disease. Thorough history-taking will elicit evidence of cultural and economic disadvantage. An encounter with the parents and child will reveal any bilingualism and may offer clues to parental incompetence or neglect (which may be corroborated by evidence from social agencies). Evidence from the parents and school reports may uncover inadequate schooling. Finally, steps should be taken to rule out possible child abuse and neglect in the course of a pediatric workup.

The second step in diagnosing a cognitive disorder is to show that the pattern of school failure is inconsistent with patterns of underachievement. In underachievement, failure may be widespread as compared to failure due to cognitive disorder. But there is one proviso. That is, that even when the failure is caused by underachievement, the failure may be more dramatic in some subjects than in others. Anxiety or depression, for example, often interfere disproportionately with arithmetic, as compared to reading performance. In addition, since even normal children have strengths and weaknesses in the abilities required at school, any source of stress or difficulty may increase the disparity between achievement in areas of strength and achievement in areas of weakness, affecting the latter more than the former. Teachers' evaluations of children's progress will generally correspond closely to the results of achievement tests. In contrast, the failure of a child with a cognitive power disorder is selective. In cognitive style disorders, although failure is more widespread than in cognitive power disorders, the degree of failure is more variable from time to time and depends more on whether the estimate is made by the classroom teacher or is based on achievement testing. Achievement test scores, though themselves variable, tend to be higher than the teacher's evaluations of the child's fund of knowledge.

Cognitive deficits are developmental and therefore long-lasting. Nearly all affected children will show some evidence of the difficulty on first entering school, and in many cases the problem will persist for years. If school failure first appears in late grade-school or high-school, and if diligent inquiry fails to reveal any evidence of a learning problem in the earlier grades, then there is reason to doubt a diagnosis of cognitive power or style disorder.

IS THE DISORDER ONE OF COGNITIVE POWER OR COGNITIVE STYLE?

The more selective the area of school failure, the more likely it is to stem from a cognitive power disorder (Table 3). If only one subject is involved — like reading and writing or arithmetic — a cognitive power disorder is particularly likely. But, particularly in older children, a more widespread failure could also have arisen from a cognitive power disorder affecting reading. This is because reading becomes

Table 3. Some Basic Behavior Features of Children with Cognitive Style and Cognitive Power Disorders

		Cognitive Style Disorder	
	Cognitive Power Disorder	Underfocused	Overfocused
Academic area involved	Specific	Widespread	Widespread
Degree of deficit	Constant in short term	Variable from test to test	Variable from test to test
Achievement test vs. teacher's report	Congruent	Incongruent	Incongruent
Child's apparent effort	Initially high	Low	High
Assignments	Completed	Not completed	Completed
Attention seeking	Average, initially	Great	Little
Discipline problem	Not initially	Present throughout	Not recognized
Effect of stimulant drugs	None	Positive	Negative

increasingly crucial for learning virtually all subjects, and also because protracted reading failure leaves a child dispirited and unprepared to make an effort in any school subject.

A child who is academically backward must have ceased to understand the subject at a definable point in the curriculum. In order to understand the material from there on, the child needs additional detailed explanations. Explanations take time, however, and the child's achievement test level will change little in the short run.

Children with cognitive style disorders differ from others in that their deviant learning style depends more on the situation, so that achievement test results may differ greatly from sampling to sampling. In general impulsive, underfocused children do better under the stress of achievement testing by a formidable stranger than in the familiar classroom setting. The opposite holds for cautious, overfocused children. So for these types of children it is harder to define what they do and do not know.

Until children with cognitive power deficits become resigned to inevitable failure, they usually try hard. Overfocused children also try hard. But impulsive and underfocused children are sloppy and facile in their work. While children with cognitive power deficits labor over their homework, as do overfocused children, impulsive children rarely complete an assignment except under continual direct threats from their parents. Children with cognitive power problems seek the attention they need. Underfocused children seek attention excessively, and overfocused children often go it alone, even when the teacher's attention is needed. Cognitive power deficits lead to disciplinary problems only after protracted failure, whereas intractibility to discipline is a primary characteristic of the underfocused child from the start. The overfocused child perseveres quietly, and this is seen as a disciplinary problem only by a teacher who likes to exert unusually tight control over the timing and direction of the pupils' classroom efforts.

Stimulant drugs prolong concentration on a single issue. Therefore, they help the underfocused child maintain a focus; but they have little effect on cognitive power problems that do not depend on maintaining attention; and they aggravate the overfocusing of the overfocused child.

Cognitive power disorders and cognitive style disorders may occasionally coexist. This confusing picture becomes clearer when drug treatment eliminates the style problem. The residual learning difficulties result from the coexisting cognitive power problem.

If, according to the above criteria, a child's problem falls into the cognitive power category, this still leaves us with a choice among the various subtypes in this category. These subtypes are discussed below.

TYPOLOGY OF COGNITIVE POWER DISORDERS
Cognitive power disorders have been classified according to their etiology, specificity, and pattern of cognitive deficit.

ETIOLOGY
A distinction has been made between *constitutional dyslexia* [2], a hereditary cognitive deficit selective for reading, and *minimal brain dysfunction*, a scattering of neurological insufficiencies attributed to early brain damage that may affect the development of reading skills. The distinction depends on finding a family history positive for dyslexia, but no history of early brain damage—or on finding a history of early brain damage but no family tendency toward dyslexia. It is hard to know what to think when family dyslexia and evidence of early brain damage coexist, or when there is no evidence for either. Also, a high incidence of family dyslexia is hard to confirm retrospectively; there are many reasons for reading problems, and one does not really know why a parent might have had such a problem many years ago. Also, no one knows how severe a history of prenatal or perinatal adversity is required to make brain damage credible as a cause of selective cognitive deficit. Thus, diagnosis based on etiology can never be better than speculative; and since such diagnosis is of no help in choosing among treatment options, it is useless in practice.

SPECIFICITY

The dichotomy between specificity and minimal brain dysfunction (MBD) overlaps the previous one. Is the deficit specific to reading, or are there also associated deficiencies caused by MBD? Here again the implication is that an isolated deficit is genetic, while a deficit cluster is the result of brain damage. This argument cannot be sustained. A limited brain lesion might well implicate only a very narrow band of the cognitive spectrum. Also, the more one examines "isolated" cases, the more one finds additional deficits. Conversely, in a case with scattered neurological and behavioral findings, genetic deficits and brain damage deficits might coincide. Finally, as in the etiological argument, the distinction has no implications for management and is therefore useless.

PATTERN OF COGNITIVE DEFICIT

Far-reaching patterns of cognitive deficit have been distinguished, either on the basis of findings extraneous to reading itself or else in relation to reading quality.

Patterns extraneous to reading

As will be described in detail in Chapter 4, the Wechsler Intelligence Scale for Children (WISC) contains two sets of subtests: those that constitute the "verbal" subscale and those that constitute the "performance" subscale. A separate IQ can be calculated for each subscale. In some children with selective reading disability there is a substantial discrepancy between the verbal IQ and the performance IQ. Often the verbal IQ is relatively low. This implies that the child is suffering from a delayed language development not limited to reading and writing. A few children show an opposite discrepancy—a verbal IQ that is high relative to the performance IQ. Such children may perhaps experience maximal difficulty with some visuo-motor ingredient of reading and writing rather than with specifically linguistic ingredients. Defective ability in learning to read would be the common end product of both types of deficits in prereading skills.

The distinction just described is most convincing when the disparity between verbal and performance IQs is profound. Discrepancies of 25 points or more seem impressive (although they occur quite often, even among people who have no school problems). Lesser discrepancies are ambiguous. In particular, children who are unable to read would be expected to accumulate verbal information relatively slowly, because much of this information is normally obtained through the written word. For this reason alone, they might show a moderate verbal IQ deficit. Or a child may have a relatively low performance IQ because of clumsiness or for other reasons unconnected with reading. Finally, and most puzzling of all, the two IQ test scores being weighed against each other are both usually within the normal range. Yet these normal scores are used to clarify the nature of abnormal academic performance. Thus, a causal relationship between an unusual WISC profile and school problems cannot be assumed. Experience shows that even some mentally subnormal children (with IQs below 75) learn to read quite well.

How, then, do we account for the role of *relatively low* verbal IQ in a clinical picture where, for instance, a child with a performance IQ of 115 and a verbal IQ of 85 has trouble learning to read? One has to argue that the IQ test is like a loosely woven net. Each actual IQ test gives only a hint of the *specific* problem existing within the verbal or performance sphere. This specific problem pulls one IQ subscale down somewhat. But if only we knew exactly how to construct a test for the specific problem, we would find that the child would score very poorly indeed on *that* test.

In summary, verbal-performance discrepancies are circumstantial evidence. They become meaningful only in the context of associated findings that have similar implications — that is, as parts of syndromes. Such associated findings are discussed later in this chapter.

Besides identifying a verbal-performance discrepancy, one can specify the individual subtests that show the most deficit. A characteristic dichotomy exists between children who show deficits on heavily verbal subtests and those who show deficits on the arithmetic subtest, block design, and object assembly [5]. In the context of correlated findings, discussed later, this becomes a meaningful distinction. At best, however, the classification by psychometric profile casts light on only a proportion of the cases of selective delay in reading. Many such children just do not show recognizable profiles on Wechsler or other IQ tests.

Reading and writing patterns
Here we may distinguish between those children who have only a writing problem, due to problems of visuo-motor control (i.e., the ability to guide one's movements according to a visual plan), and those children whose difficulties involve both reading and writing. Among the latter, two plausible dichotomies have been suggested.

One of these dichotomies focuses attention on the locus of maximal educational difficulty. The question asked is whether the difficulty centers around word recognition or around paragraph comprehension. In one study of backward readers, two groups were identified: a majority with word recognition difficulty and a minority with reading comprehension difficulty [6]. The distinction depended on the children's ability to understand printed material as compared to material read aloud to them.

The children with word recognition problems had no difficulty comprehending the material read aloud, but both their word recognition and reading comprehension of printed material were impaired. Their difficulties were not purely with respect to deriving meaning from words. They also had difficulty with repetition of meaningless auditory sequences and associations, and they had lower verbal than performance subscale scores on the WISC. Their difficulty probably involved the decoding (visual to auditory) stage of beginning reading, to which a poor auditory rote memory was related in some way.

In contrast, the children who had a problem with oral comprehension had normal WISC profiles. Their comprehension problem was at the syntactic and semantic level. Their memory problem was not with meaningless but with meaningful materials. Like aphasic adults, they were unable to use the syntax and meaning of the language to enhance their recollection of sentences and word clusters. Interestingly, these children showed no impairment on vocabulary tests, thereby demonstrating that these different linguistic components—word and sentence comprehension—are dissociable. They must, therefore, be separately represented in the brain.

The word recognition problems are no doubt heterogeneous and could arise from either perception or association problems. The paragraph comprehension difficulties (using words whose sounds are known to the child) involve both written and spoken words; they thus relate to a problem of language use that cuts across both visual and auditory modalities.

Another dichotomy arises from analysis of children's reading performance. It distinguishes between the child with relatively good sight vocabulary but poor word attack skills (i.e., good ability to recognize words quickly but poor ability to decode words) and the child with limited sight vocabulary but good word attack skills, who can decode many more words, if given time to do so, using a systematic phonics approach [1]. The first type of child supposedly has a weakness in visual prereading skill, the second in auditory prereading skill. A third type of child has both deficits. Even if these dichotomies have validity, we do not know the extent to which they are interdependent. The problem involved here becomes evident when we consider the two syndromes described in the following section.

Other patterns related to reading and writing
One pattern of this type can be called the "language syndrome." It
involves the following: a history of slow language development, a
relatively low Wechsler verbal IQ, impaired comprehension of
spoken speech (as measured by the Token Test, which samples
children's ability to carry out spoken instruction graduated in difficulty), and spelling errors mainly of the substitution type (using
letters that do not belong in the word at all, and that do not even
sound as if they should — in the manner of aphasic adults) [5].

Does a child with this syndrome have particular difficulty with
phonics and therefore lack word attack skills? Does this child do as
poorly in oral comprehension as in reading comprehension? No
information is available about this.

Another pattern in this category is the "Gerstmann syndrome."
Children affected by it have a sequencing problem. They show the
arithmetic, block design, and object assembly subtest deficit profile previously mentioned. They also have difficulty with finger
identification and right-left discrimination. In spelling they make
mostly order errors; in arithmetic they confuse the place value of
the digits [5]. Do children with this syndrome have other visuo-
spatial difficulties? Do they have trouble with drawing and design
as well as with reading? Are they the ones whose powers to visualize are in question? Are they resistant to a whole-word approach
to instruction? Again, we do not know [2].

Whereas the foregoing seek to classify children in terms of differences among them, another approach stresses differences
within a given child at different ages and developmental stages [9].
This point of view, which incriminates a general relative immaturity of the left cerebral hemisphere, hypothesizes incomplete readiness at a given age for the level of reading instruction customary
at that age. In beginning reading, perceptual-motor skills are at a
premium, and immaturity in these could account for a disabled
child's difficulty at that early stage. Some years later (perhaps
some years too late) the same child could be expected to acquire
these perceptual-motor skills, but would still be relatively delayed
with respect to peers in the more complex mental operations called
for by the nature of reading instruction in more advanced grades
(perhaps more frankly linguistic considerations). Thus, the pattern
of deficits of learning disabled children will differ according to
their age, rather than according to the particular child being studied.

Attempting to integrate these disease classifications, we arrive at
a provisional statement. This is certain to be superceded in time,
but it does represent the level of our current understanding of the

typology of cognitive power disorders relevant to reading. The statement is as follows:

Reading and writing acquisition may be compromised by unduly slow development of:

1. The ability to comprehend spoken (and in turn written) language, with difficulty in spoken naming and word-finding [3, 5, 6]
2. The ability to decompose word sounds into speech sounds and reconstitute them from speech sounds (affected children also tend to make mistakes in the sequence of speech sounds when pronouncing words aloud) [1]
3. The ability to learn to spell accurately words that can be read, which may be a residual deficit after item 2 has improved [8]
4. The ability to form letters into words skillfully, neatly, and intelligibly, which may be associated with problems in articulating spoken speech [7]
5. The ability to remember letter sequences in words on a visual basis, in association with other elements of the Gerstmann syndrome [5]

Any attempt to set up a typology of cognitive power deficits that applies the same battery of tests to all children must fail. One cannot avoid detailed analysis of each individual case to determine the basic mechanism of difficulty involved. If numerous individual analyses of this sort turn out to have a family resemblance, well and good. But we are not entitled to expect this necessarily. Reading and writing result from a complex but precise interweaving of many mental operations, every one or any combination of which is presumably vulnerable to adverse influences and capable of yielding a deficit. It must therefore be expected that instead of coming to conceive of constitutional and developmental dyslexia as a unitary entity, we will ultimately acquire a rich typology of reading disability variants. The form such a typology is likely to take can be inferred from the nature of normal mental development. Adopting the view that any child with a selective reading deficit is functioning like a younger normal child with respect to some relevant mental operation, we will in the next section consider the various reasons why preschool children find it hard to learn to read.

SELECTIVE READING DISABILITIES

Reading instruction is cumulative. Each successive phase draws upon an increasingly varied and sophisticated repertoire of mental skills. The teacher introduces new concepts when the child becomes mentally ready to handle them. Then, each new skill is practiced until the child can exercise it effortlessly. But, at any stage, a child may prove to be selectively immature in some mental operation that is necessary for progress to the next level of instruction. This is *selective reading unreadiness*. Although some unreadiness could appear for the first time at any stage of learning to read, the same children will usually exhibit unreadiness at successive levels. In other words, they will act as if they belonged to a younger stream of children when they go through the successive stages of reading instruction.

What are the readiness skills necessary for beginning reading? When we ask children to learn to read, we are asking them to do quite new things that were not required in the preschool period. Therefore, the way they handled mental challenges in preschool may not indicate how they will begin to learn to read. In order to learn to read, the child must be able to think in a way best called the *analytic* manner. Learning spoken language and learning written language are both language learning, and superficially the only difference is that one is based exclusively on sound, while the other also involves sight. But learning to speak and learning to read are very different from each other. An infant learning a spoken language is surrounded by it, can hardly avoid hearing it. The sentences at first are unintelligible to the baby; but no one, including the baby, worries about this. Then the infant begins to notice recurrent words or phrases, and they begin to make sense. Not much selective attention is needed to pick up individual words when one keeps hearing them. Also, spoken language is sequential. In contrast to things seen, which generate many stimuli competing simultaneously for attention, things heard tend to happen one at a time. Selection is then unnecessary. So, in a natural environment the beginnings of oral language come easily. It is quite another matter with respect to the finer, more abstract auditory and visual distinctions that are demanded by the processes of reading and writing [4].

VISUAL ATTENTION

Three or four months after birth, infants can see as well as adults. By then they can discriminate different colors, have a visual acuity comparable to that of the adult, and can focus at will on things near and far. They see what adults see. But they do not *look* at what they see the way adults do.

The adult is highly sophisticated in selective looking. This is necessary, because in almost all natural environments an overwhelming richness of visual impressions crowds in upon the eye. Their ability enables adults to attend selectively to any part of their surroundings. They can scan with shallow, wide-ranging attention over a wide expanse, or they can focus their attention sharply to take in some inconspicuous detail. Ignoring eye-catching, salient stimuli, they can pick out and consider nuances of location, relation, and texture. These are visual features that readily escape the attention of young children.

Adults can attend selectively not only to gross and obvious features but also to categorical details and even to relationships between visual features. Surveying a crowd, the motion picture talent scout looks for one set of characteristics, the vice squad undercover agent perceives another, and the lecturer anxious to make a good impression notices yet a third. For instance, while perhaps remaining oblivious to the colorful attire and personal attractiveness of many people in the audience, the lecturer instantly detects the slight billowing of the cheeks in a suppressed yawn, the slanting downward gaze directed at a hidden newspaper, or the involuntary drooping of the eyelids that suggests the lecture has continued long enough. To the skillful lecturer such features seem to stand out automatically from the complex scene observed. That is because they are picked out by a highly practiced, and therefore quite automatic and unconscious process.

Young children confronted with a similar scene cannot distribute their attention in such expert fashion. They may be as occupied by an irrelevant visual feature (such as a stain on the floor or a gaudy garment) as by whatever they really need to perceive. This is not to suggest that young children's attention ranges indifferently and randomly across all visual attributes everywhere. Rather, their attention is readily trapped by certain visual attributes which they notice to the exclusion of all others. These visual attributes are described as being high in the *perceptual hierarchy*. The term perceptual hierarchy is used to indicate the fact that for biological reasons one tends to attend preferentially to certain sensory attributes rather than to others. In vision, the dimensions of form and color are highest on this hierarchy. Size, location, orientation, sequence, and texture are relatively nonsalient and likely to be overlooked by immature observers, who remain engrossed in the striking forms and colors that confront them. As mental development proceeds it becomes easier to detach attention from salient visual attributes if these happen not to be what the observer is looking for. Adults can shift the focus of their attention down the perceptual hierarchy until they arrive at a critical visual feature that enables them to decide what to do next. Thus, the ability to detach and redirect attention accompanies brain maturation. What exactly is attended to is determined by experience.

Since young children's attention depends on salience, when they look at things they use strategies that are inefficient. Three reasons for this have been documented. The way young children inspect things is *incomplete:* Their gaze is arrested by eye-catching features, so they ignore other parts of the display. It is also *redundant:* Certain features are repeatedly inspected although they were understood at first glance. And it is *unsystematic:* Attention flits from salient feature to salient feature without consistent direction or any other organization. For all of these reasons the rate at which young children gather information is limited and varies from one viewing to the next.

A young child distributes attention very differently from an adult. In one study young children were asked to compare two simple sketches of the front of a house and to judge them "the same" or "different [10]." The children often judged houses that were in fact different to be the same, and vice versa. By recording their eye movements (and thereby discovering what they looked at) it was found that they sometimes looked at two different houses so incompletely that they only noticed those portions that happened to be similar, and on this incomplete information judged the houses to be exactly alike. At other times they only looked at different parts of two sketches (e.g., the roof of one, the door of another) that were in fact identical, and because they had looked from different directions at different parts, they judged them to be different. This is hard for adults to grasp, because when they look at such pictures they have the impression of seeing the whole display simultaneously and cannot imagine making such a mistake. Yet for children to do this is quite normal.

A still more striking example comes from one of our own studies. Children four to six years of age were asked to compare two adjacent straight lines for length. When the lines were on the same level and parallel, the children found it easy to judge them "the same." But when one line was moved slightly upward on the page (although not changed in length), most children judged the line further up the page to be longer than the other. Subsequent studies revealed that this was because young children base their judgments on information obtained from only one end of the two-line display; namely, the end further away from the eye. At this end one line sticks out more than the other. Based on this partial information (uncorrected by looking at the other end of the display, where there is an equal and opposite displacement of the other line) the child judges one of the two lines to be longer. An adult can hardly imagine looking at something so simple without clearly observing both ends of it almost instantaneously.

This makes it easier to conceive why children might notice only some words on a page, some letters in a word, or some part of an individual letter, thereby making otherwise inexplicable mistakes in reading (and in remembering letter names, letter shapes, and letter groupings for purposes of writing). Once this is recognized, however, the remedy becomes obvious. The instructor provides the children with the structure that they cannot provide for themselves. Thus, focusing children's attention on critically important features and removing possible distractions constitute the foundations of effective remedial education at the beginning reading level.

One type of reading and writing error that has achieved considerable notoriety is the reversal of a letter or a word. That is peculiar, because of all mistakes, the reversal is the least specific as an indicator of the type of difficulty the child is experiencing. The kinds of reversals made by children with reading and writing difficulty are exactly the same as those that most normal children make when they try to learn reading or writing at a younger (preschool) age. An average, normal 3-, 4-, or 5-year-old will reverse in copying and will remember things the wrong way around. People who wish that children were adults and who teach reading too soon come across these same reversals.

Why do normal children make reversals, and why do reversals persist unduly in some children? It is not because a child sees letters in some different way than an adult, because then the copy would also be seen in a different way, and there would be no difference between the copy and the model. Rather, the child does not know that it matters which way the shape is turned. The child is bewildered by the fact that the adults who designed our script were short of shapes, and so they used orientation to distinguish between some letters. They were so short of shapes, in fact, that they used the same form four times — for lowercase *b*, *d*, *p*, and *q*. As for other letters with unique shapes, it is adult pedantry to insist on writing a letter a certain way around; most letters are clearly identifiable, regardless of which way they are turned.

The notion that a thing's identity depends on its orientation is something children unlearned when quite young in learning about "object constancy." Whichever way mother is turned, she is still mother. From whatever angle they see their bottle, it is a bottle. Then suddenly they find that object constancy is *not* true of letters. For some reason, the older child is less surprised by this than the younger child and finds it less difficult to focus attention on orientation. Thus older children can copy simple shapes directly without making reversals. But if you ask older children to *remember* a letter shape *and* which way it is pointing, then you find that remembering a shape and remembering its orientation are separate items of mental accomplishment. The child can remember one and forget the other (as you may recall the shape of a cup but not which way it was turned).

In terms of the perceptual hierarchy, not only children but also animals give shape precedence over orientation. When mental energies are engaged in remembering, the big push is to remember the form; the orientation tends to be overlooked. The incidence of reversal errors increases with the difficulty of the word a child is trying to remember. The child may correctly orient a single letter by itself but get the orientation of that letter wrong when trying to write it in spelling a hard word. The child is trying to remember "What were those letters?" not "Which way around were they?" Basically, reversals within a word are a sign that the child is finding it hard to remember how to write the word.

The *pattern* of reversals is constant. Our data for children four through eight years old show that by far the most common errors are mirror-image reversals (∟ ⌐). Next come inversions (⌐ L), then inverted reversals (⌐ L), and last rotations (⌐ ⌐). There is something basic about this hierarchy of errors. It holds for rats learning to choose between shapes in order to get a reward, and it holds for normal adults when they are briefly shown more of these shapes at once than they can handle.

When you try to remember which way a form points (as with the letters b, d, p, and q), you unconsciously make a series of binary decisions. First, is it upright or sideways? Second, if upright, is the knob at the top or bottom? Or if sideways, is the knob at the right or left? Third, if upright with the knob at the top, then is the knob to the right or left? If sideways with the knob at the left, is the knob up or down? and so forth. There are clearly three successive decisions, of which the later ones are the most apt to get lost under pressure. This is why simple mirror-image reversal (failure of the third decision) is the most common. In Chapter 7, we shall discuss a simple way to teach children not to make reversals.

We have used a specially designed readiness test to evaluate the visual attention skills of children entering first grade. The children are shown arbitrary ("nonsense") shapes on cards and, in six separate subtests, are asked the following:

1. To tell two shapes apart
2. To remember the difference between those shapes
3. To tell the difference between two identical shapes that point different ways
4. To remember the difference in item 3
5. To tell one sequence of shapes from another
6. To remember the difference in item 5

In essence, the children are asked to discriminate between the shapes on the cards and to remember their form, orientation, and sequence. We have found no child who was unable to tell two of these shapes apart when shown them either simultaneously or successively. But some had trouble when the shapes were shown as part of two pairs (one member of one pair differing from one member of the other). These latter children had looked incompletely and had missed the crucial distinction—a problem not of discrimination but of attention (as when children failed to accurately compare two pictures of houses—see page 57). With respect to orientation, the children generally had difficulty only with the hardest (mirror-image) distinction. This problem was especially apt to arise when the matching was successive rather than simultaneous. Sequences were the hardest to handle, especially sets of three items. Most of the children overlooked differences in sequential position of the shapes on some of the cards.

Under some circumstances even a limited amount of information is sufficient for practical purposes, and so these immature ways of looking at things are no great handicap. Thus, differences among most solid objects are very overdetermined. Even incomplete, redundant, and unsystematic looking will enable children to distinguish and remember differences between most animals of different species, say, or between household utensils. This, however, is not true of letters and the written word. Minor differences along non-salient perceptual dimensions, such as the orientation of a letter or the relative positions of two letters in a sequence, may yield completely different meanings (b, d; on, no).

MEMORY

To notice critical distinctions calls for a finely adjusted analytical use of attention, and to remember these distinctions requires, in addition, a systematic and unvarying strategy of looking. This is because of the way that repeated exposure to the same information allows it to be learned. In order to recall an item of information after only one experience, one has to conjure up in the imagination major aspects of the situation (an episode) in which the item was initially introduced. So when first learning something, it is usually helpful to remember the context in which it was heard or read. One remembers the room, the lighting, the time of day, attributes of the teacher, the mood, and related mental associations. The next time the information is presented and then remembered, it may again be necessary to remember some of the context, but not as much, and the answer is apt to be more correct and to come more quickly. As the experience is repeated in different situations the contexts cancel each other out, and it is possible to recall the specific item of information without recalling these contexts. So, for instance, one ultimately knows the alphabet fluently but forgets when, where, and how one learned it.

This development of fluency relies on repeated exposure to information that was perceived in the same way each time. If a person's inspection strategies are immature, the person will notice different things about a display each time it appears. In such a case, the growth of familiarity and the decline in the need to recall the whole learning context will be very slow.

When children are repeatedly shown the same information but treat it as new each time, it is reasonable to suppose that they are unsystematically varying their inspection strategies from viewing to viewing. A teacher may show a child the word "car" five times, saying the word each time; but a very young child, or an older child with immature inspection strategies, may notice the *a* one time, the *c* another time, the *r* another, the *ca* another, and the *ar* yet another. The child will seem to have seen five different words.

It is not useful to try to distinguish between short-term and long-term memory. Information will commonly be treated in one of two ways—it will be paid attention to or ignored. What we attend to and what occupies our present awareness may be some aspect of our environment, or it may be an internally generated recollection. When attention shifts to something else, this initial information leaves the sphere of awareness. Remembering is the process of reexperiencing information from which attention had previously been withdrawn. The process of restoring this information to our awareness does not differ in principle for information that has remained unattended to for seconds or for years. Of course, the way in which it is restored to awareness by contextual reconstruction will differ in detail, because when we try to recall information after a short interval we are likely to still be in the context (room, mood, etc.) in which it was first learned; but after a long time we are likely to be in a very different context. So the contextual reconstruction becomes more difficult and fallible for remembering events of long ago.

One generally remembers best that which was experienced most frequently and paid attention to most effectively. Paying effective attention, of course, means attending to those aspects of the experience that best differentiate it from other comparable experiences. Further thoughts and associations that might accompany the experience could make it still more distinctive or even unique. Thus, both the efficiency of experiencing and the richness of what one thinks about the experience contribute toward making it memorable. These processes are largely under one's control. A degree of informed interest and curiosity is a necessary condition for remembering, and people best remember what most interests them. In fact, when people who supposedly have a good memory think about it, they realize that their memory is not universally but only selectively good; it is good for those things that they care about. It follows that one cannot regard memory as a separate process; nor is there any point in trying to think up memory exercises. The only way in which a teacher can improve a child's memory for any kind of material is by working to improve the way the child experiences the material in the first place.

The *amount* remembered also depends on how the event was experienced and the situation at the time of remembering. The more similar the context when trying to remember and the context at the time of learning, the easier it is to fill in the differences and so remember the desired episode or information. If the context for remembering is thoroughly different from that of the initial experience, the individual has to stop paying attention to the present and use imagination to reexperience the past. Detaching attention from the present means detaching attention from what is at the time most salient. This is very difficult for children, particularly young ones. So an instructor who wishes to help a child remember previous experience will make the situation for remembering as much like that of the previous experience as possible. Only after the child has successfully remembered the information several times can the teacher slowly permit the context to deviate from that of the initial experience. This can be done because with practice the act of remembering, which is initially context-dependent, becomes independent of the context, so that the item can ultimately be remembered under virtually any circumstances. At that point, a completely automatic or fluent memory has been achieved. In any sophisticated skill, such as reading, this is the ideal.

AUDITORY ATTENTION

Similar considerations also apply to remembering sounds. It is much easier to hear and reproduce a whole word than to identify its constituent speech sounds, the phonemes that build it up. The ability to say *hat* comes very early, but to say *h–a–t* is very hard and unnatural; children need specific teaching to learn to do that—they do not do it spontaneously. That is because whole words can be learned spontaneously, but breaking words up calls for an analytical listening attitude and requires a deliberate effort. Attention strategies, this time auditory, may be immature at grade-school entry. When children who are immature in this way try to break a word into its constituent speech sounds, they do so incompletely, redundantly, and unsystematically. This makes it hard for them to become progressively familiar with the breakdown, because they do not attend to it the same way each time. When analyzing a word that they hear children may completely ignore parts of it, although they may easily pronounce the whole word. They are especially apt to omit the terminal sound or syllable. The speech sounds that are noticed in the total word sound may be produced out of sequence. The child may hear the same word but listen to it differently at each hearing. In such cases, little carries over from lesson to lesson.

The reading readiness test that we designed to take account of developmental considerations includes a subset of auditory tests intended to assess the child's ability to listen selectively. The difficulty of the test is progressively graduated upward, so that children who fail the earlier subtests have little chance of succeeding with subsequent subtests. The later tests, in fact, presuppose the skills previously tested.

In these tests the children are asked first to repeat two words, and then to match two words they hear. The word pairs are all monosyllabic, and all are either identical or different with respect to one phoneme. (A phoneme is a basic speech sound, such as the sound made by *b* or *sh*.) Repeating the words is a more familiar task, and therefore an easier one, than matching them. Differences in the initial consonant are picked up more easily than differences in the final consonant. Those words that differ only at the end are misjudged "the same" by young grade-school children more often than words differing in the initial consonant.

The next two tasks are to repeat a word and a phoneme (e.g., *bat* and *k*), and then to match the word to the phoneme (i.e., is that particular phoneme present in the spoken word?). Again, the repeating is easier than the matching, since the latter calls for analytic listening. And again, the task is easier when the phoneme involved is at the beginning of the word.

The fifth test requires children to keep in mind a three-phoneme series; the sixth has them break words down into constituent phonemes; and the seventh has them put words together from their constituent phonemes. These last two tests, by far the hardest, are brief exercises in phonics. Most entering first-graders who have not been taught phonics do not succeed on these tests.

We gave our visual and auditory readiness tests to several hundred entering first-graders and repeated them at 6-month intervals. All the children performed better on both the visual and auditory tests as they got older. But it was the degree of auditory improvement—not visual improvement—that was most closely related to the rate of learning to read. This result highlights the crucial role played by selective listening in rendering normal children ready to read. That does not, of course, exclude the role of visual (selective looking) difficulties in individual children with selective reading disability.

Finally, if only to dismiss it, a surprisingly persistent misapprehension should be noted. Some young grade-school children fail on auditory word-matching examinations, such as the Wepman Test, which have them judge spoken word-pairs "the same" or "different." In has been customary to report that children who do poorly have auditory discrimination problems, as though they actually could not hear the difference between two phonemes. But we found by experiment that this was not so. The children could easily detect the difference between any two phonemes heard in isolation. It was only when the simple sounds were embedded in words that the difficulty arose.

We suspected that the problem was one of attention. Just as children shown two straight lines may only look at one end of the lines, it seemed possible that children might only pay attention to part of what adults would regard as extremely simple three-letter words. For instance, a child paying attention to only the beginnings of words would call *rib* and *rip* the same. We therefore wondered whether we could induce children with such difficulties to pay attention to entire words. In the Wepman Test the examiner pronounces the words; the child has only to say "the same" or "different." We modified this procedure by asking children to *repeat* the words the examiner spoke after saying whether they were the same or different. Under those circumstances, the children's errors were dramatically reduced (especially with respect to those words that differed in their terminal phoneme). It thus seems likely that asking the children to repeat both words added pressure which helped them maintain their attention long enough to hear both words in their entirety. Once they had done that, they generally did notice the differences in the sounds. The difficulty involved here relates to selective listening. Once one knows this, one ceases to think in terms of peripheral problems (such as deafness or inability to hear differences in sounds) and concentrates instead on listening strategies, which is a more fruitful approach.

The proper way to teach children who have a selective listening problem arises naturally from this understanding of its developmental origins. The child is unable to attend selectively in a comprehensive, nonredundant, and systematic way. The teacher, therefore, has to present the information in a way that gets around this attention immaturity—by making the information sufficiently salient to register. This is done by segmenting words for the child, by drawing attention to individual phonemes, and by building up syllables and short words (as well as longer words from syllables) to overcome poor listening strategies. Here also, the two principles of remediation apply: Make the relevant information more salient, and remove information that is not immediately relevant and is potentially distracting.

Note that this approach does not attempt to correct the disability by forcing children to act as though they could already use appropriate, effective listening strategies. There is no known way to correct the disability in such a manner. Rather, the teacher keeps in mind the primary purpose, which is to acquaint the child with useful information, not necessarily by changing the way the child thinks but by adopting whatever measures are practicable. The teacher thus arranges the situation so that the child can learn despite cognitive shortcomings. The method works, but with an important reservation. When the teaching is done, the child still lacks the underlying mental operations in question. Given further material requiring those operations, the child will remain unable to approach it the normal way. So help of the kind discussed will again be required.

CROSS-MODAL ASSOCIATIONS

Reading and writing require analysis directed at decoding the individual word (in reading) and encoding it (in writing). But analytic thinking alone is not sufficient. It is also necessary to form associations between the correctly analyzed items, pairing them across modalities (so that the way a word looks is paired with the way it sounds). Some investigators have regarded the ability to form these associations as a separate cognitive skill with its own developmental history, a skill potentially subject to selective immaturity in an otherwise normal developing child.

We know that paired associations are most easily learned when the pairs in question are similar in structure or meaning. But such similarities are absent from the arbitrary code that represents spoken language as written or printed words. That is, the convention that relates the written sign to the spoken sign is highly arbitrary. The word *sun* is not shaped like the sun. This makes it hard to remember speech-sound/letter-group combinations.

It is doubtful that the cross-modal nature of the associations has any significance aside from the fact that quite dissimilar perceptual experiences are being paired. We do not know what is called for, in addition to analytic perception of the sign and sound, in order to learn their association. Somehow the relationship has to be dramatized to render it memorable. Whatever the details of how this is done, the measure must in principle be based on some act of imagination. So again it is an attention-getting skill that is crucial at this stage of learning to read.

One sometimes encounters children who seem unable to reliably recall even the most basic cross-modal associations, such as the names of alphabet letters. Such children might have been taught this information dozens of times without success. They clearly have difficulty in cross-modal association; but in functional terms what does this mean?

Typically, such children do not simply fail to name the letter, saying "I don't know." Nor do they mistake letters for categorically different things, such as numbers or colors. Rather, they respond with the *wrong* letter name, mistaking one symbol for another. Such confusions arise from being overloaded with information in the first place. Perhaps the teacher has assigned the learning of too many (or even all) letters and letter names at once. Hence the child memorizes the letter shapes and letter names but fails to associate the two properly.

However immature the child's association ability might be, this interference of associations can be avoided by minimizing the initial amount of information given. No special mnemonic tricks are needed. One simply presents the letter shape–letter name pairings one at a time, cumulatively, as follows: *a, b; a, b, c; a, b, c, d; a, b, c, d, e*, etc., taking care to ensure that each pair is well-learned before the next is brought in, and constantly checking back to ensure that earlier pairings are not becoming confused with ones subsequently introduced.

There are two provisos. One is that the sequence must be continually varied (*a, b; b, a, c; d, b, c, a*; etc.), so that children do not merely learn a series of responses by rote. The other is that whenever the child makes a mistake, the progression is stopped, and the series in question is repeated. For example, if in going through *d, a, b, c* the child makes an error on *c*, then correct this error on *c* and avoid introducing *e* until first checking again through *d, a, b, c*. In this way, you will never be more than one item of information ahead of the student. And the student, at any given moment, will have made each of the associations involved a different number of times, a fact which makes each association more distinctive and less likely to be confused.

In a study with first-, second-, and third-graders, we found that arbitrary symbol-digit association was learned nearly twice as fast by this cumulative method than by the standard method. In the standard method the full set of items to be learned is presented time and again, until the learning criterion is met.

Note that reading — or any other task involving material that the student needs to recognize instantly — requires training beyond the "correct-but-halting" response (which still relies on reconstruction of the "episode" when the material was shown) to a point where

automatic fluency—characterized by a rapid, effortless response—
is achieved. This is the best assurance that the information learned
will still be retrievable at the time of the next lesson.

In general, this learning method should be used in building up
any automatic skill, such as building an adult's foreign language
vocabulary or assuring a pianist's command of a musical sequence.
If the individual was taught poorly and is beset by persistent confusions, the learning process must start anew at the beginning, and
the confusions must be removed by means of the differential practice inherent in cumulative learning.

LINGUISTIC FACTORS
In order to achieve up to, say, the third-grade level, children need
to be reasonably good lookers and listeners. To read beyond that
level they need additional language skills. Even a child who has
learned to decode short units (using selective looking and listening
to break words down and put them together again) can have very
poor paragraph comprehension. The child may not understand the
paragraph's content despite being able to decode each individual
word. That is where linguistic skills—involving the constraints of
the language and grammatical structure—come into play. Verbal
memory relies on a knowledge of language structure. The better
the grasp of language structure, the more easily and efficiently the
material involved can be remembered—because some of the
groupings are so familiar that they can be coded as units rather
than element by element. An older, selectively backward reader
who has progressed beyond the decoding stage may be found to
have a language problem, irrespective of auditory or visual modality.

We have developed listening comprehension paragraphs comparable to reading comprehension paragraphs. Each child is given
paragraphs to be read, and also paragraphs to be heard while
someone else reads them aloud. Then we compare the comprehension levels for those read versus those heard. We find that many
older children with learning problems comprehend no better when
listening to the text than when reading it. Such a moderate language problem—a modest difficulty in understanding connected
speech—is easily overlooked in everyday life. The problem is less
obvious when a child fails to understand a complex spoken passage than when the same child fails to understand an equally complex written passage, because we can more accurately determine
what a child is getting out of the written passage.

This suggests that remedial reading work falls into two separate
categories, one or both of which may be needed in an individual
case. One is decoding work, which emphasizes reading the words,
pronouncing them correctly, and spelling them right; that work re-

quires facility in looking, listening, and remembering. It is highly structured. The other category, less well understood, is language work. Over and above knowing the meaning of individual words, it is necessary to internalize the grammatical rules of the language so as to be able to exploit its redundancies during fluent reading. Efficient perception does not slavishly register every discernible detail but rather focuses awareness on those details critical to the task. Efficient reading (and listening) similarly focuses on the words and grammatical form enough to grasp the meaning being conveyed. To attend to more than that necessary minimum would entail a wasteful sacrifice of fluency; reading would then become slow and literal. Rather than comprehending the written words directly, the reader would have to repeat them first, so as to understand the gist of the sentence. (Skillful use of the form of the language to concentrate mental effort in the most cost-efficient manner possible is found in speed-reading). Children who read haltingly may be delayed in their acquisition of this linguistic skill. They may perceive each word separately, without grouping or coherent emphasis, in an unselective and unsystematic manner (as much younger children perceive visual and auditory information).

Fluent readers can read quickly. They can also read selectively. One sometimes reads text without any selective focus of interest and leaves oneself open to whatever information might be contained in it. At other times one reads specifically for some particular item or class of information, ignoring anything else.

We do not yet have a good way of measuring selective comprehension skill in either reading or listening. However, the ability to read selectively is a useful index of skillful reading. Young children asked to read selectively for either of two types of information have been found to take as long as when required to read for both. Older, more skillful readers need relatively less time to do the former (more selective) task. In its extreme form, selective reading is skimming, a practice that makes it possible to read text of limited interest efficiently.

SELECTIVE ARITHMETIC DISABILITIES

Any academic area may prove unexpectedly difficult for some normally intelligent children to master, because of selective immaturity of a relevant cognitive function. Second to reading and writing, arithmetic is of major concern in primary and high-school education, and many children have been found to be selectively handicapped in learning arithmetic. However, compared to reading and writing, arithmetic disability (and its remediation) has received little systematic attention. The reasons for this appear to be both historical and social.

Simple and obvious as it may now appear, the notion of selective educational difficulty is new to educational theorizing. In the past educators have been more prone to resort to environmental or emotional hypotheses to explain disproportionate failure in specific content areas. The concept of learning disability as a biological reality reached educators through the efforts of physicians, who insisted on the existence of dyslexia as a disease entity. Since this focused attention on brain-based specific learning disability, it served a useful purpose. But the misguided emphasis on a medical "disease" model disguised the fact that reading is only one of the academic areas affected by selective disability, and instead focused attention on reading to the virtual exclusion of other subjects. In addition, our educational system has emphasized reading and writing so much that difficulties elsewhere in the curriculum have seemed to lack urgency.

Nonetheless, selective arithmetic difficulty is quite common. It appears to be particularly prevalent among children with cerebral palsy and has received the most attention in that context. However, children without a demonstrable neurological deficit can be arithmetically handicapped in a manner indistinguishable from that of the cerebral palsied children.

Weakness in arithmetic is conspicuous in mental retardation and must be differentiated from selective arithmetic difficulty. An achievement test profile in which arithmetic age is lower than reading and writing age is common among mentally retarded children. This is because it is generally easier to compensate for lack of native ability by hard work in reading than in arithmetic. Much reading material can be learned by rote, as demonstrated by the occasional instance of age-appropriate or even superior reading achievement by a child who is mentally slow. The problem with this "hyperlexia" is that it tends to reflect skills in mechanical reading but not in comprehension. Indeed, there is a risk that enthusiastic and persistent training of retarded children might lead them to a uselessly high reading level, that is, a level at which they are reading words and phrases that they cannot understand. There is little risk of a comparable outcome in arithmetic (beyond rote memorization of facts about numbers), because in arithmetic mental operations have to be used which cannot be drilled into an immature child.

Disproportionately low arithmetic achievement is also prevalent among children who suffer from chronic anxiety. The explanation is similar. The effect of anxiety on behavior is to make it routine. Anxious people behave in highly familiar and predictable ways, and they fare worst when faced with an unusual situation. Although in contrast to the retarded, they do have the mental potential, their anxiety induces a state of "pseudodementia." They do not use their minds. Rote learning ability remains, but problem-solving ability (as in arithmetic) suffers.

The opposite situation is common among delinquent children who rarely experience anxiety. They are often worst at reading and writing, simply because they are not prepared to make a sustained effort.

Selective arithmetic difficulties can occur either in conjunction with reading and writing problems or in isolation. In the former category, an uncommon but well-studied type of problem is the "developmental Gerstmann syndrome." Children with this syndrome underachieve in all primary subjects, but they do worse in arithmetic and writing than in reading. The nature of the mistakes they make is revealing. These children do not lack number sense. They understand the notion of a cardinal scale and are able to arrange numbers in correct progression. Their difficulty relates specifically to the "place value" of digits in numbers with more than one place; that is, the convention that in a multi-place number the digit on the far right stands for ones, the next digit for tens, the next for hundreds, etc. These children have the greatest trouble with "carrying" from column to column, especially in subtraction, and with mental arithmetic; and they are prone to number reversals in writing down complex numbers recited orally. Interestingly, the reason that they have difficulty writing is similar: They forget the correct order of the letters. In general the problem is not one of direction. They do not tend to read or write words backward, nor are they unusually apt to make letter reversals. They might write *was* as *wsa* but not as *saw*. It is the lack of ability to order information, including letters and numbers, that is at fault.

Other children have mathematical difficulty related to drawing and spatial construction problems. It may be that these are children who have exceptional difficulty with spatial visualization, an ability that is obviously important for drawing and that has also been supposed necessary for learning certain arithmetic concepts. Still other children seem to have an isolated arithmetic difficulty which, when severe, even includes deficient number sense (not knowing which number is greater than which). These cases are poorly understood.

In the differential diagnosis of inadequate arithmetic progress, it is also necessary to consider that at grade levels four and above arithmetic problems and operations are often presented and explained verbally. Because of this, a reading problem will frequently broaden out into deficient arithmetic performance by the middle of the grade-school period.

Another factor in arithmetic problems may be the social sex stereotype that insists females are inept at mathematics. By itself this is unlikely to cause a severe deficit; but a girl who experiences some arithmetic difficulty because of selectively lagging brain development may suspend her efforts because of the stereotype, thus permitting the problem to assume an unwarranted severity.

When assessing a selective difficulty in beginning arithmetic, as revealed by achievement test scores, one separately records a child's understanding of number, understanding of place value, and facility with addition, subtraction, multiplication, division, fractions, measurements, and story problems. Readiness to perform these operations calls for the possession of certain number concepts.

Number skills are preceded by number concepts. There is an orderly succession of concepts that the child must master in order to provide a basis for the acquisition of computational skills. Teachers who limit their instruction to the rote inculcation of mechanical skills are taking for granted a repertoire of basic concepts that the learning disabled child may not command. Such deficiencies easily go unnoticed unless they are specifically sought.

The ability to group objects into sets is basic. It presupposes the ability to attend selectively to one item at a time, and to match items with each other according to some relevant perceptual dimension(s). When the ability to group and match is tested, salient perceptual dimensions (form, color) and familiar concrete examples should be used first. Only when the concept is demonstrably mastered in such terms should nonsalient classification criteria and abstract examples be used.

Relation concepts are usually acquired well before school entry. Everyday experience affords instances of smaller-bigger, longer-shorter, heavier-lighter, etc. But these and less salient distinctions cannot be taken for granted. They are acquired in the course of mental maturation and may be delayed in cases of cognitive power deficit.

Given the ability to define sets and compare individual items, the next step is to compare sets. For instance, the child assigns candies to people, shapes to spaces in a form-board, and ultimately a different numeral to each item in the set.

This last activity leads into counting. Many children memorize sequences of number names by rote before they become able to count systematically, but they omit some items and count others more than once. When they are sufficiently mature cognitively, they can count in systematic sequence.

Next, children learn additional sequences of a concrete nature — currency; relative ages of family members; units of length, weight, and time; and parts containing the same number of elements (concrete pairs, triplets, and so forth). In this way, the generality of the number concept becomes familiar.

Part-whole relationships now become subject to manipulation. Given two parts, one may infer the whole. Given the whole and one part, one may infer the missing part.

Having mastered these concepts, first in concrete instances and then in their full generality, the child is ready to operate on sets symbolically. The child can now learn the decimal system. And once that principle is understood, the child gains facility in using the notation for computational purposes. The child is then in a position to learn basic arithmetic, the vocabulary of arithmetic, the definitions and varieties of sets, the concepts of cardinal and ordinal numbers, and the basic operations performed on numbers.

THE SELECTIVITY OF UNREADINESS
Perceptual development—in the form of progressively more differentiated and flexible deploying of attention—occurs in all children. But it does not follow that the abilities to look analytically and to listen analytically develop in parallel, or even that within a modality, selective attending becomes simultaneously possible for all perceptual dimensions. Children cannot necessarily discriminate letter sequences just because they can discriminate letter shapes, for example (or remember letter sequences just because they can remember number sequences). Rather, it seems that different parts of the brain control not only different sensory modalities but even different perceptual dimensions within a modality. Thus, some children will be able to use sophisticated attending strategies in one modality, but may not achieve comparable skills in another modality until much later. Some might have difficulty in attending to one perceptual attribute but not to another, whereas with other children the reverse might be true.

The different parts of the brain, as they mature, refine their modes of processing information according to very generally applicable principles. But different parts of the brain deal with different specifics of perceptual analysis, and these parts mature at strikingly different rates in some children. The ability to process information along any one dimension cannot be taken for granted on the basis of demonstrated ability to handle other dimensions efficiently.

THE DEVELOPMENTAL PERSPECTIVE
In overview, the developmental perspective casts light not only on aspects of the detailed diagnosis and treatment of children with cognitive power disorders but also on the fundamental nature of those disorders. Such disorders seem to result from partial cogni-

tive immaturity. So the principles we have outlined with regard to perceptual and motor development apply with equal force to other aspects of intellect, such as the development of language and the ability to reason. The ability to solve any but the most elementary problems depends on being able to detach attention from the most obvious (salient) response (this response is not correct, for if it were there would be no problem) and to focus it on successively less probable (nonsalient) or even counterintuitive responses, until the answer is found. We are dealing here with a hierarchy of potential solutions, comparable to the perceptual hierarchy. The more mature and mentally agile individuals are, the more they will be able to reject the obvious but inappropriate response in favor of the subtle but appropriate one.

How do we make plans? We abstract from our total experience those perceptions that represent the situation as it is, and we mentally rearrange them in diverse combinations until the outcome fits the goal we had in mind. The usefulness of our ability to abstract is readily apparent. We can rapidly and easily rearrange abstract representations of objects, and thereby determine how they might work, in cases where it would be cumbersome or impractical to rearrange the objects themselves. The ability to abstract and mentally represent things is refined during mental development. This ability calls for (left hemisphere) skills of abstraction and (right hemisphere) skills of representation. Here, as in perceptual and mental development, we graduate from the concrete, holistic, and stereotyped to the abstract, differentiated, and flexible.

Parallel maturation of the various cognitive abilities occurs frequently but is not guaranteed. Some abilities may lag or may never fully mature. When the ones that lag relate to academic progress, school failure results. But this does not differ in its basic nature from lags in the development of other cognitive abilities that do not reflect upon the areas of learning that society gives greatest emphasis. People who experience delayed development of a mental operation not used for reading, writing, or arithmetic do not (by definition) have a learning disability; but their selective cognitive immaturity is similar from both a physiological and psychological point of view. It differs only with respect to its adaptive implication, the extent to which lack of the relevant abilities is socially embarrassing.

TYPOLOGY
What are the implications of the developmental perspective for the attempts at typology that have been discussed? It is insufficient to say that a child has trouble learning to read on account of linguistic difficulties, sequencing difficulties, visuo-spatial difficulties,

and the rest. For within each of these domains, what is the exact nature of the difficulty? The developmental approach, which regards the selectively disabled child as immature and therefore comparable to the normal younger child with respect to the mental operation in question, provides the answer. That answer is embedded in our account of principles of mental development as it normally occurs. By referring back to this account we come to understand what difficulty children actually have if they are said to have poor visual memory or trouble in learning to read by the phonics method. We can understand how the failure to apply an analytic approach to letter sequences can lead to their being dealt with as though they were interchangeable and not differentiated from each other. We can go beyond the vague generality of the word "linguistic" to a more exact appreciation of what it is about written language, or language in general, that the child fails to comprehend for purposes of learning to read or write.

What we have been discussing have been the various components of mental development that are relevant to academic skills, and the manner in which the child approaches tasks when any one of these components is immature. By studying the outcome of a comprehensive psychoeducational evaluation, including both test scores and error patterns, one can usually single out some of the crucial mental operations that a child appears not to be using properly (see Chap. 4). By means of the developmental perspective, one can then put oneself into the child's shoes, look and listen through the child's eyes and ears, and understand how the task must appear to that child. This is both the rational and the sensible route to doing something effective about the learning difficulty involved.

REFERENCES
1. Boder, E. Developmental Dyslexia: Prevailing Diagnostic Concepts and a New Diagnostic Approach through Patterns of Reading and Spelling. In H. R. Myklebust (Ed.), *Progress in Learning Disabilities*, Vol. 2. New York: Grune & Stratton, 1971.
2. Critchley, M. *Developmental Dyslexia*. London: Heinemann, 1964.
3. Denkla, M. B., and Rudel, R. G. Naming of pictured objects by dyslexic and other learning-disabled children. *Brain Lang.* 3:1–15, 1976.
4. Kinsbourne, M. Looking and Listening Strategies and Beginning Reading. In J. T. Guthrie (Ed.), *Aspects of Reading Acquisition*. Baltimore: Johns Hopkins Press, 1976.
5. Kinsbourne, M., and Warrington, E. K. Developmental factors in reading and writing backwardness. *Br. J. Psychol.* 54:145–156, 1963. Reprinted in J. Money (Ed.), *The Disabled Reader*. Baltimore: Johns Hopkins Press, 1966. Pp. 59–71.
6. Lavers, R. A. Auditory Verbal Deficits Associated with Two Types of Reading Disorder. Ph.D. dissertation, McGill University, 1971.

7. Mattis, S., French, J. H., and Rapin, I.   Dyslexia in children and young adults: Three independent neuropsychological syndromes. *Dev. Med. Child Neurol.* 17:150–163, 1975.
8. Nelson, M. E., and Warrington, E. K. Developmental spelling retardation. In R. M. Knights and D. J. Bakker (Eds.), *Neuropsychology of Learning Disorders.* Baltimore: University Park Press, 1976.
9. Satz, P., and Sparrow, S.   Specific Developmental Dyslexia: A Theoretical Reformulation. In D. J. Bakker and P. Satz (Eds.), *Specific Reading Disability: Advances in Theory and Method.* Rotterdam, The Netherlands: University of Rotterdam Press, 1970.
10. Vurpillot, E.   The development of scanning strategies and their relation to visual differentiation. *J. Exp. Child Psychol.* 6: 632–650, 1968.

SUGGESTED READING
Gibson, E. J.   *Principles of Perceptual Learning and Development* New York: Appleton-Century-Crofts, 1969.
Knights, R., and Bakker, D. J. (Eds.).   *The Neuropsychology of Learning Disorders: Theoretical Approaches.* Baltimore: University Park Press, 1975.

4. Diagnosis

When a child is brought in because of school failure, it is necessary to determine through testing whether or not the child really is failing. If the failure is real, the extent and elements of the failure must be determined. Whether or not the child is actually failing, it is also essential to understand family interaction patterns. How much have the child's relationships with parents and siblings contributed to or aggravated the child's failure experience? If there turns out to be no objective academic failure, have some interactions in the family created a situation where the child is mistakenly thought to be failing, to be falling below a standard the family has established or supported? Careful interviewing, and both psychological and educational testing, are crucial to making a differential diagnosis and determining the nature and dimensions of the problem.

INTERVIEWING
When a physician talks to a patient about a physical complaint, the dialogue is usually directed at communicating facts. "How long has your arm been hurting?" "Where does it hurt?" "What makes it worse?" When a psychotherapist talks to a patient about an emotional disturbance, the sessions may continue for years and consist primarily of explorations of feelings, with the therapist usually exerting much less control over the conversations' content and form than if the complaint were primarily physical.

When a learning disability specialist talks to patients and their parents, the interaction falls between these two types. The specialist has an initial interview and an interpretive interview in which to communicate with those involved. In the former, the specialist will mainly listen for facts and feelings; in the latter, some facts (test results) and some recommendations ("Here's what I think should be done about those facts") will be communicated in the hope that the recommendations will be accepted. Because school failure sometimes has emotional causes and usually has emotional consequences, parents are more likely to feel guilt and anger and to have inappropriate rescue fantasies than when their child hurts an arm or leg. Of course, the specialist may try to follow up on these cases and may refer some for psychotherapy; but the initial and interpretive interviews must be carefully handled if many parents are to hear and to remember what is recommended. Some interviewing problems may arise in both interviews. The ones that relate primarily to the initial interview will be discussed in this chapter, and those relating principally to the interpretive interview will be treated in Chapter 5.

Interviewing is a science and an art. It is an art insofar as it is made fruitful by an interviewer who can put people at ease, listen well but not intrusively, and sense the hidden messages or concerns behind what the interviewees are saying. It is a science insofar as the interviewer can encourage the patients or parents to express themselves freely without giving them clues about what the interviewer approves of, disapproves of, hopes to hear, or hopes not to hear. The less intrusive the interviewer can be, the more accurate a picture is likely to be acquired from those being interviewed.

In the case of a child with school problems, the interview is the time to learn the role that the child and the failure play in the family, how the parents and child feel about each other with respect to the failure, and what aspect of the school problem is most disturbing to the child and to the parents.

Even before the interview begins, observe the patient and the patient's parents. In the waiting room, are they talking to each other or not? Are they sitting next to each other or separately? Do they look relaxed, concerned, anxious, self-conscious, scared? Do they seem to be a unit sharing the same purpose and concern, or adversaries, or bosses and bossed? Use these preliminary impressions as hypotheses to be supported or dismissed.

On the basis of these observations, you can construct a tentative picture of how the patient and parents deal with anxiety, because waiting for a doctor to see a child who is having school problems is typically an anxiety-arousing situation. That they seek a consultation indicates that at least one of the parents has acknowledged or believes that there is a problem—that the child is less than perfect, less than normal, or—at best—unusual. Karen Horney has described three ways in which people respond to stress: They can move toward, against, or away from other people. Which style best characterizes what the patient and parents seem to be doing? Under stress, do they draw closer and try to face the problem together? Do they react to stress by acting aggressively toward each other? Or do they withdraw and become isolated from each other?

When you are ready to begin the interview, who should be present—the parents, the child, or both? Some assume the child should not be present while the parents talk about the child's problem and failures. We prefer to ask both the child and the parents, in a relaxed, natural way, to come into the office together, for two reasons. One is that it makes clear to child and parents the doctor's intention to keep all information out in the open; it suggests that there is nothing so shameful about the child that it must be hidden; and it implies that the doctor finds nothing shocking or embarrassing about the problem. The second reason is that it gives the physician an opportunity to observe—often quite dramatically—how the child and parents feel about the matter. The parents' reaction to this suggestion that the child remain during the interview may show that they have talked to the child about the school problem as though it were either a shameful handicap or a culpable fault. Or there may be a striking disparity between the parents' real feelings about the child's problem and how they present the problem to the child. Some parents actually deceive the child about the reason for the visit, saying, for example, that the doctor is going to do a physical examination for camp. As will be discussed in detail later, it often happens that many of the psychologically disturbing consequences of a child's school problem result from parents, teachers, or society branding learning difficulty as shameful. It could be devastating if the child's physician supported this view. On the other hand, it could be a turning point for the child's self-regard when the physician says calmly and straightforwardly, "Let's all go in and discuss the problem."

Conducting the Interview: How to Act and What to Keep in Mind

As a family counselor, a professional often feels pressed to console patients and their parents as quickly as possible. If accustomed to taking an efficient, well-organized history, the professional may find it difficult to postpone such active questioning. But in cases of school problems this postponement is necessary. It allows one to observe some clues about the nature of the family situation that will be helpful in making a diagnosis and in explaining one's findings and recommendations to the parents in a way that they are likely to accept and implement.

It is suggested that the interviewer begin by looking directly at each person in turn while asking simply "What brings you here today?" or "Can you tell me what the problem is?" After this initial question, the interview should have two parts: a "blank screen" (passive) portion and a portion in which the interviewer does more active questioning. The blank screen part follows a common psychotherapy practice. It keeps the interviewer's personality, biases, and feelings from intruding into the interview at this point; and this in turn maximizes the probability that the patient or parents will say what is on their minds rather than what they perceive the interviewer wants or does not want to hear. This is particularly important when the parents are very anxious or worried, because they are then most likely to be concerned about making a good impression on the doctor, rather than expressing their real concerns or any feelings that they believe are "wrong," such as anger or resentment toward their child.

The interviewer's silence and nonintrusiveness during the first part of the interview serves an additional purpose. As the interview progresses, one naturally begins to form opinions about the nature of the problem. Unlike many (physical) presenting complaints, there is no definitive, certain test for the interviewer's suspicions of "guilt-ridden parent" or "extrapunitive parent." Therefore, the interviewer, upon hearing each new remark from the speaker, conscientiously considers all possible interpretations of that remark and notices how it affects the overall picture that is emerging as the speaker continues. What the parents and child say during the interview are the raw data for the interviewer to use in constructing hypotheses about the nature of the family interaction, possible family problem areas, and the effect all of this has upon the child.

What easily interferes with a less-than-vigilant listener's attempt to acquire an accurate understanding of the situation are the listener's own standards, preconceptions, and past experiences. Therefore, one must be quick to note when one has made an assumption while the parents are speaking. Then one must ask honestly, "What was the basis for my assumption?" Was it what the speaker said, how the speaker looked when saying it, how the child looked while the remark was being made? Equally important, was the assumption to any degree the product of the listener's own need for achievement, fear of failure, biases (e.g., "It doesn't matter so much if it's a girl who can't read"), or childhood experiences (e.g., "My own parents were furious if I got anything less than an A on a report card, so these parents are probably putting too much pressure on their child," or "I was lazy when I was seven years old, so the child probably is lazy also"). If interviewers are afraid or reluctant to acknowledge these feelings in themselves, then the information the parents are offering is obscured by the glue and feathers of the interviewer's past and personality, and the interview is less valuable as a result.

WHAT TO LISTEN FOR IN THE "BLANK SCREEN" PORTION
First, you can notice nonverbal signs. Eye contact, or lack of it, is important. Gaze avoidance by the people you are interviewing can mean that they are intimidated by you or ashamed of their child. When either of these feelings is so strong that they cannot bear to look you in the eye, those feelings may later keep them from taking in and dealing with what you have to tell them. They will remain steeped in their intimidation or shame unless you can make the interview less formal and can indicate that learning disabilities

are neither shameful nor a product of inadequate parental discipline.

Where do the parents and child sit? Who sits next to whom? Does one of them take charge of the seating? This can reflect family alliances: whether the parents are allied with each other and reject the child, whether one parent "sides" with the child, or whether parents and child act as a unit. It can also tell about their attitudes toward the physician. If they worry about the doctor's approval of where they sit, it may be desirable to put them at ease some time before the interpretive interview. Otherwise, their efforts to please or "obey" may interfere with their hearing what is said about their child. One well-educated but anxious-to-please mother of a patient listened carefully as a plain-speaking unforbidding physician explained his findings to her. She nodded repeatedly, said she understood, and even said "God bless you for helping us." But afterwards she confided to one of our female technicians "That doctor is so nice, but I didn't understand a thing he said."

Other parents are at the other extreme. They arrive angry and seat themselves with defiant postures, having come out of desperation or because the child's teacher insisted, already certain that the doctor can do nothing to help—and in fact intends to blame them for the child's trouble and take their money. With such people, one must clarify the situation: "We are all here for one thing: to figure out the best way to help your child. All of the talking and testing we do here will have that as its primary purpose. We are not very concerned with how the problem arose, because we want mainly to know what to do *now* for the child." Such a statement helps to allay the parents' fears that you will blame them for the trouble, and it defines the doctor's relationship to them: Everyone here is on the same team; the goal is not to prove what good, hardworking, strict, permissive, or moral parents they are, but rather to give information that will enable the physician to help their child.

Do the parents think they already know the solution to their child's problem? Even the best of parents hate to lose face. If they are allowed to make too much of telling *their* solution (whether in this interview or in the interpretive session), they may so desire to prove themselves right and the doctor wrong that they will not help implement the latter's recommendations. So if they burst forth with their solution before it is established that the purpose of this visit is to *find out* what to do, then it is desirable to shift their focus. Simply saying "But that is what we are here to find out" is inappropriate. In response to such a comment, parents may become silent, and their bottled-up energy may come out later as

anger toward the child or physician, or as failure to hear suggestions. To give them an alternative use for that energy, one might
say "You seem to have given a lot of thought to how to help your
child. For parents who try hard, it is especially frustrating when
the child's problem continues. Your strong desire to help will be
very important later when you and I discuss what our tests can tell
us about helping the child."

How about the general pattern of the parents' response to the
initial question of what they believe to be the problem? Two features of this response are particularly important:

1. *Do they talk more about the child's experience or about their own
   reactions to the child's failure?* Parents who are preoccupied with
   their own feelings about the child's failure may respond well to
   a professional's statement that the parents cannot (and should
   not try to) make a child with learning disability perform at an
   average level. If making it clear that the parents and child are
   not regarded as one does not succeed in relaxing the parents,
   then they may need psychotherapy later in order to encourage a
   less close and destructive identification with their child's failure.
2. *How large a part of the relationship between parents and child is
   consumed by the child's school problem and its shock waves?* Even
   in the warmest, best-adjusted of families a trouble-spot begins
   to draw upon the members' time and energies. For the families
   with fewer problems, it may suffice to alert them to this danger
   and to explain that the parent-child relationship must transcend
   reading and writing, agonizing, or even offering reassurances
   about failure. It is crucial to strengthen the other aspects of the
   relationship: time spent in purely enjoyable activities, the exchange of warmth, and dealing with the everyday and life crises
   that all children continue to encounter. As with any other dis-
   proportion in the family relationship, if too great an investment
   in the school problem persists, psychotherapy is indicated.

Toward the end of the blank screen segment of the interview,
ask "What would you like us to do? What would you like to know
from us?" Responses to these questions can give quick, clear insight into unrealistic expectations. These responses can range from
"Teach her to read like other children her age" through "Send his
teacher a note saying he really is smart after all" to "Make my
marriage happier." In any case, the answers will give a good idea
of where to begin (and which parental fantasies the interviewer
may need to declare an inability to fulfill) at the interpretive session.

History-taking is best done during the interview in the child's absence. Ideally the child will not wait in idle suspense during this time, but will be occupied with something such as psychological testing. However, at the end of the interview the child is called in. The clinician explains the purpose of the discussion with the parents and summarizes for the child what the main problems seem to be at a level the child can comprehend. The child should then have an opportunity to enlarge upon, amend, or disclaim any of these statements. The feeling of openness that is generated by this step will be of great use at a later stage when information is interpreted to the child.

After the parents and child have been interviewed together, it is a good idea to speak separately to the parents and then to the child before testing begins. The interviewer tells the parents that their child will be asked to do a variety of things that will permit a more detailed understanding of the best way to help the child have an easier time in school. The parents may be asked to fill out a questionnaire or behavior checklist at this time, and should be told approximately when the testing will be completed. If the parents have information or fears that they are too anxious to discuss in front of the child, this is when they usually bring them up.

The child should be told the same thing about the testing as the parents—that it is done in order to find the best way to help. "We do not want you to feel too worried about getting questions right or wrong, but if you do your best, we can learn more about how best to help you." At this time, make sure that the child understands the purpose of the visit. Simply asking for an explanation—in the child's own words—of what is understood to be the reason for the visit and what the child thinks likely to happen during the day will usually bring out any hidden misconceptions or fears. Younger children in particular may need to be told that they will not be given injections. Some children may need to be told that they have not been brought because they have been naughty or have sinned. And children from some kinds of religious backgrounds may need to be dissuaded of very primitive notions—such as the idea that a devil lurking inside them keeps them from learning.

HISTORY-TAKING

Most of the information in this section relates to the cognitive style disorders discussed in Part III, as well as to the diagnosis of cognitive power disorders.

Although unstructured "blank screen" interviewing can provide important information, it soon produces diminishing returns (often after 15 or 20 minutes), and it then becomes time to begin taking a systematic history. Answers to some of the questions in the history, such as questions about school experience, will probably bear directly on the ultimate assessment and recommendations. Others, such as answers to questions about perinatal traumata, may have research interest only or may be clinically relevant only because they reveal areas of parental guilt or concern.

The following outline indicates the items typically covered in taking the history of a school problem case:

I. Summary of problem presented, with ramifications concerning:
   A. Learning of school subjects
   B. Classroom behavior
   C. Emotional problems of child, such as ones resulting from fear of repeated failure
   D. Relationship with peers
   E. Relationship with parents and siblings
II. Learning problems and hyperactivity in parents, grandparents, and siblings
III. Pregnancies and births
IV. Developmental milestones before school entry
   A. Motor development
      1. Gross
      2. Fine
   B. Language development
   C. Other cognitive development
V. Sleeping and eating patterns since birth
VI. Interpersonal style since birth
   A. As baby—cuddly or rigid? overactive or underactive? tantrums? rocking? headbanging?
   B. As child—relationships with peers and siblings?
VII. School history
   A. Basic school subjects (the three R's)
      1. Has any teacher recommended special help for the child?
      2. Has the child ever received special help?
         a. In or out of school?
         b. From whom?
         c. How long was each session, and how many did the child have?
         d. What was the child's emotional response to it?
         e. Did the child make any progress because of it?
VIII. Family relations
   A. Number and ages of parents and siblings
   B. Who lives in the home?

C. Who is close to whom?
D. Does child have own room?
E. Amount of time each parent spends with child
F. Nature of each parent's relationship with child
G. Each parent's goals for child
H. Each parent's disappointments with child

IX. Child's strengths
A. Skills
B. Personality

X. School circumstances
A. What kind of classroom is the child in?
1. Structured
2. Open
B. What is available?
1. Is any other kind of classroom available in that school?
2. Is any special help (small-group or individual teaching) available in that school?

XI. How many professionals have been seen before and why? What were their verdicts? (This should be explored right away, if necessary, to expose parents' feelings of guilt, of ignoring the child's needs, and of assuming the interviewer to be omnipotent)

XII. Who instigated the visit (school, parents, child, or physician)? Why (what was the immediately precipitating factor)?

XIII. What decisions need to be made?
A. Official-educational and medical decisions
B. Family-related decisions involving reality-testing, expectations, existing pressures, help with homework, etc.

It should be stressed, however, that in helping the child to learn better, most of the history and physical examination make little difference. This is important to keep in mind while considering the meaning of the history.

A part of the brain may be slow to mature in a given child for many reasons, including damage before, during, or after birth. If an area of brain helping with one function (e.g., a learning function) is impaired, it seems likely that some other area may also have been affected. That seems to be why some children who are learning disabled are, for instance, also clumsy. But for purposes of both diagnosis and remediation that relationship is irrelevant. This is because no physical therapy improves reading or any other cognitive function, and no improvement in reading makes a child walk gracefully or draw neatly. The brain simply does not work that way.

Furthermore, many clumsy children have no learning problems, and vice versa. So, if it is learned that the child was anoxic at birth, how does that help in diagnosing or prescribing for that child? It does not help at all. For regardless of a positive or negative history of trauma, the need is to find out whether the child is actually clumsy and, if so, to prescribe physical therapy or to wait and see if the child outgrows it. There is also a need to find out whether the child has a reading problem and, if so, to recommend tutorial help or some other appropriate measure. However, one problem has, operationally, nothing to do with the other. (There is only one obvious exception—give a child attention, or a success experience in *any* way, and it may improve the child's general self-confidence or motivation; but this is purely motivational; it does not involve modifying one ability by working on another.) Hence a focus on etiology only leaves the door open for unproductive blame and guilt at best, and for costly time-consuming quack remedies at worst.

With these reservations in mind, we shall comment on what can be learned from history items that is relevant for decisions about management.

The problem presented will most commonly relate to learning school subjects. To document the complaint, we question the parents and the child and also assemble the necessary documentation from the school before the consultation. In addition, we inquire about the child's classroom behavior and peer relationships. The child's classroom behavior may give a hint about the reasons for the learning failure. As will be discussed in detail, an impulsive approach to problem-solving may account for much or all of the difficulty, as may its opposite, the compulsive or overfocused approach. If the child's learning tempo departs grossly from that of the group, the manner of instruction for the group may not be suitable for the individual. Or again, the child may be anxious or timid, or may be acting out a response to protracted failure and consequent teacher and peer disapproval. This information is needed in order to counsel the teacher and parents on how best to react toward the child's failure and in order to justify moving the child to another setting if that should be necessary.

Ramifications of the problem for family and peer relationships are common and important. The child's social adjustment may be grossly undermined by painful failure, and the degree to which this occurs is a more important indicator of the severity of the problem than is the amount of academic failure itself. The highest priority is to safeguard the child from maladjustment. The second highest priority is to render the child capable of improved achievement.

Knowledge of a child's behavior in the home and with peers

helps distinguish a disordered style limited to the classroom (that arises out of the classroom problem) from a disordered style that pervades the child's approach to the task of living. A child may be disorganized and impulsive (or timid and overfocused) in the classroom because the work is found too hard. In that case, those styles will not be apparent in nonstressful situations outside the classroom. However, if either of these styles is a stable personality trait, then it is important to know this, as the trait itself might go far toward explaining the learning problem. If it is a personality trait, of course, then similar behavior should be manifested outside the learning situation.

Both learning disability and hyperactivity are often inheritable, and it is useful to document their presence in the immediate family. But even as one finds it difficult to diagnose either of these conditions in children under immediate scrutiny, one finds it impossible to do more than guess whether relatives were once similarly affected. The fact that a parent had difficulty learning to speak or read, or constantly got into trouble and fights at school, is never more than suggestive. However, inconclusive though it is, such information is useful in interpreting to parents, and it helps the clinician present the child's predicament as something that is not unique and extraordinary, something that has features in common with situations faced by other family members.

Adverse events during pregnancy and delivery could have caused brain damage. But given the present state of knowledge, one cannot be sure whether a particular adverse event caused the learning difficulty or not. However, any pertinent information should be recorded, if only so that it can be discussed with the parents who have questions about it.

Developmental milestones passed before school entry should be ascertained to the extent possible, as a preliminary screening procedure to differentiate general mental retardation from the selective cognitive problems with which we are concerned. The use of the Denver Developmental Screening Test is recommended. Note that the details of motor development, although useful, are less relevant to intellectual problems than details of language and other cognitive development. The details of motor development will, however, cast light on clumsiness where that is a complaint.

Details about sleeping and eating patterns since birth can reveal an impulsive personality trait as well as allergies causing irritability. This line of questioning is also a good way of beginning to hear what parents have to say about their children and what attitudes the parents' words convey.

The child's interpersonal style is an important indicator of the presence of temperamental deviations, such as impulsive or compulsive extremes. Again, the parents' response to the child's style is in itself something important for the clinician to know about.

Such history of events at school as can be obtained is, of course, directly relevant to the problems and the range of remaining educational options. The recommendation that the child receive special or individualized help will sound quite different to a parent whose child has never received such help than to one whose child has repeatedly and uselessly travelled that route. If various treatment modalities have been used and have failed, then it is important to document their exact nature so that the same mistakes not be repeated.

Details of the family interrelationships are needed for counseling parents about the healthiest attitudes to take toward the child and the problems. *This is relevant.* When family dynamics are seriously disturbed, then this information can be handed on to a designated counselor. However, in many cases one, two, or three interviews with learning clinic personnel will suffice to enable family members to achieve the necessary perspective.

Knowledge of the child's strengths is essential, both for educational or vocational guidance and for the purpose of restoring some balance to everyone's attitudes toward the child (including the child's self-image).

Details of the child's situation in the classroom are important because they might suggest useful alternatives. What are the school's resources? Recommendations which involve the child in changes within a school are preferable to recommendations which necessitate switching the educational setting. It is not justified to move the child unless it is certain that the necessary resources cannot be mustered in the school the child is attending already.

Some information about previous assessments and advice is necessary, not so much to make use of them (because presumably if they had been useful the child would not have been brought in), but rather to explore what has failed and what attitudes the parents and child have assumed with respect to those failures. The cliniciag must never be seduced into expressing value judgments about previous encounters with professionals as these encounters are related by the parents, but should take note of the way the parents describe the interaction. If that description is unfavorable, the clinician should take care that the present interaction with the parents not be similarly stigmatized. Furthermore, if the parents express distaste for some particular category of professional, it is important to know that. This is not because clinicians should be deterred from recommending the same kind of professional again, if it seems advisable. Rather, this knowledge is a warning that any such referral back to that kind of professional must be done with circumspection and an unusually detailed explanation.

It is necessary to know who instigated the visit and why it was instigated at this time. The reason is so that information can be sent to the appropriate individuals. Also, the timing of the referral often relates less to the child's school progress than to other important family events that might not spontaneously come to light.

Finally, the parents should be asked specifically what help they want and with what decisions they would like assistance. The clinician should note this, and then use this information to remind the parents of it during the interpretive interview at the end of the assessment.

In the course of history-taking, the clinician should be an active listener and should interact in a lively and attentive fashion with the parents, reacting to their answers in a supportive but not judgmental fashion. Active attention by the clinician while the parents recount the history signals a lively and humane interest in their predicament. It is essential, however, that the clinician give no preliminary clinical opinions at this stage, even if, as is very commonly the case, anxious parents demand it. Jumping to premature conclusions renders the rest of the assessment senseless.

THE PHYSICAL EXAMINATION

PURPOSE

Any agent that damages one part of the nervous system is quite likely to damage another part of it as well. So it is worthwhile to check for signs such as clumsiness or other motor deficits traceable to the spinal cord and brainstem; and if you find such abnormality, you may regard it as somewhat more likely that the cognitive problem also has an organic origin. But many physically normal children have learning disability that is developmentally (organically) based, and many children with nervous system damage do *not* have learning disability; so the physical examination cannot be used in any individual case to determine whether the school problem is due to learning disability.

In theory, one part of a neurological examination could be relevant to beginning reading—that is, examination of the association areas of the cerebral cortex. But there is no such physical examination.

Why, then, conduct a neurological and general physical examination on a child who presents a learning problem? It is not because the physician feels comfortable doing this or believes it will reassure the parents to see a doctor acting like a physician. Rather, it should be done in order to rule out coexisting physical abnor-

Table 4. Minimal Brain Dysfunction (MBD) Terminology

Terms Synonymous with MBD	Behavioral Disorders Attributed to MBD
Association deficit pathology	Aggressive behavior disorder
Cerebral dysfunction	Aphasoid syndrome
Cerebral dys-synchronization syndrome	Attention disorders
Choreiform syndrome	Character impulse disorder
Diffuse brain damage	Clumsy child syndrome
Minimal brain damage	Conceptually handicapped
Minimal brain injury	Dyslexia
Minimal cerebral damage	Hyperexcitability syndrome
Minimal cerebral injury	Hyperkinetic behavior syndrome
Minimal cerebral palsy	Hyperkinetic impulse disorder
Minimal chronic brain syndromes	Hyperkinetic syndrome
Minor brain damage	Hypokinetic syndrome
Neurophrenia	Interjacent child
Organic behavior disorder	Learning disabilities
Organic brain damage	Perceptual cripple
Organic brain disease	Perceptually handicapped
Organic brain dysfunction	Primary reading retardation
Organic drivenness	Psychoneurological learning disorders
	Specific reading disability

malities. The physician who examines a patient for display purposes is likely to be inattentive to the results of the examination, and to fail to note abnormalities if there are any. Furthermore, doing an examination in order to reassure parents of one's medical status may mislead them to suppose that their child's physical characteristics may have caused the cognitive problem, and that physical types of therapy will improve cognition. This is particularly risky in the case of parents who tend to respond to gimmicks, or who wish to deny that their child is having trouble with some aspect of thinking.

A frequently offered rationale for the physical examination of children with school problems is need to search for signs of minimal brain dysfunction (MBD). (Synonyms for MBD are listed in Table 4.) A bewildering miscellany of minor and trivial abnormalities has been grouped together with the cardinal disorders of cognitive power and style into this dubious disease category. Most of the signs in question are neurological but at levels of neural organization other than those relevant to the symptoms presented.

Why examine for irrelevancies? Ostensibly because the presence of MBD signs increases the probability that the disordered behavior is brain-based rather than emotionally or environmentally determined. But to draw such conclusions in any individual case is grossly unwarranted. MBD signs may be absent in strikingly selective cases of cognitive deficit, and they are often present in children who have no school problems at all. Nevertheless, the examination for signs of MBD is compelling for many clinicians, particularly those who like to exercise their physical examination skills rather than puzzle over more complex behavioral issues.

Viewed out of context, the examination for MBD seems so irrational and useless that one might wonder why it was ever introduced. The reason arises out of a long history of misunderstanding between medical and psychoeducational specialists interested in the school failures of normally intelligent children.

Physicians, notably neurologists, deserve credit for introducing the idea that a child might suffer selective school difficulties on account of constitutional shortcomings, at a time when educators and psychologists were not inclined to look beyond more obvious emotional and environmental factors. Unfortunately, however, physicians persistently couched their explanations in terms of disease models. Thus, a selective reading failure would be taken as evidence of a developmental or constitutional dyslexia. But the fact that the child was dyslexic was inferred from the presence of a selective reading problem. This circularity did not escape detection and criticism by psychologists and educators disinclined to accept neurological hypotheses. The same criticism applies to the notion of organic or developmental hyperactivity or hyperkinesis. Here again, physicians inferred a diseased brain state from the presence of a behavioral anomaly but were not able to offer any evidence outside the very presence of this behavioral anomaly as support for the neurological hypothesis.

It thus became necessary to look for additional evidence of brain involvement. Neurologists and other clinicians did this by performing increasingly careful physical examinations, particularly examinations of the nervous system. By this means they uncovered minor evidence of neurological deficit and immaturity in a substantial number of children with selective school failure. However, they were also compelled to admit that such signs could also be found in a smaller proportion but substantial number of children who had not failed in school. Furthermore, the pattern and distribution of abnormalities turned out to be so miscellaneous as to be different in every child. People doing this work were therefore confronted with a tantalizing situation: They could convince themselves that the disorder was brain-based but could not convincingly argue that it was a unitary disease.

One solution for this dilemma would have been to give up the unitary hypothesis and admit the immense individual variation, not only with regard to associated findings in these children but also with regard to the detailed nature of the target behavioral symptoms. Although this would have been the practical thing to do, it was not done. Instead the term "minimal brain damage" or "minimal brain dysfunction" was introduced to impose verbal unity on a very diverse situation. This move was, in fact, effective, in that it greatly stimulated interest in brain-based hypotheses with regard to children's learning and lent support to investigatory efforts in this direction. However, the drawbacks outweighed the gains. The single label tended to blur distinctions among the different practical problems that different children experienced and laid the field open to simplistic solutions which supposedly were applicable to "children with MBD," as if they were some homogeneous group which could be expected to respond to some homogeneous therapy. That tendency to look at school problems in a unitary fashion and to seek panaceas for these problems is still with us today. In our view, it is the single greatest obstacle to a proper understanding of what these children need.

The term MBD, despite its flagrant shortcomings, is nearly universally used, so that one might question whether there is any point in opposing its use. But sin, which is also nearly universal, still has vocal opponents, and we advocate equally dedicated opposition to the use of the term MBD.

PRACTICE

Inpatient assessment
Admitting a child to a hospital for routine assessment of an apparently uncomplicated learning disability or hyperactivity is unjustifiable. The diagnostic steps that are usually necessary can be taken readily on an outpatient basis. Only in the context of clinical research and the specialized study of drug and other chemical responses may admission be needed. Even then, or when the investigation will take more than one day and the child comes from out of town, it is preferable for the child and parent(s) to stay overnight in a hotel. In this way children are spared the admission routine, contact with personnel uninformed about school problems, contact with sick children, and the idea that they themselves are medical "cases." The goal is not to diagnose children's diseases but to determine what is required to help them learn.

Physicians sometimes admit learning disabled children to a hospital so that the family can take advantage of a health plan that provides inpatient but not outpatient coverage. It is hard to argue with people's economic limitations, but pressing relevant agencies to refrain from biasing families and their medical advisers toward admitting children to hospitals unnecessarily is very justified. Other physicians admit children either because they are unduly influenced by a "disease model" of school problems, or because they are personally uninformed in this area and hope their hospital colleagues or residents will "sort things out." Clearly, only informed physicians should take charge of such cases, and they will find hospitalization unnecessary.

Outpatient assessment

Direct observation of the child in the context of a school failure has three purposes: (1) detection of any disease or disorder contributing to the school failure or coinciding with it; (2) detection of signs of brain disorder over and above the learning problem itself; and (3) observation of the child's behavior in respects relevant to the school failure.

A variety of diseases can produce school failure as one of their symptoms, and occasionally confusion with learning disability is possible. Anemia, malnutrition, parasite infestation, and other debilitating conditions will make a child listless in the classroom. In all such cases history-taking reveals a definite change in the child's behavior. The same is true of disorders specific to the brain itself. In rare cases a child progressively loses ground in school as an early symptom of a progressive brain degeneration. Other common features of brain degeneration—such as epilepsy, paralysis, and sensory defects—might have a later onset. Such a child, in effect, has a falling IQ. In this case, the degree of school failure is in proportion with the child's intellectual potential at the time of failure, and thus the condition does not qualify as a learning disability. Furthermore, the progressive nature of the deterioration ultimately becomes apparent.

One rare simulator of chronic inattentiveness is the epileptic variant, status petit mal, that produces momentary lapses of consciousness. During these lapses the child is unresponsive for only a second or two at a time; there is no loss of balance or any motion, except perhaps for a turning upward and outward of the eyeballs. These minor lapses, which come in "showers" of tens or hundreds, may be so frequent as to simulate mental dullness and inattentiveness, and this may be the complaint presented. The physician, however, will observe the momentary arrests of movement, the episodic unresponsiveness, and often very minor twitching of small muscles such as muscles in the head. Electroencephalography easily confirms the diagnosis.

In summary, so many pediatric conditions could affect learning in school that a full routine examination is necessary and should not be bypassed. However, when school failure is the condition presented, it is more usual for any disease found on examination to be coincidental than for it to fully explain the school failure itself.

A routine pediatric examination includes examination of the nervous system. Performed in the traditional manner, like examinations of the other bodily systems, this only occasionally reveals a disease state responsible for the school failure. However, neurological examination of children with school problems has another use — not to localize lesions, but rather to detect disordered or immature neurological development. When a physical sign of neurological abnormality is detected, this is treated not as a clue to the location of the damage, but rather as an indication that nervous system damage exists. For if damage exists elsewhere in the nervous system, might it not also exist in areas inaccessible to the traditional neurological examination, namely the parts of the brain that involve skills related to school achievement?

A variety of minor physical signs indicating abnormality or immaturity of the central nervous system frequently accompany learning disability, and some physicians use their presence as an argument favoring an organic as opposed to a functional explanation of school failure.

Whether an abnormal neurological finding is classified as a hard or a soft sign depends on whether the observed phenomenon is ever normal (for instance, in a younger child) or is abnormal regardless of age. Hard signs are those that indicate pathology regardless of age. Paralysis and movement disorders (choreiform or athetoid signs) are hard signs and are abnormal at all ages. In contrast, such soft signs as clumsiness characterized by synergisms and associated movements occur normally in every young child. Essentially, a soft sign is a neurological manifestation that the child should already have outgrown. The fact that the child has not done so is thought to be significant.

Hard signs of minimal brain dysfunctions become apparent during the traditional neurological examination. Often these indicate very mild cerebral palsy; a mild spasticity, ataxia, or athetosis might have caused no obvious handicap and could have escaped medical notice. Such a disorder might differ only in degree from a finding typical of full-blown cerebral palsy. Other hard signs, such as concomitant strabismus or a tendency to toe-walk, are harder to

classify, and there are also a number of minor congenital anomalies, mostly not affecting the nervous system, that are claimed
to be more frequent in children with school failure, but that are
hard to evaluate with regard to their relevance and implications.

INDIVIDUAL SIGNS

Asymmetries

Asymmetry may be detected with respect to (1) the growth of the
two sides of the body, (2) neurological signs on the two sides, and
(3) preference for the use of a particular hand, foot, eye, and ear.
Taken by themselves, the configurations of both bodily halves,
their reactions, and the manner in which they are used may be,
and usually are, within normal limits; nevertheless, a detected
asymmetry could be regarded as indicating an abnormality of one
or more parts (i.e., their divergence from the plan laid down by
the child's genotype).

ASYMMETRY OF BODILY PARTS. One side of the body, or part of one
side, may be larger than the other. This usually indicates abnormally slow growth of the smaller side rather than accelerated
growth of the larger side. Damage to one cerebral hemisphere at
an early age can cause delayed growth of the opposite side of the
body, both of the soft tissues and of the bones (as shown by ra-
diographs indicating delayed bone age). This phenomenon, which
may be striking in hemiplegic cerebral palsy, can occur in minor
form in otherwise normal children. The physician is then at liberty
to speculate on the existence of early minor lateralized cerebral
damage.

Often only some bodily parts on the affected side are implicated.
In particular, one side of the forehead may slope more precipitously than the other side when viewed from above and behind
(unilateral frontal recession). The palm of one hand or the sole of
one foot may be wider than the other. One limb may be longer
than its mate. Or one side of the face may be larger than the other.

Bodily asymmetries, unless gross, are hard to evaluate. Slight
asymmetries are very common in the general population, and there
are no norms by which the clinician can judge how marked an asymmetry must be before an inference of brain damage can be made
with reasonable confidence.

ASYMMETRICAL NEUROLOGICAL SIGNS. Any of several tendon reflexes
may be more brisk on one side than on the other. When this is so
in the absence of detectable weakness, abnormality of tone, or abnormality of coordination, then the side with the brisker reflexes is

under suspicion. The same is true if tone is increased, but the reverse is true if tone is decreased or if there is incoordination on the brisker side. In the first instance we are describing a mild corticospinal deficit; in the second we are describing a mild impairment of cerebellar function.

Minor asymmetries of the plantar response are particularly frequent, variable, and ambiguous in their interpretation.

MIXED PREFERENCE. Departures from the regularity of right-sided hand, foot, eye, and ear preferences constitute a special type of asymmetry that has long been under suspicion of having some relevance to learning disability.

Hand preference is usually established by answers to a series of questions about hand usage. As determined in this way, such preference turns out to be a matter of degree. Whereas most people use the right hand for most specific and skilled one-handed acts, a minority (about 10 percent) use the left hand for some, most, or even all, and there is no real discontinuity between ambidextrous and lefthanded individuals. Contrary to general belief, neither lefthandedness nor ambidexterity bears any relationship to learning disability when this occurs in the absence of gross brain damage.

What then is the relationship of handedness to cognitive skills? There is an unduly high proportion of lefthandedness among the mentally retarded, the brain-damaged, psychopaths, and the criminally insane. But this is due to the high incidence of cerebral damage in these special groups (which may shift the hand preference of genotypic dextrals from right to left) and is irrelevant to children in the general population. Therefore, unusual handedness characteristics occurring in otherwise physically normal children are best regarded as neither hard signs nor soft signs, but rather as the harmless products of normal individual variation. In contrast, when they occur in children with neurological deficits (e.g., cerebral palsy), they could naturally be secondary to asymmetrical neurological damage. For instance, whereas an otherwise physically normal lefthander is so for genetic reasons, a lefthanded child with right hemiplegic cerebral palsy could well have been a genotypic righthander who shifted to "pathological lefthandedness" to compensate for a useless right hand.

Foot preference is usually on the same side as hand preference, and when it is not this fact is uninterpretable. Eye dominance is more complex, because each retina projects to both cerebral hemispheres, so that the preferred eye does not indicate which is the "dominant" hemisphere. Eye preference is more often right than left, but up to 30 percent of the general population has left-eye dominance. The main influence is probably a differential acuity of the two eyes based on peripheral factors, and there is no validated relationship between eye dominance and learning.

All in all, the folklore about hand preference and mixed dominance is not supported by recent competent studies. Certainly these preference factors appear to be poor indicators of cerebral dominance for language. Non-righthanders can have language dominance in either hemisphere, and some even seem to have language represented in both hemispheres.

Sensorimotor soft signs

Soft signs have two aspects. On the one hand, a soft sign represents persistence of a primitive form of response. On the other, it represents failure in a certain kind of performance. The child fails to do something which, at that age, most children can do. A simple test will help to illustrate this. The child extends both hands, and wooden sticks (or ballpoint pens) are placed between the fingers of each hand. The child is then asked to drop each stick singly, in turn. A 3- or 4-year-old child is apt to drop not only the indicated stick but others as well—most likely an adjacent stick in the same hand and the mirror-image stick in the other hand. The easiest one to drop singly is the stick between the index and middle fingers, and the hardest is that between the middle and ring fingers. A 6-year-old should not drop more than five extra sticks in the course of the six trials.

This test has two useful features. One is that the objects fall to the ground, and it may entertain the child to see you dive for them in the midst of a rather solemn examination. The other is that you are studying associated movements in a way that goes beyond clinical impressions. You do not have to say "It is my clinical impression that two sticks dropped." You can say "Two sticks dropped." The test demonstrates the nature of associated movements. The child who fails the test has not yet become able to abduct two fingers while leaving the rest in place; there is still a mass response of general abduction. In the course of motor maturation, selective finger abduction differentiates out. The same applies to contralateral associated movements. Motor overflow to the opposite side gradually comes under inhibitory control. In this way, movements become more precise, clearcut, and skillful.

A wide variety of sensorimotor immaturities can be detected by examination. The motor immaturities generally involve overflow from primarily involved muscle groups to muscle groups that are synergically linked but whose action is not called for by the test. An example is the pronation of the wrists that a young child will show when asked to walk on its toes. The overflow may be due to synergisms in the same limb or to the counterpart of the primarily active muscle group in the opposite limb. Thus, a forcible grasp by one hand may lead to an associated grasping movement by the other hand. Associated movement is itself a developmentally normal phenomenon (in that all young children manifest it). How much a particular pattern of synergic and associated movement represents an excess for a given age is a matter of judgment. Here there are no generally useful objective measuring devices. Therefore, the physician should select two or three such tests (arbitrarily, as no one test has been shown more important than any other) and should become familiar with age-related changes in the performance of these tests by normal children (as well as with the range of normal variation at any given age). The physician will then have an internalized standard of reference for judging whether the patient's degree of synergic or associated movement qualifies as a positive soft sign.

The fact that synergic and associated movements represent a developmental stage does not mean that they are totally absent once the nervous system has fully matured. The readiness with which they appear is a function of the degree of effort invested in the primary movement. During strenuous effort, even normal adults manifest synergic and associated movements.

A tendency toward synergisms and associated movements can be much exaggerated by gross central nervous system damage. In essence, the incapacitating motor disorder of athetosis represents the uncontrollable intrusion of synergisms into the patient's attempts to move in a precise and discrete manner. Patients with hemiplegia of early origin show more associated movements than normal children the same age.

A good example of a sensory soft sign is "extinction" of one out of two simultaneously applied stimuli. For instance, a child with closed eyes may be lightly touched on both hands. Although children are readily aware of each touch when it is given in isolation, they usually miss one if both are given simultaneously, and it is usually the one on the left. Again, one needs to have extensive normative experience before being in a position to judge whether the amount of extinction found in a given case is more than age-appropriate and therefore constitutes a soft sign.

Clinicians wishing to perform a more comprehensive and quantitative motor examination, for which age-related norms are available, have for years used the Oseretsky test battery or its more recent modification, the Lincoln-Oseretsky test battery. These tests involve 36 items of increasing difficulty and are applicable to children 6 to 14 years old. However, the tests are very time-consuming, and some of the items are uninterpretable. Another test, the convenient and adequately standardized Test of Motor Impairment, represents an improvement. Incidentally, this test indicates that motor impairment is relatively more prevalent among children in impoverished families and among children described as maladjusted, especially those who show lack of impulse control. However, even in these categories the majority of children exhibit no motor impairment. This confirms the view that motor impairment is relevant only to motor symptomatology and should not be considered as supporting evidence for a cognitive or emotional diagnosis.

Strabismus

Except for concomitant strabismus, definite cranial nerve abnormalities are rare in children who are not obviously brain-damaged on other grounds. Strabismus itself is so common that when it coincides with school failure there is no way to be sure that the association is more than coincidental. The possibility that the strabismus or the visual failure (amblyopia ex anopsia) associated with it account for a learning disability has been studied repeatedly with negative outcome and can be discounted.

Cognitive soft signs

The examination of higher mental function (neuropsychology) can also be considered to yield both hard and soft signs of abnormality. Hard signs would be manifestations—such as anomia, visual distortions (metamorphopsia), or spatial hemi-neglect—that do not recapitulate any stage of normal development. Soft signs would be evidence of delays in cognitive development that render the patient no better able to perform the task in question than a much younger child (by virtue of the same limitations on performance, and therefore the same pattern of errors). A proponent of the delay (developmental lag) model of learning disability would regard all cognitive deficits in this situation as soft signs by definition. However, among tests that are helpful in the elucidation of learning disability, only a few are derived from the efforts of neuropsychologists. Two of these are the Token Test for receptive language and tests for finger-order sense.

In the Token Test the child is shown five cut-out squares and five cut-out circles. Each shape appears in five colors. At the first level of difficulty, the child is asked to successively identify a series of single items, specified by color and shape (e.g., "Touch the red square"). At the second level, an alternate set of ten "tokens" is added to the display; they differ from the first set, being of smaller size. The child is then asked to point to tokens specified by size, color, and shape (e.g., "Touch the small green circle"). The third level recapitulates the first but uses double instructions (e.g., "Touch the red square and the yellow circle"). The fourth level recapitulates the second (e.g., "Touch the large green circle and the small yellow square"). The fifth and final level introduces function words, such as "with" and "under." The Token Test is thus a test of verbal decoding, in which the load on the individual's memory is gradually increased, while the vocabulary, at least through the first four levels, is strictly limited. Finally, at the fifth level, the vocabulary is expanded to include function words. Token Test performance improves with increasing age among normal children. Norms are available, so that a grossly substandard performance for a given age can be ascertained with confidence. Deficient Token Test performance in a child with reading disability incriminates the spoken language system as a relevant area of difficulty.

Another way to examine the nervous system for a cognitive "soft sign" is to elicit "finger agnosia," more correctly known as "disordered finger sense." Usually acquired around six or seven years of age, this is the ability to differentiate certain sequences. These sequences are the relative positions of the fingers on the hand and their relative positions in terms of right and left. Immaturities in the development of this ability are often accompanied by immaturities in learning both to spell and to calculate. These two skills are affected by the same type of mistake. The relative positions of the fingers are what distinguishes them from each other. Children who cannot identify the fingers' relative positions fail to recognize them, and hence cannot identify right and left in terms of their relative positions. (Front and back are different because you cannot see in back. Up and down are different because you fall down, not up. But right and left look alike and are relative concepts.) The same children make order errors in their spelling, mix up the place value of the digits (e.g., confusing 54 and 45) in arithmetic, and have trouble carrying over numbers from column to column.

The best tests for disordered finger sense are very simple and employ a minimal number of words. In the "Finger Differentiation Test you make sure the child's eyes are closed and then touch the child in two places at the same time, either on the same or on two adjacent fingers. The child is then asked "Am I touching you on two fingers or one?" Another test is the In-Between test. You touch the child on two different fingers and ask how many fingers are in between the ones you are touching. Only a child who has the concept of sequential finger position can tell how many are in between. The Finger Block test approaches the same problem from an ostensibly different perspective. You may, if you wish, refer to a publication which tells you more exactly how to do these finger order tests[1].

Interpretation of soft signs
Observers often disagree about the reality of any individual soft signs. Disagreements about signs, of course, often crop up in the traditional neurological examination. There an additional validity check is provided — for it is possible to see whether the signs cluster meaningfully with respect to clinical experience and to known neurological structure and function. But this source of information is not available in the case of soft signs, because they are taken to indicate neither selective damage to any neurological location or system nor the action of any particular noxious influence on neuronal function. Thus, soft signs taken together do not signify more than the individual signs. Soft-sign counts have been suggested from time to time, but their clinical usefulness for learning disability has not been demonstrated. Mean aggregate scores are equal in normal, retarded, and epileptic children and are significantly higher only in children who can be classified as neurologically impaired on other grounds. When the results of special investigatory techniques (such as EEG) are added in, the basic uncertainty of interpretation remains.

Electroencephalography in learning disability
Although this method of investigation has been widely used in testing children with developmental disabilities, its applicability is very specific and limited. Two kinds of EEG findings are relevant. One is the presence of spike discharges, indicating epilepsy that might be subclinical (in that no overt seizure activity is observed). In a very few cases behavioral and learning abnormalities are relieved when the paroxysmal spike activity in the EEG is corrected by anticonvulsants (notably Dilantin).

The other relevant EEG finding is an excess of slow wave activity for the tested child's age. In the normal course of events, young children have a predominance of slow wave activity in the delta (below 4 per second) and beta (4 to 7 per second) ranges. As the nervous system matures, the dominant frequencies are increasingly concentrated in the alpha (8 to 13 per second) range. Some children with learning disabilities have an excess of slow wave activity (especially posteriorly); this presumably indicates either some immaturity of brain development or failure of brainstem centers to facilitate adequate cerebral cortical activity. It has been reported that administration of stimulants to hyperactive children, besides causing behavior improvements, simultaneously shifts dominant frequencies from the beta to the alpha range (i.e., makes the EEG become more normal for the child's age). Quite how precise and reliable a guide this is remains to be determined.

Furthermore, the conventional EEG is a difficult tool to use in making these delicate judgments. A far superior technique is power spectrum analysis. This is a method for quantitatively determining the child's relative distribution of different wave form frequencies within a given time frame. This technique, however, requires both specialized skills and a computer. Further investigation will show whether power spectrum analysis is sufficiently useful to justify its relatively high cost, and whether other useful information might be learned from the electroencephalogram.

THEORETICAL BASIS OF THE PHYSICAL EXAMINATION
The brain basis of learning disability
The presence of hard signs, of soft signs, and of neither, point respectively to each of three possible models of brain involvement in learning disability. The "deficit" model, which regards the affected child as lacking some school-relevant ability or abilities, is best illustrated by cases with demonstrable structural damage. The presence of hard signs would be one indicator of such damage. The deficit model of learning disability would place the symptomatology in accord with general neuropsychological symptomatology (i.e., regarding the behavioral deficit as brought about by focal damage to the brain). The only departure from general neuropsychological symptomatology would involve the age at which the lesion was incurred (presumably very early, as in the perinatal period). Whereas acutely brain-damaged adults lose abilities which they can be presumed to have had prior to the insult, if they were previously normal, brain-damaged newborns may not demonstrably have lost anything; that is, they may appear normal upon examination. But they may subsequently fail to develop abilities related to the damaged brain area.

The "delay" model, like the deficit model, deals with central nervous system abnormality incurred at a very early age. But it differs in its emphasis upon the time parameter of development. Selective lags in neurological development, according to this model, do not necessarily arise from structural damage (although structural damage can cause just such lags). They could easily have genetic causes, or else they could be due to changes at the molecular level that are not observable with present neuropathology methods. The model regards neither examinations nor investigations as likely to reveal evidence of gross damage, and considers the underlying abnormality, in effect, an inference based on the phenomenon one is trying to explain: the unexpected delay in maturation of certain mental abilities which, in the learning disabled child, happen to be necessary for coping with normal school problems. Unless the causative agent of delay is remarkably selective, neurological systems other than the one that determines cognitive development will frequently be affected as well. For example, sensorimotor immaturities arise that are detectable in the form of soft signs upon neurological examination. What was evidence of immaturity at a lower, sensorimotor level of integration is taken to indicate that the school failure itself is likely to derive from developmental immaturity, even though different brain areas are responsible for cognitive and sensorimotor activities.

The third model is the "difference" model. This does not rely upon an inference of structural or even molecular abnormality, but rather treats the child's predicament as arising from individual variations in the pattern and timing of the development of cognitive skills. These variations are not in themselves abnormal, but they are inconvenient in view of the rigid demands society imposes upon the child. One would not expect such individual variations, presumably genetic in origin, to be accompanied by neurological abnormality (although soft signs can in their own right be expressions of "difference"). The emphasis here is on accommodating the child to the environment and vice versa, rather than on pathology and possible treatment.

Each of the three models can fit many situations; more important, it is rarely possible to prove that one model is more applicable to an individual case than the other two. Whereas the presence of hard signs might arguably support the deficit model, a proponent might see their absence as merely suggesting that the structural damage was too localized to generate hard signs, even though such signs could be detected by other methods. The presence of soft signs is easily attributable to structural damage, since the typical effect of early structural damage is to retard the onset of development of those functions which are normally the responsibility of the damaged brain section. The delay model views hard signs as coincidental and the absence of neurological soft signs as indicating a narrowly focused delay with regard to cognition only. The difference model would regard the presence of hard signs, neurological soft signs, or both as coincidental and unilluminating.

The effect of these considerations is to highlight the uselessness, with respect to school failure, of the much-discussed MBD phenomena. Inferences made from the presence or absence of signs of one or another kind are at best problematic in nature. Worse still, the probabilities attached to each finding are quite unknown. This type of information is not useful in the individual case. Only when the finding relates directly to the school failure is it of interest. Thus, when clumsiness is one cause of a child's difficulty in the classroom, then soft signs of motor immaturity are relevant to the complaint. The same applies to selective cognitive deficits and to cognitive style abnormalities, but these are better regarded as primary complaints than as associated findings.

The analogy with adult brain damage
The ability to read, once acquired, is vulnerable to focal brain damage like any other cognitive skill. Whether a focal brain lesion interferes with reading skill depends not only on its severity but also upon its localization; for only part of the cerebral cortex is specialized to support reading skill, the rest being preoccupied with unrelated activities. However, there is no single reading center in the brain. Rather, different cerebral areas each contribute in different ways to the complex integration of mental operations that makes it possible to read and write fluently. Therefore, lesions in several different cerebral areas will lower overall reading ability; but depending on the area, the nature of this impairment (as inferred from the characteristics of the mistakes made) will differ.

Reading and writing skills clearly have major nonlinguistic components. These abilities include certain discriminatory, spatial, and executive skills which, though put to linguistic use, are not restricted to that purpose. As language function is lateralized to the left cerebral hemisphere in roughly 19 out of 20 people, impairment of the specifically linguistic component of reading and writing will usually result from acquired damage to the left cerebral hemisphere. The right hemisphere in these people is specialized to establish a spatial framework, within which the specific decoding and comprehension activities occur. Certain posterior right hemisphere lesions will disrupt reading, because of a general spatial deficit through which people lose their way on a printed page or fail to notice its left side. These, of course, are not selective or specific alexias. The reading problem is thus only one part, and sometimes a minor part, of a more general cognitive disability.

The cerebral locus of attentional development is uncertain; but in terms of current understanding of the relative roles of the two hemispheres, there seems more reason to attribute it to the left than to the right hemisphere. This is not because attentional development is in any sense specifically linguistic, but because it is an analytic and disjunctive process, in which specific attributes are picked from a set of alternatives. The left hemisphere appears to have primary control over differentiation of this type. Thus, one might postulate a slower maturation of the left hemisphere than of the right in some children. This could then quite reasonably be expected to involve, at school entry, immaturity in just those perceptual skills that provide the underpinnings of the efficient looking and listening abilities required for beginning reading. Such children might acquire those abilities after a little delay, but might then encounter trouble again in the third or fourth grade, because the level of instruction given presupposes certain additional linguistic skills. And again, because of delayed left hemisphere maturation, these skills might not become available at the customary time. Thus a person may have continued selective reading backwardness for reasons that change over the years and that involve a changing pattern of mistakes. Whether some of the many selectively delayed readers are suffering from delayed left hemisphere maturation remains uncertain. Some studies have suggested possible left hemisphere immaturity in such children based on right versus left comparisons of such indicators as average evoked potentials. But the evidence is flimsy, and at this point we do not know whether the suggested sequence of events occurs or not.

Even very limited lesions in adults, if strategically located, can disrupt fluent reading skill. Patients who are aphasic usually have difficulty with reading and writing that is similar to their difficulty with auditory comprehension and spoken expression; but their reading and writing deficits are, if anything, more severe (possibly because reading and writing are more recently acquired and less overlearned). More interestingly, there are a number of rare but well-described syndromes in which the reading or writing process is selectively implicated with little or no general language disturbance. These are the pure alexias, the nature of which remains controversial. They may represent a subset of the visual agnosias in which people are able to see and physically describe, but not recognize or correctly interpret, what were familiar items (three-dimensional objects in visual object agnosia, faces in prosopagnosia, colors in color agnosia, and letters in pure alexia).

Another interesting disorder is simultaneous agnosia — in which people are able to identify individual letters, but only so slowly that they have to pick through each word letter by letter. They say the words' letters to themselves aloud or under their breath and then listen to the letter string, blending it into a word. In this manner they painstakingly proceed along the sentence. This "spelling dyslexia," like visual agnosia, indicates a left posterior (anteromedial occipital) lesion, at least in righthanders. Focal lesions elsewhere in the left hemisphere can selectively disrupt oral spelling ability while leaving written spelling as well as reading relatively intact; or they can disrupt the ability to shape letters correctly (apraxic agraphia), or the ability to choose the correct letters for writing (even though letter shapes are correctly executed, and even though the ability to spell aloud is retained).

Still another intriguing selective deficit is one associated with the so-called Gerstmann syndrome. In addition to finger agnosia, right-left disorientation, and difficulty in calculating, this involves a characteristic spelling difficulty consisting of confusion in letter sequence without substantial confusion in letter choice. Affected individuals reverse letter positions or introduce a letter too soon or too late in the word.

At present there is controversy and uncertainty concerning the extent to which these well-documented selective syndromes of acquired focal damage in adults and older children have congenital or developmental counterparts. (Of course, one cannot expect a developmental deficit to resemble an acquired one in precise detail, as it arises under such different circumstances. Specifically, in the case of an acquired deficit one might retain a body of knowledge which one could not have acquired if the deficit had been developmental.) An analogy has been drawn between the reading difficulty that accompanies aphasia and that of delayed language acquisition. A comparison has also been made between the spelling problems of the Gerstmann syndrome in adults and a comparable situation in children (who, however, have a reading as well as a spelling difficulty). There is less reason to suppose that the other syndromes mentioned above (e.g., prosopagnosia, simultaneous agnosia, color agnosia, alexia) are represented among the population of selectively disabled readers. Perhaps this is because localization of functions or the degree of specialization of functions in young children is different (i.e., less tightly knit) than in adults. Or perhaps cerebral specialization in children is just different from that in adults. The simplest view is that the localization of functions in children is the same as in adults. According to this view, the dearth of clearcut selective syndromes implicating reading in children with developmental disorders is due to the fact that losing a component process used in an already functioning skill (adult reading) has different residual function implications than does loss of that process before the skill is learned. In the first case, the skill might continue to be used, though in a characteristically imperfect manner. In the second case, learning of the skill cannot proceed properly without one of its integral components; so the behavioral manifestation broadens out from that dictated by the selective nature of the deficit into a general failure to learn to read or write. This may be why analogies from adult neuropsychology have been remarkably sterile in helping us to understand the problem of selective reading unreadiness. Localizing hypotheses about the brain basis of affected children's difficulties are moot in most cases, and even if correct they have little practical implication. This is because we are not dealing with a potentially treatable structural lesion, but rather with a delay or imperfection in development that we do not begin to know how to approach at the neurological level. It is thus safest to abstain from neuropsychological analogies, because they tend to impose too rigid and simplistic a constraint on our analysis of what these children really find it hard to do. At the present stage of knowledge, the insights of developmental psychology are more helpful than are the insights of clinical neuropsychology. Presumptions about which brain structures might be immature are of no use whatever in planning to improve a child's learning. For this reason, neuropsychological test batteries seeking to localize lesions, such as the Halstead-Reitan battery, do not contribute to the practical management of children with school problems.

PSYCHOLOGICAL TESTING
It is never good practice to diagnose a cognitive power disorder without documentation from psychological testing. Even the most careful interviewing, combined with the physician's usual list of questions, is not an adequate basis for diagnosis. The following situations help to illustrate some of the reasons why psychological testing is necessary.

1. A father and mother said their 9-year-old son was failing to read at the fourth grade level. "How is he doing in math?" they were asked. "Marvelously," the parents replied, handing over their copy of the achievement test results from his school. "It's all in here," they continued. "He cannot read, but in math he's actually above average." The test results were: "Reading Achievement: Grade 2.8 (nearly third-grade level); Math Achievement: Grade 1.5 (halfway through first grade level)."

Note: Because schools and society place greater emphasis on reading than on mathematical abilities, a child's failure to read may understandably be perceived by adults as more serious than failure in math. This may lead to unintentional misreporting of a child's pattern of abilities and problems.

2. The teachers and parents of a 10-year-old fifth-grade girl referred her for treatment of what they called her failure to learn at her grade level. Her grades in school ranged from well below average to failing. On achievement tests, however, she scored at the fifth-grade level. Further questioning of her parents and teachers revealed that her school drew its students from a population of uni-

versity faculty families. The average IQ of children in that elementary school was far above the national average.

Note: On the basis of her grades and the opinions of her teachers, her parents, and perhaps even herself, this child's school performance might have been classified as a learning disability (average IQ but achievement below that of her peers, in the absence of evidence of motivational difficulties), or as a case of underachievement due to emotional disturbance. Psychological testing made it clear that not only her intelligence but also her achievement were average. The disparity between these test results and the reports of her parents and teachers made further exploration necessary; this resulted in discovery of the highly competitive school in which her performance level suffered by comparison. A less competitive school was found, and she was reassigned there.

3. A 10-year-old boy was brought by his mother, who said he was not learning the material in his fifth-grade class. Testing revealed that his achievement was in fact at the fifth-grade level. Intelligence testing indicated, however, that he was retarded. He was nervous, timid, and tearful in even the most relaxed situations. His well-educated parents were embarrassed and angry that their son was not bright, and it was only under tremendous pressure from them that this retarded child had managed to keep up with his classmates.

Note: Parents' attitudes can force some children into academic performance that appears average. This can happen only at the cost of the child's happiness. Psychological testing can give an idea of how much a child should be encouraged to attempt. (An interesting side-note is that the parents' deep shame about their child's slowness led them to fear his academic failure so much that they believed he was not learning enough when he was actually overachieving).

Although it is discourteous for a physician to simply tell a psychologist what tests to give, a physician who is well-informed about the relevant tests can certainly request specific ones, accompanying the request with a brief statement explaining what information the physician hopes to get from them. (Once a physician and psychologist have established a good working relationship, they can of course exchange this information very efficiently.)

It is wrong to assume that any child is failing or falling behind in schoolwork unless standardized, individually administered tests reveal that to be the case. Such tests allow one to find out approximately how much the child *could* learn at best (in a very general sense) and approximately how much the child has in fact learned at the time of testing. Relying on parents' or teachers' reports of a child's failure allows too many extraneous factors to interfere with the attempt to answer the crucial first question: "Is this in fact a case of school failure?"

Intelligence or IQ tests primarily indicate the child's general ability to learn and think about a variety of matters. Achievement tests show how much the child has actually learned in particular subject areas. Specific learning disabilities tend to cause children disproportionate difficulty in learning certain things (e.g., reading, spelling, arithmetic), without preventing them from learning most other things much more easily. As this is a relative rather than an absolute matter in psychological terms, it could be reflected by average IQ test results combined with one or more achievement test scores substantially below average; or by a superior IQ result combined with only average achievement; or by a below-average IQ result combined with even poorer achievement.

In many cases an emotional problem of the child or the family may interfere with the child's functioning so seriously that you will ultimately recommend psychotherapy. In some cases you may wish to leave all formal personality or projective testing to the therapist. But the emotional problems may be mild enough, or the parents' refusal to consult a psychotherapist may be strong enough, so that you will want to try to straighten out some of the problems in your interpretive interview or in some sessions of your own that are limited in number and frequency. In this case some personality and projective tests given by a psychologist may help pinpoint the trouble-spots.

We shall now seek to describe some of the various tests mentioned and to explain their uses and limitations.

INTELLIGENCE TESTS

Among psychologists two basic schools of thought prevail; these involve what are known as the "multifactorial" and "unitary" theories. Proponents of the multifactorial theory say that many different abilities make up intelligence, with the usual corollary that within one person the level of each factor may vary widely. Thus, one person may have a superb memory for digits but poor ability to learn a code; another may have the opposite pattern; a third may be good at both; and a fourth may be deficient at both. Other psychologists regard intelligence as one basic property, called "g" for "general intelligence." According to this theory any given person has more or less "g" and is either able or unable to do most kinds of thinking well.

Be that as it may, a few abilities correlate very well—both with other abilities and with external standards of intelligence. In general, the better a person's vocabulary, general information about the world, and ability to identify similarities between superficially different things, the better is that person able to perform most other mental operations. People who have superior abilities in these areas also tend to do well in formal schooling and in careers that require careful thinking. That would support the "g" theory. But that support may be qualified by knowledge that the above is only a rough rule, not a precise one. We know from everyday experience that the best speller is not necessarily the best multiplier, memorizer, or logician. The correlation is not perfect.

An intelligence test could be composed of tests for any abilities that the test designer felt like calling measures of intelligence. It is fortunate that the subtests of the IQ tests, such as the Wechsler Intelligence Scale for Children (WISC) and the Stanford-Binet test, actually give an excellent idea of a child's general learning potential in school. The items on the various subtests of these IQ tests turn out to tap a wide range of mental abilities that are necessary for adequate school performance. By and large, a child who scores very low on these IQ tests will have trouble meeting cognitive school requirements, while a child who scores near or above the average level will not. In addition, most of the questions on the test do not require the child to read. Certainly there are enough subtests that a child can score well on without ever having read a word to give us an idea of those aspects of the child's intelligence that have not been limited by reading failure.

One objection to IQ tests has provided a hotbed of controversy; this objection is that they are not culture-free. Some people have claimed that it is unfair to give IQ tests to culturally deprived children whose at-home dialect may differ from the more normal English used in the tests. They have further objected that a wide range of middle-class experiences are necessary to score well on an intelligence test. They allege, for instance, that poor children who may not play with blocks at home will fail on the WISC block design subtest simply because they are not accustomed to using blocks.

There are two answers to this criticism. One comes from research with tests employing "nonstandard" black language that tap the same mental abilities as the standard tests. Results from such tests showed that both black and white children performed better when standard test language was used. William Raspberry, a black columnist for the Washington Post, criticized these "black" IQ tests in a *Time* essay published September 23, 1974. He said such tests measure "knowledge of a specialized vocabulary." He also said "the tests that are the despair of disadvantaged blacks — the tests that keep them out of the good tracks in school, the good colleges and the good jobs — are those that purport to measure skills, aptitudes, achievement and reasoning ability."

For our purposes the standard IQ tests are ideal, simply because they so well represent the skills needed for good performance in a typical school situation. WISC scores, as well as standard achievement test scores, are good predictors of inner-city children's school achievement. Schooling in North America is basically a middle-class enterprise. It involves the traditional middle-class values of delaying gratification, restraining impulses, and learning basic cognitive skills. Most of the children referred for learning problems are in traditional schools. By and large, in fact, children who are having trouble learning do even worse in schools that are run in less "middle-class" ways. If placed in unstructured settings, they are so confused by the many options offered that they never do choose to try to read, or write, or add, or whatever they have trouble doing. As we shall discuss in Chapter 7, it is more individual teaching, even more highly-structured teaching, that is most likely to help these children. Children who are failing in school usually desire (or have parents and teachers who desire) that they learn what might be called white, middle-class subjects but what are in fact useful, usually necessary tools for getting along in the world. Parents who want their children to learn ghetto lingo or pottery and farming instead of the three R's do not need the help of learning specialists; they need to move to other cultures or found new ones. For most children with learning problems, then, the traditional IQ tests give a good picture of how the child, with the existing background and home situation, could learn in most schools.

We shall now discuss how IQ tests are constructed and what mental abilities their various components tap, using the WISC as an example. We have chosen the WISC because we have found it to be the most useful, informative, and comprehensive of the intelligence measures, and also because of the wide range of its subtests. In addition, Wechsler revised the test extensively in 1974, so that the 1974 version, the WISC-R (Revised) is more culture-free and less sex-biased than the 1949 version.

Whatever IQ test is used, though, must be administered absolutely individually. Group tests, given to whole classes at once, or tests in which the child goes into a room alone and marks the answers, provide the least amount of information about a particular child. That is partly because a good psychologist will note important aspects of a child's cognitive approach and other behavior during the testing period, and this affords invaluable, irreplaceable information.

Complex testing and statistical procedures were used in deciding what questions, out of the infinite number possible, should go into the WISC. Basically, however, Wechsler chose items that tapped a wide range of mental abilities and that differentiated well among children ranging in ability from very superior to mentally deficient. In arranging the questions, he made sure that the easiest question within each subtest came first and that the questions then became progressively more difficult. For each subtest there is a "discontinue" note, such as "Discontinue after four consecutive failures." This ensures that no child will experience massive failures that might interfere with thinking on later subtests.

When the test is scored, two things are taken into account: how many questions the child answered correctly and the child's age. An intelligence quotient is a comparative statement. You do not learn from a child's IQ score how that child compares to all other children of all ages. Instead, you learn how that child performed in comparison to other children of the same age. However, it is true that beyond the age of five or six years a given child's IQ tends to vary rather little with age.

The WISC-R is composed of subtests. The so-called verbal subtests are entitled "Information," "Similarities," "Arithmetic," "Vocabulary," "Comprehension," and "Digit Span." The so-called performance subtests are entitled "Picture Completion," "Picture Arrangement," "Block Design," "Object Assembly," "Coding," and "Mazes." Digit Span and Mazes are optional subtests not required for computing a full-scale IQ.

The best way to begin to learn about the WISC is to have someone give the adult version of it (the Wechsler Adult Intelligence Scale, or WAIS) to you. Barring that, if you look at each of the subtests, many of the capacities that contribute to performance on each will become obvious.

The Information subtest poses a series of questions that ask for information, including bits of useful everyday knowledge ("What must you do to make water boil?"), historical and geographic items, and simple scientific facts. Each answer is scored 1 or 0, right or wrong. Good performance on this subtest depends on alertness, awareness of what goes on around one, memory of such facts, and easy recall of them. This is one of the subtests that is the best predictor of overall IQ, perhaps because alertness and memory — obviously basic to most cognitive tasks — are both involved here. If one could only give a few subtests for some reason and needed to get an idea of a child's general level of intelligence, this subtest and one or two others we shall mention would be the ones to administer.

The next subtest, Similarities, is another excellent predictor of overall IQ. Here the child is asked how pairs of things are alike, beginning with concrete items like "wheel" and "ball," going through "pound" and "yard," and proceeding to the last pair, "salt" and "water." Answers are scored 2,1, or 0. A child who can think abstractly, search systematically through possible answers, and choose the most appropriate one will score well. An answer which names a category that is pertinent and abstract enough to cover both items in the pair ("apple and banana are both fruits") but that is not unnecessarily large (e.g., "apples and bananas are both things to eat") is a two-point answer.

The Arithmetic subtest items are straightforward primary-school problems. They start with simple counting of trees and end with a complex multi-operation problem. Although this is more like an achievement than an intelligence subtest, most theorists believe that performing mental operations with numbers is an aspect of intelligence, and often the test can indeed give a rough indication of a child's arithmetic difficulties. Besides operations directly related to arithmetic (counting, adding, subtracting, etc.) optimal performance also depends upon a child's ability to focus and maintain attention, to hold relevant numbers and facts in the short-term memory, to choose the appropriate arithmetical operation, and to prevent anxiety (which sight of the stopwatch often elicits) from interfering with cognitive processes. The examiner reads the first 15 problems aloud, but the child is told to read the last 3. Therefore, a reading problem can obviously impair performance on questions 16, 17, and 18.

The Vocabulary subtest consists of a list of 32 words. In each case the examiner asks the child "What does _____ mean?" These items are scored 2, 1, or 0, depending upon the accuracy and completeness of the response. A high score indicates many of the same abilities as a high score on the Information subtest—abilities including general alertness regarding what is said, heard, and read, as well as memory of material with a highly verbal content. An understanding of what constitutes an adequate definition, rather than a superficial one, also increases the score, so that the child's appreciation of the nuances of language is relevant.

The Comprehension subtest contains somewhat miscellaneous questions. It includes some items requiring common sense ("What is the thing to do when you cut your finger?"), some dealing with general information, social customs, and understanding of those customs ("Why is it usually better to give money to a well-known charity than to a street beggar?"); and some that are highly moralistic ("Why should a promise be kept?"). In addition to the alertness and memory required on the previous subtest, this one requires greater depth of thought and some reasoning ability. Because the questions are scored 2, 1, or 0, some judgment of one's own answers is helpful. An overly brief, overly concrete, or insufficient response will earn only one point or no credit at all. Nonintellectual factors that can interfere with a maximum score are psychopathic traits or freedom from concern about conforming to expectations when that is carried to the point of negativism. For example, a psychopathic child asked "What is the thing to do if a boy (girl) much smaller than yourself starts to fight with you?" might answer, "Beat him (her) up, teach him (her) a lesson." Such an answer does not indicate unawareness of what most people would consider appropriate. In fact, many such children might give a two-point answer like "Walk away, don't fight" if the question were phrased "What do grown-ups think kids should do if smaller children try to fight with them?" Also, an angry or impulsive child may care less about giving the correct answer than about responding impulsively and aggressively. When interpreting a low score on the Comprehension subtest, therefore, one must look at the child's responses to each item in order to understand whether intellectual limitations were at fault or whether mood or personality factors were responsible.

The optional Digit Span subtest consists of asking the child to repeat progressively longer sequences of digits, first forward and then backward. The primary intellectual capacity required is short-term memory for numbers, and the primary attitude needed is sufficient motivation combined with little or no anxiety. This subtest is particularly subject to interference arising from anxiety.

The first of the performance subtests is Picture Completion, in which children are shown a series of drawings and asked to tell what is missing from each one. Here again, general alertness to surroundings and memory of them, this time with less verbal content, contributes to a high score. And again, an understanding of the elements' relative importance is helpful. For example, on picture 1 (a picture of a comb) the correct answer is that a tooth of the comb is missing. "Brush" would be a related answer but obviously not the most relevant.

The Picture Arrangement subtest presents the child with pictures printed on 13 sets of cards. The pictures in each set tell a story. The order of each set is scrambled, and the child is asked to put them in the right order. These items are timed, and scores depend partly on the order of arrangement and partly on the length of time the child takes to achieve the correct order. Basic to good performance on this subtest are some general spatial sense; logical thinking; some social sensitivity and reality-testing (so that the child does not make up a bizarre story to justify an illogical arrangement); and the ability to visualize, symbolize, and mentally rearrange symbols into sequences.

For the Block Design subtest, the child is required to use blocks to reproduce two-dimensional designs that are drawn on cards. Each block has two red sides, two white sides, and two sides divided diagonally into red and white halves. In addition to a general spatial ability, this subtest also demands that the child analyze and then synthesize, first analyzing the flat picture into its parts and then arranging the blocks to form the same design. Because extra points are given for speed of correct performance, anxiety and distractibility can markedly reduce the score.

The Object Assembly subtest is composed of four items, each of which is an object (e.g., a horse) cut up into parts like pieces in a jigsaw puzzle. Children are timed while putting the pieces together and can receive bonus points for speed. There is a good deal of variation in the speed with which they realize what some of the later items are supposed to be. Some general spatial abilities are necessary; these are particularly helpful in mentally arranging and synthesizing the parts, and in mentally putting them together enough to recognize the object. The ability to analyze each part and its potential relationship to the others is also helpful. An overly compulsive person will often hesitate too much to make the cognitive leap ("Ah, it's a horse!") and will proceed only by moving each puzzle piece around each other piece. This physical manipulation obviously takes much longer than doing much of the manipulation in one's mind.

The Coding subtest requires a child to draw appropriate lines in spaces below geometrical shapes, for example, a vertical line below each star, an equals sign below each circle, etc. (For older children, lines are used as a code for numbers rather than for shapes.) There are several rows of shapes, and the child is told to correctly fill in as many rows as possible in the 120-second time limit. The code is at the top of the page, so the child can refer to it, but of course the more of the code the child memorizes the less time will be wasted looking back and forth. Therefore, the ability to memorize paired symbols rapidly is one contributor to good performance on Coding. Perhaps that is why children who have trouble with beginning reading (which includes learning paired symbols—letter shapes paired with their sounds) often score lower on Coding than on the other subtests. Naturally, good coordination of the hand and finger muscles also improves speed. Compulsive children often score low, not because they answer incorrectly, but rather because they spend too much time rechecking correct answers.

The optional Mazes subtest consists of nine mazes in which the child must find and draw the correct path. The score depends on ultimate arrival at the end of the maze and the number of errors made (blind alleys entered) on the way. Ability to plan and spatial memory are the two most important intellectual requirements for this task. Among the nonintellectual contributory factors are a physical one (hand-eye coordination) and one involving personality and cognitive style (impulsiveness). Regarding the latter, an impulsive child may ultimately find the right path but will lose points by thoughtlessly entering too many blind alleys.

Three IQ scores are computed: a verbal score, a performance score, and a full-scale score. The verbal is based on the verbal subtest scores, the performance on the performance subtest scores, and the full-scale on all the subtest scores. They are expressed in terms of their relationship to an average score of 100. That is, the average child of the same age as the child tested scores 100. Differences of a few points are not relevant, because no intelligence test is accurate down to the exact point score. The WISC, however, tends to be accurate within a few points, so that no child who scores around the average mark can have intelligence below the average range; and only an extremely anxious, pathologically unmotivated or negative child can have average intelligence and score well below average. The pattern of IQ scores seems to follow a normal distribution, with a standard deviation on the WISC-R of 15 points. That means that close to 64 percent of the children at any age will have IQs between 85 and 115 (i.e., within a range 15 points below to 15 points above the mean). Wechsler notes in the WISC-R manual that the highest one percent will have IQs of 135 and above, the lowest one percent IQs of 65 and below. He further explains:

. . . the mean (100) and standard deviation (15) which have been chosen will give IQs which, on the whole, are fairly close numerically to IQs of other well-standardized tests like the Stanford-Binet. This will make comparison with IQs of other scales, at least at the numerical level, a not too unreasonable procedure.

Wechsler also inserts an important cautionary note:

However, as the scales are not identical, individual interpretation must always be in terms of each test.

A score of 100 on the WISC-R, for example, is not precisely equivalent to a 100 on the Peabody Picture Vocabulary Test, because all of the Peabody items ask the child to choose correctly the one picture out of four that illustrates the vocabulary word named by the examiner. Nor is the WISC-R 100 figure precisely equivalent to the average score on one of the least verbal of all intelligence tests, the Ravens Progressive Matrices.

After considering some of the intellectual capacities that contribute to a high score on the WISC-R, one has some appreciation of the range of abilities that the test measures. It will be noticed, however, that almost nothing on the test measures reading ability (the Coding subtest and the last three Arithmetic items excepted). There is certainly no breakdown of the reading, writing, or spelling processes into their components; and a child who has never read or written a word can, if intelligent, score well on the WISC-R and on many other IQ tests. The limitation here is that some IQ tests, like the WISC-R, do not measure or require reading ability, and therefore do not help to diagnose a reading, spelling, or writing problem. Other intelligence tests require the child to read or write in order to understand the directions or to answer questions. Such tests would make a bright child with a reading, writing, or spelling problem appear to be extremely unintelligent.

What, then, are the uses of intelligence tests in evaluating children with learning problems? The first, most basic use has already been mentioned. It is to rule out retardation, to make sure that the child under study has at least average intelligence. The second is to detect learning disabilities affecting a child whose achievements in one or more areas do not measure up to the child's IQ potential: that is, a child with a very high IQ and only average achievement test score. In any case, the intelligence test score gives one an idea of the child's basic, general intellectual capacity.

There is another kind of information the WISC-R affords. A comparison of the verbal and performance IQs can suggest which general types of learning problems some children have. Children with reading problems who score substantially higher on the verbal scale have trouble reading for different reasons than children who score substantially higher on the performance scale. Minor differences between verbal and performance IQs are common and uninformative. But a difference of more than 25 points is usually due to a selective deficit, either among verbal or visuo-spatial mental skills. Either kind of deficit could lead to a reading disability, and therefore such a verbal-performance discrepancy deserves further exploration.

What we have already said about the importance of analyzing the components of the reading, writing, spelling, and arithmetic processes strongly suggests that an even more detailed look at the WISC-R results can be helpful. The term *subtest scatter* refers to the pattern of one child's scores on all subtests of a test such as the WISC. The WISC-R test sheet includes a space for graphing the child's score on each subtest, so that high and low points are easy to spot. Different people will show more or less scatter, of course, and it is rare to score at exactly the same level on each subtest. But major differences in relative performance on the various subtests help suggest what the child's weak and strong points are. One can search for patterns: Does this child perform poorly on any test requiring short-term memory for numbers (e.g., Arithmetic and Coding)? Is there some ability that all of the child's "good" or "bad" subtests share? If the "bad" subtests do so, is that ability a component of whatever function the child cannot perform (reading, arithmetic, etc.)? In a similar way, by noting the child's strengths, one can develop an idea of what eventually to advise the child's teachers. For example, you may learn that the child has a relatively easier time with spatial than with verbal tasks. If such a child has an arithmetic problem, the teacher might want to represent arithmetic problems with drawings ("See this picture of six trees") rather than with words ("There were six trees in a field").

It is essential to insist upon an IQ score from an individually administered test rather than a group test. When the goal is to understand the cognitive nature and the emotional components or results of a learning problem, there is no substitute for individual testing by an observant examiner. Such an examiner can tell you whether the child's test scores represent optimal performance or whether the child was so anxious that the scores probably underrepresent existing abilities. The examiner can tell on what subtests, or what items, the child became particularly frustrated, upset, or anxious. Sometimes a child's comments in passing can tell you about cognitive functioning ("I need to count on my fingers," or "I can't remember the numbers when I have to read the problem, too") or about emotional problems, as when a child mentions personal experiences in defining vocabulary words like "seclude" or "nuisance."

EDUCATIONAL TESTS

Educational tests can be divided into those that are norm-referenced and those that are criterion-referenced. The norm-referenced tests tell *how much* a particular child has learned in comparison to other children the same age. Achievement tests are norm-referenced. The criterion-referenced tests tell which of a number of skills the child has trouble with (e.g., remembering letter sequences). If a child has trouble with one of these skills, that will be likely to lower performance on achievement tests. Therefore, one administers achievement tests in order to find out how much the child has learned, and if the child has learned less than one would expect on the basis of that child's IQ test results, then one uses criterion-referenced tests to examine individually each of the skills that, if limited, would have made it difficult for the child to learn to read, write, spell, or calculate. We shall discuss these various types of tests in some detail.

Achievement tests

Once you know from intelligence testing that a child's basic intellectual abilities do not account for a learning difficulty, you need to make sure that there is, in fact, a learning problem. Some parents and teachers mistakenly diagnose a learning problem. Some children, because of shyness, negativism, or even brain-based deficits in communication, may not seem to be learning even though they really are. Other children may be learning at the same rate as average children their age but may be in a school filled with unusually bright children. In such a setting, the average children might seem to have learning problems, whereas in fact the problem would be the excessive pressure put on them by their environment.

Achievement testing is usually quick and simple to administer, and the results are easy to interpret. "Can this child read, or do arithmetic, like an average child of the same age?" The tests sample the child's ability to work at various levels of schooling (e.g., reading and understanding paragraphs of varying difficulty, working arithmetic problems of graduated difficulty, etc.). If the child has a physical handicap that interferes with test performance (e.g., cannot speak or hold a pencil) it is easy to modify the tests. For example, instead of marking the correct answer, a paralyzed child may be able to speak it, and a child who cannot speak may be able to mark the correct answer or nod yes when you point to it.

Many achievement tests serve the important function of measuring what a child has learned in reading, spelling, and arithmetic. Among the most useful are the Metropolitan Test for reading and arithmetic, the Spache Test for reading comprehension (mostly for children beyond the second grade) and the Wide Range Achievement Test (WRAT). The latter has the merit of being individually administered. It requires the child to *read words aloud*, rather than to mark the correct word from a choice of four while the examiner does the reading. Most achievement tests were designed for administration to entire classes at one time, and so the questions require written responses, usually multiple choice, that do not permit an observant examiner to hear the individual child actually read. The WRAT arithmetic section has the advantage of including no story problems such as "Jane has three marbles and wins two more, etc." Thus it truly separates reading from arithmetic achievement. From a practical standpoint, of course, children in school are asked to do mathematical problems that are posed in words. But the *first* thing you need to know about children reported for failure in arithmetic is whether they can do the pure arithmetic when it is uncontaminated by words.

Achievement tests are necessary — not only to confirm that a learning disability exists, but also to indicate the level at which the child should be taught. The achievement age indicated by an achievement test, however, often overestimates that level. Taught at achievement level, a child becomes frustrated; teaching should be at a rather lower level, and independent work by the child is best done at a lower level still.

Hardly any achievement tests provide information that has practical application for a child who is behind in achievement. Why is this so? Well, a reading achievement test, for example, may indicate that a child scores at a grade 1.4 level (fourth month of first grade) on sight vocabulary and at a grade 1.2 level on oral reading. That tells you nothing about *why* the child has a low sight vocabulary or reads aloud poorly. Some of the tests try to go beyond that, by including error checklists or even charts for counting various error types. These are helpful if they tell you more than the child's teacher has already noticed. But if a teacher refers a child, saying "She can't read because her sight vocabulary is so small," you would hope to offer the child and teacher more than the statement, "Yes, you are right."

Let us look at some commonly used error categories. The Gray Oral Reading Tests cover substitutions, omissions, and repetitions of words. Although children with a reading problem may make such mistakes, that tells us nothing definite about the reasons for them. Children may substitute, omit, or repeat words because they have trouble recognizing or remembering letters or letter sequences, or because of anxiety. And children who are aware of their trouble with reading, for any cognitive reasons, may accordingly become nervous and commit additional errors they know how to avoid. Educators must therefore rely on their experience and common sense to draw their own inferences. None of this brings us any closer to advising the teacher about what teaching strategy to use, because norm-referenced achievement tests reveal the subject in which the child is behind but not the child's specific strengths and weaknesses or how the child should be taught.

There is a wide range of achievement tests to choose from; different educators have their own preferences and are familiar with different instruments. We mention here some tests that can be useful but do not imply that others might not do as well. Thus, we are merely illustrating the composition of a comprehensive educational assessment.

Auditory aspects of the reading process can be evaluated by use of several tests, as follows. The ability to blend letter sounds is assessed by the Gates-McKillop Reading Diagnostic Test. Auditory memory, which is involved in writing dictation, is tested by the

Detroit Test of Learning Abilities. Children's ability to remember sentences and to follow spoken directions are also measured by the Detroit Test, and their command of vocabulary is measured by the Peabody Picture Vocabulary Test. The Detroit Test also samples expressive language in terms of free associations and verbal opposites, and tests basic visual skills in terms of copying designs and of memory for designs, for pictures, and for letters. Reading comprehension can be measured by the Gates-Basic Series, writing by the Picture Story Test, and spelling by the Gates-Russell Spelling Test.

Spoken response to visual information is an essential part of reading, and this is sampled at various levels of detail by the Gates-McKillop test. This includes recognition of nonsense words, of initial letters, of final letters, and of vowel sounds. The opposite process, essential for writing, is sampled by the Gates-Russell test in terms of spelling words and syllables from dictation.

Oral reading can be measured by the Wide Range Achievement Test, syllabication and the combining of word parts by the Gates-McKillop test, and oral spelling by the Gates-Russell test.

Arithmetic computation and problem-solving are evaluated by the Metropolitan Arithmetic Achievement Test.

Tests of prereading skills and reading unreadiness

Many tests purport to measure a child's cognitive readiness to learn to read, write, spell, and calculate. In practice they are usually of little use. Readiness tests attempt to probe the child's ability to begin to learn to carry out certain mental operations and then sample the child's inventory of information gathered by performing those operations. Ideally, there should be a test that could determine, for example, whether a child could tell letters apart or could learn to do so if taught right now or in the near future. But in practice, two types of failings afflict readiness tests. First, they test a child's *readiness* to perform operations by asking the child to perform those operations. This is achievement testing in disguise. Second, they include various tests that are fun or interesting but in fact have little or nothing to do with a child's current or future ability to learn to read, etc.

An example of a test with the first shortcoming is the popular Lee-Clark Readiness Test, which includes items testing whether the child knows the names of letters. As others have also shown, a child's ability to write letters rapidly and correctly is an excellent prognostic indicator of the ability to make good progress in grade-school reading. However, although this empirical information might be of some use, little is learned about the nature of the difficulties of the child who *cannot* perform this task. Obviously, if you have already begun to do something, you are more likely to go on learning to do it better than if you have not yet begun to do it at all. And there may be many different reasons for this.

Other sections of readiness tests currently marketed sample what purport to be preacademic readiness skills — such as a variety of perceptual judgment and manipulative skills involving non-letter materials. It is claimed that these tests tap skills necessary for readiness to learn to read, write, spell, and calculate, but all the tests have drawbacks of the second variety that are serious enough to render them useless. No evidence is offered that the arbitrarily selected operations tested really bear a determining relationship to readiness to learn. In no case has it been shown either that being able to do the "readiness" operations involved is sufficient for, say, reading readiness, or that any of these operations are necessary; that is, it has not been shown that a child lacking the ability in question cannot learn to read. Therefore, using these tests risks an unknown but quite possibly high proportion of both false-positive and false-negative results: children pronounced ready when they are not and pronounced unready when they are. These risks make the tests an unacceptable basis for any decision-making. There is one further subtle but real danger. This is that teachers will teach "readiness;" that they will waste children's time with procedures related to the test items and teach them skills for which there is no possible use (rather than teaching them what they need to know).

Probing the ability of children to do certain things is subject to serious error, in that children's previous experience with the kinds of material offered is not controlled. Particularly when socially heterogeneous groups are being tested, assumptions cannot be made about any uniform level of prior experience, and occasional sampling of behavior may be grossly confounded by the reaction of some children to an unfamiliar situation or task. The logical way to overcome this important difficulty is for the tests to be tests not of knowledge, but of ability to learn. The ideal format of any tests for learning disabilities would therefore be an arrangement which is in some respect a microcosm of the reading instruction process at a particular stage. More revealing than determining whether a child can discriminate between orientations is to see which children can be taught to do so rapidly and which cannot. More revealing than probing for a child's ability to segment words into their speech sounds is knowing which children can do this after logically organized exposure to a limited set of simple test words, and which cannot.

Few tests explore the rate of learning rather than the existing fund of knowledge and problem-solving skills. One reason is that it takes longer to teach (and determine whether something was learned) than merely to test the existing cognitive structure and fund of knowledge. The challenge is to design learning tests which will be valid and reliable without being excessively time-consuming. Attempts have been made, including one by ourselves that will be described subsequently, but these tests are not ready for general use.

Even more important than the results of psychological and educational tests are teachers' observations concerning the manner in which particular children respond to teaching and the way in which teachers find themselves instructing in order to have particular children respond. The teacher should teach systematically (i.e., should know how the teaching has been done) and should record the child's response to that teaching. The resulting information as to what it would take to meet that child's learning requirements is much more pertinent than that which arises from any compartmentalized psychoeducational evaluation, however comprehensive and expertly done.

Popular tests of presumed prereading skills include the Frostig Developmental Test of Visual Perception, the Purdue Perceptual Survey Rating Scale (by Roach and Kephard), the Bender Visual-Motor Gestalt Test, the Perceptual Achievement Forms Test, the Motor-Free Test of Visual Perception, and a number of motor tests recommended by Ayres.

Diagnostic educational testing
In order to discover exactly what an individual child finds unduly difficult, and therefore needs additional help with, teachers use criterion-referenced tests that tell them whether or not the child reaches some criterion of "sufficient" skill on each of a range of individual operations called for by the instructional process. The definition of "sufficient" and the detailed nature of the skills sampled are arbitrarily determined by the designer of the test. This form of testing is intended to yield information about what exactly the child knows and does not know, can or cannot do, is or is not sure of, in a particular instructional area. Like achievement tests, these formal diagnostic instruments first enable a general level (e.g., for word recognition) to be established. Unlike achievement tests, however, these criterion-referenced tests classify the types of mistakes the child makes at the current instructional level in order to reveal particular problem areas (i.e., the most prevalent types of error). An instructional prescription based on these findings directs the teacher's attention to those subskills that need to be strengthened.

An example of a diagnostic reading test is the Queen's College Educational Clinic's Sample Word List. This is intended to help assess specific weaknesses in word calling and word attack. The student's errors are recorded under headings such as omissions, whole-word reversals, letter confusions, substitutions, added or omitted endings, confused initial sounds, confused ending sounds, confused medial vowels, and omitted medial syllables. The Gates-Russell Spelling Diagnostic Test measures oral spelling, word pronunciation, methods of word attack, auditory discrimination, etc. The Zaner-Bloser's Evaluation Scale assesses cursive and manuscript handwriting with respect to legibility. Both Diagnostic Tests and Self-Helps in Arithmetic assess the child's ability in various arithmetic component skills and provide corrective self-help exercises. In addition, inventories for each academic skill can be constructed by teachers from readily available guidelines to meet the needs of individual children.

Diagnostic educational testing differs fundamentally from readiness testing. Readiness tests examine supposed precursors of academic skills and pave the way for training programs in these precursors, rather than in the defective skills themselves. The definition of these readiness skills reflects nothing more secure than the test designers' theoretical preconceptions, and the training does not necessarily strengthen the academic skills in question, as it is supposed to do. Nor has prereading training been shown to lessen the difficulties of children who would otherwise have had definite trouble when beginning to learn to read. Therefore, it is recommended that diagnostic teaching be used to locate the child's specific difficulties in the academic area of failure. Then, using existing knowledge of children's mental development (outlined in Chap. 3), the teacher can infer which is the best way to clarify for the child the particular matter that has not yet been grasped. In this vein, diagnostic educational tests are best viewed as providing teachers with a systematic framework for classifying and recording their pupils' performance in academic areas. As teachers gain experience, so they will become increasingly capable of relating particular portions of a child's test performance to particular teaching approaches and needs.

Thus, a comprehensive educational assessment will sample the child's ability with respect to the auditory, visual, and auditory-visual cross-modal foundations of the reading and writing process, as well as the child's ability to perform a range of manipulations inherent in that process. The choice of activities sampled is necessarily empirical and is based on informed intuition rather than secure knowledge. But the results do afford an opportunity not only to know what children can and cannot do, but also to observe the manner in which they go about their successful and unsuccessful attempts at these various component activities. The error patterns that emerge are often very revealing in terms of what the child does not know and needs to know. The same is true of arithmetic achievement and diagnostic testing.

PERSONALITY TESTING

Checklists and the MMPI

In some cases you may want to investigate the child's emotional life. You may wish to gather some impressions about the child's major areas of concern or conflict in order to reassure or explain certain things to the child in the interpretive interview. Or you may suspect parent-child problems that are severe enough to warrant mention during the interpretive interview but simple enough so that there seems insufficient reason to recommend psychotherapy or family therapy right away. In such circumstances it might be advisable to suggest that the father spend more time with the child, that the parents stop being the child's reading tutors, or that someone reassure the child that a learning problem does not signify general worthlessness or sinfulness. Sometimes parents or children tell you about these worries spontaneously; but many times you may need to request personality tests for this purpose. On rare occasions, a previously undiagnosed psychosis or borderline personality may be interfering with the child's learning.

The simplest, most straightforward kind of personality test is the checklist. Children are asked to check spaces labeled "yes" and "no," or "always," "usually," "sometimes," and "never" in response to a series of statements describing themselves. The statements may include interests and preferences ("I'd rather take walks alone than go to a party"), feelings ("Sometimes I feel like running away from home" or "I feel like people are always telling me what to do"), or self-descriptions ("I am ugly," "No one likes me," "I make friends easily"). One of the most useful of the checklist tests is the Self-Observation Scales (SOS) devised by Stenner and Katzenmeyer. The results of the SOS are computed as scores on four scales: (1) self-acceptance (including the degree to which the children tested feel happy, important, generally competent, and valued by peers, family, and teachers); (2) social maturity (including whether the children know how they are supposed to feel in a variety of social situations, whether they understand the importance of ideas like fair play and helpfulness, and whether they are likely to behave in selfish, inconsiderate, or immature ways); (3) school affiliation (whether they consider school a positive and happy experience); and (4) self-security (their level of emotional confidence, stability, sense of control over life, and time spent worrying about possible troubles).

The SOS seems to be the best personality checklist for children in the early grades. At present it has the drawback that the test protocols have to be scored by computer, and there can be a substantial delay. When the scoring key becomes available to the people who buy the test and administer it to their patients, this drawback will be removed.

What about a personality checklist for older children? Personality tests for adolescents are difficult to design, and good ones are few. This is partly because what may be normal feelings or behavior for an adolescent are often considered disturbingly pathological for younger people or adults. In addition, some theorists believe that there is more normal variation in adolescence than at any other time of life. So it is easier to describe a typical normal child or a typical normal adult than a typical normal adolescent. There may simply be more normal patterns of adolescent development than there are for other age groups.

For a 16-year-old of average intelligence, or an unusually intelligent or mature 14- or 15-year old, a helpful checklist is the Minnesota Multiphasic Personality Inventory (MMPI), which was originally an adult test. Recently, though, some useful gathering and interpretation of adolescent norms has been reported. The patients check whether or not each of a long list of statements applies to themselves. Therefore, there is a large but not infinite number of ways in which people can respond to it. Specifically, there are 566 items on the test, a large enough number—and a varied enough collection—so that many different kinds of emotional disturbances can be reflected in many different patterns of response. The MMPI has recently been revised and updated by introduction of computer scoring and analysis of the patterns of response produced by large numbers of people. Interpretation of this test depends to some extent on the psychologist's experience with and knowledge of the MMPI. However, a system of interpretation that is easy to use is the system of two-point codes, which can be described briefly as follows:

The standard scoring of the MMPI includes the plotting of a kind of graph for each patient. Of the 566 items on the test, various groups of items are included on more than one scale. In addition, the test includes a number of built-in safeguards to minimize the effects of lying or trying to falsify responses. These scales allow the psychologist to know, before making further interpretations, how much each patient probably lied, exaggerated, or covered up, and whether a given patient lied so much that the whole test is in-validated (this latter situation almost never arises). Each scale is given a name (the names are misleading in some cases) and a number, as shown below.

The "clinical" scales:

1. Hypochondriasis
2. Depression
3. Conversion hysteria
4. Psychopathic deviate
5. Masculinity-femininity
6. Paranoia
7. Psychasthenia
8. Schizophrenia
9. Hypomania
10. Social introversion

The way in which the test is scored and the graph of results plotted means that the higher a score, and the higher its position on the graph, the more pathological or atypical is that factor. Using the two-point code method of interpretation, the psychologist notes the highest and second-highest scales and their numbers (e.g., one common pair of high scores is 2–7, and another is 4–6). Depending upon the extent of personal experience, then, one may use MMPI reference books to see what characteristics 2–7s tend to share, or else draw on one's own experience to make that inter-pretation, or do both these things. Because reliable MMPI norms for adolescents are lacking, the test should only be interpreted by a highly experienced, cautious psychologist when the patient is an adolescent. There are some modifiers, of course, including the magnitude of the two scores and also the difference between the score on the 2 scale and the score on the 7. For example, a score of a certain magnitude on the 8 scale indicates schizophrenia with fair certainty; but a higher score, for various reasons, would rarely if ever come from a true schizophrenic; instead, it would be more likely to come from a severely anxious person who desperately wants some help. One further modifier is the test interpreter's knowledge of the patient's history and current life situation. For example, someone who scores very high on the hypochondriasis scale may be hypochondriacal or may have just had surgery or a stroke. Some people who may appear pathologically paranoid, par-ticularly adolescents, turn out to be marijuana users who have good reason to suspect that they are being watched by law enforcement officers. But taking these modifying factors into consideration, one begins with the two-point codes and then looks successively at each of the next-highest scales to consider what additional information each affords. For example, for a 2–7 patient, a third-highest scale of 9 would indicate something very different (often suicidal tendencies) than it would for a 4–6 patient (perhaps a likelihood of committing some grossly antisocial or illegal act).

The Missouri Children's Picture Series, designed for use with even young children, produces some of the same general types of information as the MMPI. Children are asked to sort pictures of activities into those they think are fun and those they think are not fun. Scoring produces ratings of Conformity, Masculinity-Femininity, Maturity, Aggressiveness, Inhibition, Activity Level, Sleep Disturbances, and Somatization.

Personality checklists are quick and easy to administer and to score. If a child answers truthfully, they can give a good picture of that child's personality and worries. But if a child is very shy or defensive, the checklists may not give a true picture. Many children who are not ordinarily defensive may become reticent when they know that a stranger is trying to find out about feelings they consider embarrassing, worrying, or unusual. (That drawback is mostly averted on the MMPI, but the test unfortunately cannot be used for young children and many adolescents.)

Projective tests
Projective tests offer a partial solution. A set of inkblots or pictures is shown to the child, and the child is asked either to tell what the blot looks like or to make up a story about the picture. Projective tests make it much harder for people to know what they are revealing about themselves by the responses they give. One characteristic of the tests that makes them hard to interpret, however, is that, in contrast to checklists, there is an unlimited number of possible responses.

The theory of projective testing is as follows: No two people have identical life experiences, personalities, or cognitive styles. Two people witnessing an automobile accident rarely retell the event in an identical way, probably because of the differences in where they looked, their own personalities, their memories, and their habitual strategies for remembering and learning. Similarly, prison bars may evoke fear in a criminal but a feeling of being protected from criminals in a law-abiding citizen. The effects of these individual differences are much more pronounced on projective tests because the elements of the tests are designed to be vague and evocative. The best of the projective tests are those with the fewest recognizable details, because the patients' responses then come more from their own emotional life than from the stimuli. Patients look at the stimulus card and see only an inkblot or a few people or animals, perhaps a bit of scenery, and must then draw on their own feelings, imaginations, and biases to produce a response or create a story.

Projective tests have been criticized. This criticism has been based mostly on their improper use. Some psychologists once believed they should be able to read someone's test responses and then, on that basis alone, to correctly identify the patient's age, sex, race, social class, and personality traits. The function of projective tests, however, is to suggest areas of conflict, concern, pleasure, or shame, and to indicate the nature of relationships that the patient has with parents, peers, or siblings. No projective test response should ever be taken as *proof* of anything. It is merely a way to gather impressions and insights, to accumulate bit by bit the information one needs to have about the patient. It may be information that supports hunches you had before the tests were given, or the test material may suggest avenues that you want to explore later in interviews, or that you believe a psychotherapist should explore further.

Two of the projective tests commonly given to children are the Children's Apperception Test (CAT) and the Rorschach Inkblot Test.

THE CHILDREN'S APPERCEPTION TEST. There are two ways to "score" the CAT—a children's form of the Thematic Apperception Test. One way sounds more systematic and scientific than the other; it is to use the test manual's list of themes, count the number of times each theme appears, and add up the number of happy, sad, or neutral outcomes. This quantifies or confirms the impressions the psychologist may have gathered as the test was being given. But the psychologist may happen to like or dislike the patient, may have preconceived ideas about the patient's problems and concerns, or may have unusually strong feelings about some issue or other. These things can make one of the patient's stories or sentences loom unjustifiably large in the psychologist's evaluation, or make it so insignificant as to escape notice, thereby rendering the scoring unsystematic.

However, such scoring should not be accepted as the sole basis for interpreting the test results. A skilled, experienced psychologist will note qualitative aspects of the test results that may be more informative than the formal scoring. For example, children may be so defensive that they only mention some "negative" emotion such as self-loathing or resentment of parents in one story, but do so with a tremor in the voice and tears in the eyes, and end that story with a disaster. The formal scoring of that child's test might include only one instance of such an emotion and only one story with a miserable outcome; but it could be crucial to appropriate management of the child for you to know how the psychologist tends to weigh and interpret responses.

For that reason, the two most important qualities to look for in psychologists are astuteness and sensitivity to people's feelings and ways of expressing them, and experience with the tests being used. The former traits are important for obvious reasons. They involve the more intuitive, empathic aspect of projective testing. Experience with the tests being used involves the more scientific aspect of such testing. The more times a person gives any test, and the wider the variety of emotional disturbances and diagnostic categories of the patients who take the test, the better basis the tester is likely to have for judging responses to be bizarre or ordinary, and for hypothesizing that certain responses tend to signify emotion X or conflict Y.

What can one learn from the CAT or TAT (the Thematic Apperception Test, used for adults)? In one sense the answer to that question is limitless, because of the number and variety of stories a patient can create. But four major facets about which information can be obtained are: (1) cognitive style, including the patient's response to more or less structure; (2) emotional style; (3) specific feelings, issues, and fantasies that trouble the patient; and (4) self-image. Though we shall briefly discuss a few examples of how test material relates to each of these, it should be noted that many other themes, issues, and explanations of patients' responses are possible.

Cognitive Style: The psychologist has asked the patient to tell about the present, past, and future of the story on each card, and to tell the characters' thoughts and feelings. In considering cognitive style, as with all aspects of projective test interpretation, the key is *differences* among patients. Some patients, or even untroubled people, will remember the initial directions, and others will ask to have them repeated several times. That may tell you that the former have a better memory, are less anxious, or both. Some people will organize each story differently, whereas others will scrupulously tell first the present, then the past, then the future, and then the characters' thoughts and feelings. Still others may consistently forget one or another of those story segments. This gives an indication of the compulsiveness of their cognitive style (and this of course overflows into emotional style as well). In the case of the patient who consistently forgets story segments, or forgets them on certain cards, this may indicate that the patient's own past included something too painful to remember, or that the patient has disturbing fears about the future. The content of the rest of a story from which some part has been omitted may help to interpret the omission. A story about loneliness for which the patient does not volunteer to give the outcome suggests fears of separation, desertion, or death. These tests thus provide circumstantial evidence for hypothesis formation, evidence that requires confirmation by further testing, interviewing, and observation. They must not be used alone to make diagnoses or recommendations.

A corollary of this is that no single response can be assumed to reveal the same thing about any two people who give it. For example, two patients may both tell stories in which a son has hurt his mother's feelings and is apologizing to her. In one case the story may reflect the patient's strong, still-current feeling of responsibility for his mother's happiness. In the other it may reflect a situation that the patient finds saddening but which indicates more about that patient's sensitivity to other people's feelings than it does a neurotic degree of concern about guilt and responsibility. Both of these patients' stories, then, must be interpreted in the context of what they say on the rest of this and other tests, and on the basis of what else the psychologist knows about their lives and problems.

Other characteristics of cognitive style can appear in projective testing. A person's tendency to think things through, to be logical and complete, may be reflected in the completeness and cohesiveness of the stories. This is also related to the extent that the patient is aware of and sensitive to the tester's presence. Psychotic patients, or many kinds of people who have trouble with interpersonal relationships, may speak their thoughts without much attempt to make them clear and comprehensible to the listener.

Another source of information concerns the patient's response to more or less structure. This is an aspect of both cognitive and emotional style. One usually gives projective tests last in a series of tests, after the more objective tests like IQ and achievement batteries. Thus, the testing begins with a great deal of structure. The patient knows, or senses, that there is only one correct answer, or at most a very limited set of correct answers, to each question, and indeed the questions are worded in a way that is intended to focus the patient's attention on particular kinds of information. With projective tests, on the other hand, instructions are minimal and are intended to ensure that the responses are dictated, as much as possible, by the pressures of a patient's emotional life and a hierarchy of the patient's present and past worries. Obviously, there are no correct or incorrect answers on a projective test, for all answers tell one something about the responder.

So as patients progress from the objective through the projective tests, they move from a great deal of externally imposed structure to very little. Some people are flexible enough to take this progression in stride, giving their imagination and feelings more and more play, keeping within the structure when it is clearly important and then opening up as the psychologist reduces the structure.

What can interfere with the patient's making this adaptation? One thing is a rigid compulsiveness. Compulsive people may do one of two things. They may, in essence, treat the projective tests as though they were objective tests, giving very limited, careful answers, the content of which is defensive and reveals little other than their fears of self-revelation. Or they may disintegrate as the structure diminishes; being unable to tailor their answers to less highly structured directions, they may lack the capacity to remain calm in the face of that obstacle. In such cases, the inadequacy of response typically takes one of two forms. Either the patients say literally or virtually nothing (e.g., "It's a picture of three chickens eating something"), or else they become overwhelmed by feelings that well up when not rigidly suppressed. In the latter case, patients may say something like "This is a picture of a mother's rage with her children, who hate her so much that they will throw at her the food she worked all day to prepare," their emotions overwhelming any attempt they might make at telling a story in a calm, logical way. Patients like this often show physical signs of the difficulty they have in regulating their flow of feelings. They may quiver with rage, dig their fingernails into their palms, bite their lips, become tearful, etc.

The borderline or psychotic personality's response to diminishing structure may be similar to this. Such a person may perform very well on IQ and achievement tests, in which the questions by and large have little emotional significance. But faced with projective tests composed of stimuli intended to evoke feelings (particularly troublesome ones), their self-control falls away, and they, too, either resort to exceedingly defensive, rigid answers or become awash with uncontrollable feelings. With borderline and psychotic patients, the content of the TAT stories tends to become even less logical and communicative, particularly on cards that they find especially threatening. They may then say things like "This is mother-son hatred," becoming so absorbed by the feelings that they do not go beyond that level of abstraction to create the requested narrative. A variation on this response is given by a patient who, having responded to a very upsetting card, then tells the same or virtually the same story, or relates the same emotion, for succeeding cards where it is inappropriate. One then suspects that the patient has little capacity to handle feelings in a way that allows an adequate response to the next card. This is a sign of extreme anxiety, often of rigidity, and sometimes of psychosis.

Emotional Style: Much of what we have said about cognitive style also applies to emotional style. In addition, several other aspects of emotional style are revealed on projective tests. A few of these are as follows: Patients who tend to repress feelings to an unusual extent often give very defensive responses on projective tests. This tendency is exaggerated by the patients' awareness that they cannot be sure how the psychologist will interpret their TAT stories; so, in effect, they cannot be sure how much they are expressing any time they speak in that situation. Such patients often tell stories that are either very sparse or strikingly lacking in emotional content. Paranoid tendencies often appear in a patient's production of stories where the main character is harshly and unfairly judged while in fact being an admirable person.

People who have trouble regulating the flow and expression of feelings, notably borderline or schizophrenic patients, may find it necessary to put some distance between themselves and the stimulus cards. They may accomplish this by beginning the stories with "Once upon a time" or setting them in a distant location or historical period (e.g., "In ancient Egypt there was a girl. . . ." or "This takes place in the jungles of darkest Africa"). The use of such settings should not be taken as proof that someone is schizophrenic or borderline; it simply indicates that the patient is having trouble becoming involved in the feelings the card arouses and has a primitive way of dealing with that trouble. This may indicate an extreme neurotic striving for control or something more serious, but in any case it is an indication of a need for further investigation. It should also be noted that the use of fairy-tale settings or far-off times and places is less unusual for children than for adults, and thus in young children it alone does not constitute cause for alarm.

The other way that trouble regulating emotional expression manifests itself on apperception tests is through overinvolvement in the stimulus cards. Occasionally a patient will inspect a card exceedingly closely, not as if to observe some previously unnoticed detail, but rather as if expecting one of the pictures on the card to move or somehow reveal further information. More often a patient with such trouble will become so involved in one or more of the stories created that it becomes unusually hard to get away from the card; the patient draws the story out endlessly, often dwelling on some particular aspect long past the point at which its content has been clearly communicated.

Feelings, Issues, and Fantasies: For the most part, the ways the patient's feelings, issues, and fantasies appear in projective test stories are self-evident. A surprising number of troubling feelings or wistful thoughts and fantasies appear as striking parts of the narratives (e.g., "This boy feels guilty because his parents gave him a violin but he doesn't like to play it," or "This girl is looking out the window, wishing she were old enough to see her boyfriend whenever she wanted," or "This little bunny is lonely, but she knows that her daddy will come back some day and take her to live in a big castle"). Much of the content in these categories is interpersonal and illustrates trouble-spots the child experiences in dealing with parents, siblings, and peers (e.g., "The monkeys are whispering to each other about how stupid the little monkey is," or "The mother bear and baby bear are trying to pull the rope away from the father bear, and they will win because the mother bear always beats the daddy").

Self-Concept: Here, too, much of the material is self-explanatory. Children often feel that one of the characters is telling another about some embarrassing or shameful trait or behavior of the main character, who usually represents the patient. Children with school problems often represent the main figure in their stories as stupid, trouble-making, or ostracized by family, teachers, and peers.

THE RORSCHACH INKBLOT TEST. The Rorschach Test has much in common with the TAT and CAT. It, too, is a projective test, and Rorschach selected the ten cards that now comprise it using similar criteria: the blots tend to elicit fairly rich emotional imagery, and there is enough variety among them so that the test tends to tap a wide range of feelings within a given patient. But the Rorschach is even less structured than the TAT and CAT. Rather than being asked for stories, the patient is simply told, "Look at this and tell me what you see" or "what it looks like." If a patient gives one response to the first card and then stops, the psychologist says, "Anything else?" but usually says nothing after that. As with the other projective tests, the examiner's reticence is intended to ensure that most of the response has to do with the patient's needs and feelings rather than with the patient's style of interacting with the psychologist. The patients who ask if it is permitted, or required, to turn the cards upside down or sideways, or to give a large or small number of responses to each card, are told that they may do whatever they choose.

The psychologist gives the patient one card at a time and records the responses to each. Then the psychologist says "Now we're going to go through these again, and I want you to tell me what it was that made it look like each thing you saw." The psychologist checks to see what the patient said about the first card and says, for example, "Here is the first one. You said it looked like a mask. What made it look like a mask?" After the patient answers, the psychologist asks the same question about the next response on card one and continues in order through all ten cards.

Virtually everything we have said about scoring and interpretation of the TAT and CAT applies to the Rorschach. There are several additional points, however, that should be mentioned. The first of these concerns scoring. The mathematical scoring of the Rorschach is far more complicated than the quantitative scoring of the apperception tests. To begin with, there are two main categories of Rorschach information that must be considered. The first category consists of content, or what patients say they see on the cards. The second category is composed of determinants and some related characteristics. As already mentioned, after the patient has responded to each card, the psychologist asks what it was about each blot that made it look like those things. The recording of the patient's answers to this inquiry is extremely detailed. The psychologist notes the determinants (e.g., Does the patient say it was the shape, the color, the shading, the texture, or the location of the inkblot that made it look like a mask, an animal, or whatever?). Then the psychologist notes where on the card the patient saw each thing. Was it on the blot or in the white space around it or in the middle of it? Did it include the entire blot or just part of it? If it included only part of it, was it a large part (called D for large detail) or a small part (called d for small detail or, occasionally, for a segment not usually noticed or segregated as a single response)? In addition, the psychologist scores each response for something called "form level." Form level classifies responses as either good or bad, sometimes on a scale ranging from 0 to +4, depending on the extent to which that blot, or part of a blot, really looks like what the patient said it resembled. To some extent, judgment of form level depends on experience with the test. There are some responses that would not occur to the tester, but that would seem more understandable after the tester has had the experience of hearing several patients give the response in question, or after having inspected the blot in question while a patient explained why it looked like that. The psychologist, in short, must be able to lay aside preconceived notions about what the blots look like and to consider as objectively as possible whether their form really justifies the label the patient chooses to give them.

What do we mean by "justifies?" There are two basic determinants of any Rorschach response—the blot itself and the patient's needs and fears. An extremely anxious, hypochondriacal, or angry patient may see blood and gore on every blot, regardless of the blots' shapes and colors. A very defensive patient may call every blot a cloud or a map, even though most people would notice other things clearly suggested by the form. Some very upset patients may see whatever is on their minds but may inspect the blots carefully enough before responding so that they are able to choose sections that really resemble the objects of their worries or fantasies. If such a response is unusual but somewhat justified by the form of the blot, then the psychologist will note that the patient seems to be feeling pressure from some strong emotion. If the relation to the form is very poor, however, the psychologist will begin to suspect that the patient's methods of dealing with strong feelings are so primitive as to preclude a reasonable response. This may indicate a borderline or psychotic disorder.

This provides an example of how qualitative considerations combine with something more quantitative (How common is the response, and how far justified by the blot?) to suggest interpretations of the Rorschach. What about the mathematical scoring methods alluded to earlier? There are many such formulae and handbooks for interpreting them. They include such things as tallying up the ratio of the number of color responses to the number of movement responses (i.e., How many times did the patient say color made the blot look like the thing seen, and how many times did the patient say that the thing seen looked as if it were dancing, waving, jumping, etc.?). Some theorists believe that a high ratio of color responses indicates hysteria or even schizophrenia, particularly if the form level is poor. Some believe that a certain number of texture responses (e.g., "It looked like a bearskin rug because it looked soft and fuzzy") indicates anxiety, whereas others interpret this merely as a sign of rich emotional life.

It is particularly difficult to resolve such issues because of the dual problems of patient selection and test interpretation. Even if one collects 25 obsessive-compulsive housecleaners, the fact that the number of possible Rorschach responses is infinite makes it difficult to find many similarities among the test protocols of those 25 people. And even when one finds such similarities, some are likely to simply reflect "popular" responses, or responses that many or most people give. The proper next step, then, would be to compare the responses of the 25 obsessive compulsives to those of 25 schizophrenics of acute onset, 25 lifelong schizophrenics, 25 psychopaths, etc.

Overly strict adherence to mathematical exercises with the Rorschach implies *erroneously* that the Rorschach is a scientific instrument. As with the CAT and TAT, some kind of tallying may be helpful to guard against grossly inaccurate misperceptions. But once the tallying has been done, a careful qualitative interpretation is best.

With respect to the qualitative interpretation, much of what was said about the four categories of information on the apperception tests applies here. There are also some additional sources of information on the Rorschach. One of these involves the symmetry and nonrepresentational quality of the inkblots. Unlike the CAT and TAT cards, the Rorschach cards do not need to be held right-side up. If their own rigidity does not preclude it, patients are free to turn the Rorschach cards sideways and upside down, and indeed many new responses often suggest themselves after such turning. This is another indication, then, of rigidity. Do various patients even ask about turning? Do they worry about whether the tester will allow it, or do they take the initiative and do it on their own? Do the additional possibilities produced by turning push them into compulsively turning each card and trying to come up with many more responses on each one? Or does this possibility, by further widening their options, push them toward disintegration in the face of too little externally imposed structure?

A second aspect of the inkblots is that they seem able to tap more unconscious material, often things of which the patient is not aware, than can the TAT, CAT, or checklists. One reason seems to be that, like unconscious fears, the blots are not clearly defined, not tied to any conscious logic or any reality. Being non-representational, they provide fewer objective details which the reticent patient can describe in order to avoid allowing emotions to be evoked by the cards. One of the striking characteristics of many unconscious fears and other feelings is an absence of clear outlines or limits and sometimes even of clear definitions. The Rorschach inkblots often evoke such feelings. Furthermore, the test itself provides little opportunity or guidance for the patient seeking to organize or clarify the feelings and associations evoked. Creating stories (as on the CAT and TAT) or writing poetry bring many such unconscious feelings under control by embodying them in a structure, modifying and limiting them by virtue of including them in a story line or a poem. But the inkblot test does not offer such limits, except by asking the patient to express what is seen in one or more words. So more unconscious material often comes through.

By and large, for the reasons just outlined, the Rorschach is usually harder to interpret than other tests. It requires more experience and greater care. A really good Rorschach interpreter follows this principle: Associate very freely to what the patient says, but draw conclusions very conservatively. The reason that it is good for psychologists to "associate freely" to the patient's responses is that this allows them to draw on the widest possible range of their own experiences, feelings, and professional training. Because the Rorschach is aimed at revealing individual differences, it makes good statistical sense that the more feelings or situations a psychologist has seen at least one person associate with, for example, a bat (one common response to one of the inkblots), the more likely the psychologist is to interpret what significance a particular patient's responses have in comparison to all others. But because of the nature of the test, for obvious reasons, the psychologist should make sure that any conclusions are based on at least two indications from the test material, or on at least one indication that would seem justified by its intensity or by other comments the patient may have made.

SUGGESTED READING
Bellak, L. (Ed.).   *The T.A.T. and C.A.T. in Clinical Use.* New York: Grune & Stratton, 1971.
Bert, C. L., Touwen, B., Heinz, S. R., and Prechtl, H. *The Neurological Examination of the Child with Minor Nervous Dysfunction.* London: Heinemann, 1970.
Johnson, O. G., and Bommarito, J. W.   *Tests and Measurements in Child Development: A Handbook.* San Francisco: Jossey-Bass, 1971.
Mehrens, W. A., and Lehmann, I. J. (Eds.).   *Standardized Tests in Education.* New York: Holt, Rinehart & Winston, 1969.
Purkey, W. W.   *Self Concept and School Achievement.* Englewood Cliffs, N.J.: Prentice-Hall, 1970.

5. Interpretive Interviews

WHAT TO SAY

Many elements of the initial interview serve as important preparation for the interpretive interview with parents. The single most important thing in the interpretive interview is to make sure that the parents hear your conclusions and recommendations. A person's mere physical presence and unimpaired hearing do not guarantee that the person understands, accepts, remembers, and carries out prescriptions for treatment. How many times have doctors made recommendations and found later that the patient did not understand, was too frightened or threatened to listen properly, or failed to remember and implement the recommendations? This is certainly true of even the simplest directions, such as "Take this pill when you have a pain right here."

The possible sources of interference are increased substantially when the problem is not purely physical, has important implications for social acceptability (how one's child is performing in school), and has many emotional components. Some parents are so ashamed of their child's inadequate school performance that they cannot settle down to focus on what to do about it. Others are so frightened of (or awed by) the physician's social standing and authoritative position that they are afraid to admit when they are not understanding what is being said. Still others are too absorbed by their frustration at encountering a situation they cannot totally control, a problem they cannot solve alone, that their resentment of the "interfering" doctor gets in the way. The more of these feelings that you can acquaint yourself with, beginning in the initial interview, the more you will know about the tone of voice, the words, and the order to use in presenting your findings and suggestions to the parents.

In general, it is simplest to take a straightforward approach, assuming that the parents are prepared to hear what you have to say, regarding you simply as a source of information. After all, if it takes much special wording, soft-pedaling, or "coming on strong" to get through to the parents, then individual or family emotional disturbances are likely to be causing severe obstructions. The appropriate recommendation, then, would include psychotherapy, and you cannot do much of that in a single interpretive interview. In addition, trying to do so wastes time and is likely to anger the parents more, the longer you go on. So in most cases we briefly review the presenting complaint, report the relevant test results, explain them simply, and follow this by making our recommendations for management.

At the early stage of reviewing the presenting complaint, it is useful for the parents and physician to reach an explicit agreement—not only as to what the problems are, but also on their relative importance for the life of the child and the family. It should be clear to all which are the major impediments to a fulfilling life (inability to read, to concentrate, to relate straightforwardly to other children, etc.) and which should be regarded as matters of little significance (minor degrees of clumsiness, questions about irrevocable past events, attribution of guilt to either parent) or of no significance at all (lefthandedness, mixed dominance, etc.). The problems affecting the child should be focused upon in such a manner that a clear aim emerges: the welfare and happiness of the child. This focus can then be maintained throughout the interpretation and recommendations that follow. Questions relative to parents' hopes, fears, guilt, and unrealistic aspirations must naturally not be shirked, but it must be understood throughout by all concerned that although these may be important issues, they are not the primary issue. The same naturally applies to issues involving the physician's sense of professional status, the need to be respected or even obeyed, and areas of agreement or disagreement with colleagues and other professionals. An explicit and specific focus upon the welfare of the child in question tends to deemphasize the innumerable distractions that threaten to becloud the quality of thought about highly charged issues with social and psychological as well as medical implications.

When we review the presenting complaint, we note the way the parents describe it and whether the teachers made the same complaint or a different one. We also tell the parents the extent to which their child understood the reason for visiting the clinic. Naturally, this must be done without any suggestion of blame or disapproval if the child has not been dealt with straightforwardly. We simply mention that we have explained to the child, for example, that parents and teachers are concerned about the child's trouble with reading.

Some of the complaints are often minor or unrelated. It is frequently useful to deal with these first, to get them out of the way of the main discussion. Examples might be the presence of a strabismus, the possible relevance to the school problem of some coincident disease or disability, the possible relevance of historical episodes such as a prior concussion or seizure, or indeterminate findings on an EEG tracing. Also, it is useful to make clear from the outset that, while you take every possible step to acquire all relevant prior information, you feel under no obligation to explain, defend, excuse, or assail the opinions that other professionals may in the past have voiced about the case. It is a thankless task to qualify the opinions of others, and a treacherous undertaking to improve upon them. Nor is it ever clear how much the parents' account relates to what the expert actually said. Instead it is preferable to point out at this time that you are the one being consulted, and you are now shouldering the responsibility. The recommendations will then be yours alone. It is up to the parents, after due consideration, to decide whether they will be guided by your recommendations or not.

Physicians conversant with psychological and educational tests are in an ideal position to minimize trouble when it comes to interpreting to parents. They can pick out the points relevant to each child's case; and being looked upon as authority figures, they are likely to feel free to dispel parents' needless obsessions about exact test scores or unjustifiable milking of test results for clues about their child's long-term future. In general, we report test results in the order in which the tests are given: intelligence, achievement, educational, and personality.

When discussing *intelligence tests,* it is best not to volunteer a child's score. We tell the parents the most important thing, that is, whether the child's general intelligence is far below average, low average, about average, or above average, and that is the background against which we discuss the other results. Some parents press for exact scores, and then we tell them; but this information *must* be accompanied by a clear, emphatic explanation of the extent to which the score is literally accurate. One might say, "These IQ scores vary by a number of points in their accuracy. They do give us a good idea of the general range within which your child's overall intelligence falls, but they are not exact. So your child, whose IQ is 92, is not necessarily smarter than a child whose I.Q. is 91, or even 87. Nor is your child necessarily less smart than a child whose IQ is, say, 97. The main thing is that your child's general intelligence is around the average, or slightly below the average level." Nor is it any cause for surprise or reappraisal if repeated psychometric evaluations yield scores differing by several IQ points. In fact, most parents do not misuse or grossly misinterpret the meaning of the test scores if the meaning is carefully explained. But even if they do, they have a legal right to know what those scores are. Some people are so troubled that they will misuse whatever information you give them, but that sad fact cannot lead us to deny them information to which they are entitled. Furthermore, suspicious, angry parents are frequently intractable *until* shown their children's test scores, after which they realize that no one is manipulating them, keeping relevant information out of their hands, or acting as though they were too stupid or irresponsible to be trusted with the facts.

If IQ test results show a child's general intelligence to be well below average (around IQ 75 or less), we explain that this means that virtually everything that children of the same age usually learn is probably too difficult for this child, and hence the child should be placed in a special classroom for such children.

If a child's IQ test results reveal about average or above average intelligence, we explain that the child is likely to be able to do some of the work performed by age-mates, but that work calling for certain skills (such as reading, or spelling, or arithmetic) will be too hard. Before making any recommendations about placement in such cases, we explain that our next step was to give achievement tests to find out the general areas in which the child seems to have had trouble learning thus far.

We next discuss the *achievement test* results. These are usually straightforward. Since they tend to be expressed in terms of grade-level equivalents, there is not much that needs to be interpreted to parents, and it is harder for parents to misunderstand or misuse them. We say, for example, "We gave your child a series of achievement tests. These tell how much has actually been learned in a number of subjects. We found that your child can read aloud at the third-grade level, but that understanding of the meaning of what was read is relatively poor, being only at the first-grade level. So despite recognizing and figuring out words as well as most children the same age, your child has a lot of trouble understanding and remembering the meaning of sentences and paragraphs that are read. In arithmetic, the child can do problems that involve only numbers, but not problems explained with words, such as, 'If Jane had four trucks and gave one away, how many would she have left?' "

We explain the extent to which IQ and achievement test scores are related to each other. Intelligence tests give us an idea of how well the child can do some basic kinds of thinking—such as using logic, noticing what happens and remembering it, and thinking analytically; these abilities are necessary to learning almost everything. So a child's IQ results show about how much that child *should* have been able to learn in school. We explain that the achievement tests tell us how much the child has in fact learned in various school subjects. When a child is failing to learn, some analytical educational tests tell us *which* skills the child lacks that are preventing reading, etc. Without the IQ test abilities, it would be hard to learn school subjects, but these abilities are not the only ones necessary for learning the three R's. Each school subject requires some additional skills, and a child who lacks one of these additional skills will fail to learn. So we look at achievement test scores to see *what* the child knows, and if we find a deficiency of knowledge we give educational tests to pinpoint the reasons (such as poor memory for sounds) *why* the child has failed to learn.

By and large, when the achievement tests show that children display a level of learning on the subjects tested that is consistent with their ages, it is appropriate to reassure the parents. But when a child performs poorly on an achievement test, say in reading, we then move to the educational tests.

The *educational tests* give a fine-grained analysis of the child's capabilities in the various academic areas. The results can be used to acquaint the parents with what their child knows and does not know, and to illustrate for them the kind of thing the child finds exceptionally difficult. This places the emphasis exactly where it belongs, namely in the arena of individualized education.

Regardless of whether the educational tests have revealed cognitive power deficits, if we have given *personality tests* and found anything noteworthy we discuss it with the parents. If the findings are simple and the parents not unduly defensive, we tell them, for example, that their child fears being rejected because of school failure, or desires more time and attention from the father, or thinks the parents prefer their other more intelligent child. But if the parents are very angry or defensive, or if the projective and self-image tests suggest severe personality or family disturbance, we present these findings in outline only and stress the need for individual or family therapy. We explain that emotional problems can make it much harder for a failing child to keep trying, and that untreated individual or family emotional problems can keep even a child with no cognitive deficits from learning. If children with learning disability have worries and fears that are not dealt with early and adequately, then they may outgrow their cognitive deficits but never learn to read because of the emotional traumas associated with failing to learn and then fearing to fail.

It is usually a good idea to check up on the parents' understanding of the recommendations and findings. One must at all costs avoid sounding patronizing, so the wording must be carefully chosen. Something like the following can be helpful. "Now, I have just presented you with a lot of information, some of which is fairly complicated. If there is something you are unclear on or confused about, then I need to do a better job of explaining it to you. Can you tell me what your understanding is of what I have said so far, and whether you have any further questions?"

The interpretive interview is also the time to tell the parents that, with their consent, you will write to and talk with the child's teachers, principal, school board, prospective tutor, etc., in order to see that your recommendations are implemented and to ensure a good relationship between the school, the parents, and yourself.

Discussing the prognosis for a child possessing a cognitive power deficit with that child's parents can be a delicate matter. Children with cognitive process disorders are often said to have brain damage. This implies that the child had a normal brain which, at some point, was damaged. This causes many parents to spend time and energy blaming themselves, wondering whether it all happened that time they let the baby roll out of bed; also, they often interpret "damaged" as meaning the child is not normal in any way, or as meaning the child will never improve and the deficiencies will never lessen. For parents to think these things can have tragic consequences, because many children have problems that are limited and likely to lessen with time. They will suffer if treated as completely abnormal and hopeless cases. The fact is that most of these children do show some improvement as time goes on, and some of them even become as capable as their age-mates in the area of their former failure. But the main point about prognosticating here is that it should not be done. If you tell a parent or teacher that a child will make rapid progress, the probable consequences will be too much pressure and added frustration for the child, plus further disappointment and anger for the parents and teacher. These are disastrous consequences, typically resulting in serious emotional disturbances. Some people, including many remedial reading teachers, ignore these dangers, arguing that the most important thing is to offer "hope." In our experience, this attitude does *not* increase children's progress and only increases their motivation briefly, until they experience a few more failures in the face of increased expectations, or compare their recent work with that of peers and find themselves as far behind as ever. This attitude of offering "hope" is similar to that of oncologists who would be unable to work if they admitted to themselves that they could not save many of their patients. But in the case of children's learning problems, the teacher's or parents' desperate belief in the child's imminent progress is self-indulgent, blinding them to small steps the child may be taking. If, on the other hand, you say that there is no hope, the child's performance will certainly drop below even what could be achieved with the already limited ability.

It is often good to discuss prognosis using the analogy of physical growth. We explain truthfully that development of cognitive power in a child with a deficiency in one or more relevant areas is as unpredictable as a child's physical growth. We know the average height for an adult female or male, and we know that some short children become short adults, others become average-sized adults, and a small number get their growth late and become tall adults. Likewise, we know that some children with deficits in one or more of the three R's can never perform those cognitive operations very well, others acquire average skills, and still others reach even above average levels. However, as with physical growth, we cannot predict what level any given child will eventually reach, whether the course of that child's development will be gradual or go by fits and starts, and whether most of the development will come sooner or later.

What implications does this inability to make an accurate prognosis have for treatment? From the standpoints of both remedial educational and management of emotional ramifications, it is important to stress the single most important point: It is crucial for parents and teachers to teach the child an individualistic approach. Neither the parent nor the child should compare the child's progress in school with the progress of any other child (any more than the parent or child should be furious to see that the child was shorter than other children, or should expect the child to be able to grow taller just because the others are taller). Parents must teach their children that they should try as hard as they can, using what cognitive power they have, and should feel proud of that effort ("That's wonderful! I can see you did your best! "). When the child has done as well as possible, the parents must make it clear that they are not disappointed that the child still cannot read, or write, or add as well as others the same age. Parents and teachers should also be encouraged to tell children that, after trying their hardest, they should then go outside and play, or help with a constructive job, or do something they consider fun, just as children without learning problems are allowed to do.

PROBLEMS IN INTERPRETING

Now we turn to eight types of problems parents frequently present. This is certainly not a comprehensive list of problems, nor is the discussion of our approach to each type intended as anything more than a brief sketch of the approaches involved.

Hostile, "know-it-all"

Proper handling of the initial interview can help prepare for the interpretive interview with hostile parents who enter your office believing you have nothing to offer that they don't already know. The most effective refutation of this attitude is a physician's manifest competence and concern throughout the phases of consultation. Much of this was discussed in Chapter 4 (Interviewing), but a crucial management element in such cases bears repeating: You must make it clear immediately that you naturally consider the parents and yourself to share an identical concern—how best to help their child. Then, throughout your subsequent contacts with them you can allude to that alliance, stress your respect for the active aspects of their personalities, and emphasize your expectation that their strength of character will be invaluable in ensuring that the recommendations you make will be properly implemented.

Self-blaming
Another problem arises when parents have become embroiled in self-blame, which sometimes includes self-pity. These are the parents who ruminate continually about whether something they did caused the current school problem. You may need to make any or all of three points to such parents. First, it is not known what causes cognitive power deficits; there are only some very rough hypotheses, and there is at this time *no* way to find out what caused any particular child's deficit. You may want to mention specifics here. For lefthanded parents who fear that their handedness genes produced the child's reading problem, you can explain that many lefthanders have lefthanded children with no such problem, so one could not possibly conclude that parental hand preference was the culprit. In a similar vein, most mothers who were given prenatal and perinatal anesthetic do not bear children who cannot do their schoolwork.

Second, dealing with cognitive power deficits, nothing currently known about their etiology tells us how to choose treatment or to increase the accuracy of prognosis. Therefore, the child's interests are not served by the quest to allocate responsibility.

Third, time spent on self-blame, or blame of the other parent, should instead be spent in paying warm attention to the child. Furthermore, self-blame and recrimination by parents damage a child's emotional state and can wind up needlessly hindering already limited cognitive functions. A child in this position sometimes becomes guilt-ridden, assuming responsibility for the miserable self-blame of the parents because the school failure is felt to cause the parents' unhappiness. Had they never existed, such children believe, their parents would have nothing to make them sad. Another possible reaction by children of self-blaming parents is anger at being labeled the cause of such powerful negative adult feelings. In short, adult time spent in self-blame or blame of the other parent is at best useless and self-indulgent, and at worst pernicious for the child.

Blaming the child
Some parents attribute their child's failure to insufficient motivation or effort. They accuse the child of not trying hard enough. This is understandable when the child has in fact quit trying, out

of frustration, but less so when the child is trying very hard and still not learning. In either case, we explain that the original cause of the failure to learn was completely beyond the child's control. We also point out two major harmful effects of telling such a child that reading or arithmetic could be learned by trying harder. One effect is to further frustrate and anger a child who has been trying hard, especially when the parents are seen freely abandoning attempts to learn things such as dancing or fishing when they have no success. Another possible effect — one that is more complex and devastating — is to confuse children deeply about their own feelings and abilities. Part of a parent's responsibility is to help growing children label their emotions, identify the effects of the different elements in their behavior, and come to understand the way they interact with each other. Parents who have children with cognitive power deficits, and who nevertheless attribute the children's failure to lack of effort, can produce serious confusion. Children, especially ones with low self-images, will learn always to label their own best efforts as inadequate. This drastically distorts the child's mental rating system; that is, if a best effort is far from sufficient, how should lesser efforts be rated? This confusion may produce either neurotic and excessive striving for perfection or a throwing up of the hands and cessation of all effort.

Clinic-hopping

These are the parents who have prejudged what is wrong with their child. When the first professional they consult does not come up with their diagnosis, they decide the professional was stupid, insensitive, or money-hungry, and they go to another, and so on. This sometimes happens when a child is actually retarded and the parents cannot bear to think that their child will never go to college or otherwise compete effectively on the basis of intellect. They take the child from one place to another, hoping for a diagnosis of learning disability, or imperfect vision, or insufficient motivation. Moreover, children with cognitive power deficits may have parents who do not want to hear that having made sure their child receives special educational help each week they must then wait, not knowing what the outcome will be, without exerting pressure on the child or trying any special gimmicks.

Parents with this tendency are often active and usually achievement-oriented. They have trouble accepting the child as anything except a vehicle for carrying out their ambitions. Such parents are exceedingly difficult to stop, because their clinic-hopping represents an inability to accept reality, combined with an extreme aversion to being out of control in any way. These are neurotic traits that often require extensive, long-term efforts to reduce. But we do try to appeal to whatever genuine warmth such parents feel for the child. It is necessary to confront them directly with the fact that they have taken the child through many different consultations and, even after your talk with them now, appear ready to arrange for yet another.

We also ask what they wish were the reason for the child's problem, what they would find easiest and least upsetting to deal with. Once we have some idea of that, it is easy to express sympathy with them and assure them that all parents find it saddening and frustrating to have a child who is not normal in every way. Then we appeal to their concern for the child. We point out that responsible parents would certainly take every reasonable step to make sure that no opportunity is being missed to help the child. This might well involve consulting more than one professional, particularly in areas of disability that are controversial and not well understood. Up to a point, children appreciate that these multiple consultations and examinations derive from their parents' love and concern for them. But if the process is prolonged unduly, the message that the child receives changes radically. It becomes increasingly obvious that the parents cannot accept the child as is. They want the child changed to conform to their own aspirations, and they will not rest until this is accomplished. That message amounts to a crushing rejection of the child, who is made to feel unloved and unwanted, regardless of any amount of protest to the contrary. So it is essential for the child's emotional welfare that the parents come to terms with reality.

Preoccupation with bizarre remediation
A phenomenon that one frequently finds related to clinic-hopping, perhaps as a different symptom of the same parental disturbances, is a fascination with bizarre remedial methods. Some parents wish to avoid using their own abilities to think logically about ways to help the child. Preferring not to confront the failing child and their own sadness, they engage in displacement activity, focusing their energy and attention on finding complex-sounding, often unduly comprehensive methods of "treatment." For some reason, such parents find it hard to do the simple straightforward thing of acknowledging their child's deficiency and arranging for treatment that is clearly relevant and to the point. If they instead can find a weird, unusual treatment program, they will feel that this attests to extraordinary efforts on their part. They can then shift their own attention and the attention of others from a less than perfect child to a fascinating "remedial" method. And they can shift their emotions from the child to their new identification with an intriguing treatment. This is particularly true when the method is one of the kind

that requires hours of volunteer time each day. Then a sense of moral fervor is added to the fascination: "I am the parent who convinced 30 people to give of themselves each week for the sake of my child." It becomes a crusade, as when a community collects money to finance kidney dialysis for an impoverished patient. But there is a difference. In the case of children's learning problems, evaluation of the treatment program usually gets lost in the shuffle. The focus is on what the adults are doing, rather than on whether the child is benefiting.

When parents tell us they want to try some bizarre method, we first try the most straightforward approach of explaining why, in our experience, that method is unlikely to work. Many people are so uncritically excited by what reaches them through the media that they believe things work simply because public relations experts and salespeople say they do. If the parents are truly conscientious and concerned about their child, they quite rightly want to consider anything that might help, and our task is then to underline the crucial difference between *considering* something and actually *trying* it. If the former is done in a logical, thoughtful way, it may do no harm. But the latter puts a strain on the child's time and energy, and usually the parents' as well, not to mention the family's money and stability. Strange methods can make the existing deficit seem stranger to the child than it is. What child, after all, would not be confused by having a difficulty in telling one letter shape from another treated by being flipped around in a hammock, being given vast amounts of vitamins each day, or being made to exercise their eyeballs?

Here one also confronts a problem of professional mystification. The people who push bizarre remedial methods typically speak with authority and self-assurance, implying that people without special training cannot understand why these methods work. In fact, the reason for this behavior is likely to be a lack of any supporting evidence. When purveyors of such methods use language that sounds too technical for most parents to understand, the parents are unlikely to ask for explanations.

The most effective way to help parents evaluate the merits of committing their child to an arduous and protracted remedial regime is by comparing costs and benefits. Children with a learning disability, whatever its specific nature, are always in the following predicament: They take longer than other children to acquire certain types of information. Thus if such children are to catch up or keep pace academically with unaffected peers, they must always work more intensely and longer. And whereas customary schooling leaves the normal achiever with plenty of extra time and energy, these things can be minimal for a learning disabled child.

Hence such a child's time and energy are precious resources, to be jealously guarded for purposes of keeping pace and not to be squandered on immaterial procedures. Time and energy expended fruitlessly could instead have been used constructively for the undramatic but steady advance that even a severely learning disabled child can make in an area of weakness with steady application. Wasting months or years on pointless remedies may permit the achievement gap to widen to a degree that makes further efforts to close it unrealistic. Thus the urgency underlying cost-efficient treatment is the same as the urgency underlying early diagnosis: both permit the situation to come under control before it is too late.

When parents exhibit knowledge of a wide range of remedial offerings, speak in familiar or "name-dropping" ways about noted or notorious self-styled experts, and counter the clinician's commonsense approach by reiterating the claims such people make, they are not necessarily contesting the interpretation; instead they may merely be testing it. In such cases, calm and patience on the part of the clinician is rewarded. As the clinician reiterates reasonable doubts about the claims and places them into the perspective of the well-being of the whole family (avoiding invective and extreme statements), it may become apparent that the parent was actually playing the "devil's advocate," and in fact is on the way to accepting reality and to working with the situation as it is. But the parent has to work this through. After a little time, it may become apparent that the parent had already half-formulated what is now being told, but needed to hear it cogently presented from the lips of a clearly concerned, impartial, and sane adviser. A clinician who permits this process to unfold may be rewarded with more significant progress toward a sensible adjustment than had at first seemed possible. (See also Chap. 7, Talking to Parents about Irrational Methods.)

Using money and time, not good sense and warmth
Similar to the parents described in the two preceding sections are parents who are willing, even anxious, to spend any amount of money to "help" their child. Expenditures of time may follow the same pattern if the time is spent in displacement activities like the ones described above (e.g., finding large numbers of volunteers to help the child, or rushing the child from one evaluation or remediation team to another). Some parents will do anything rather than think logically about what will help the child, and some find the most difficult thing to be spending time with the child in a relaxed and affectionate manner. Such parents may be basically reserved people at best, or they may be self-centered and cold. We

have found well-educated, well-heeled parents to be most prone to this avoidance.

We point out to these parents that spending a lot of money, or spending time making arrangements for the child instead of interacting warmly and directly, does not help the cognitive problem and only creates or exacerbates emotional difficulties surrounding the idea of parental rejection. If this seems to fall on deaf ears it is then crucial to get the child into some kind of supportive psychotherapy, or at least to arrange for regular time to be spent with a loving adult. Parents who cannot make a show of being warm to their child in a doctor's office are even less likely to do so in everyday living; so the child must be assured of some warm attention on a regular basis.

Obsessing about school achievement
Even people who defend the right to do one's own thing find it hard not to insist that the "thing" be done well. Parents often find it disturbingly difficult to stop thinking of a child in terms of school achievement. It may be fairly hard to explain that a child with a learning problem needs to spend time with parents doing neither work in the subject of difficulty nor work in areas of successful learning. The child needs, more than most children, to believe that an important part of life has nothing to do with the whole dimension of success and failure, but rather with love, relaxation, fantasy, and enjoyment. Children who do not learn this lesson grow up without a stable core of self-esteem, because they feel that they are what they do, and therefore they can never rest.

Denying
Some parents deny their child's problem. They act as though nothing is wrong, telling only about the child's good points or areas of accomplishment. They may say that the teachers do not understand the child and are mistaken in thinking there is a problem. When the parents act this way, they are often covering up marital problems or insecurities in themselves. Such denial is often a sign of hostility (hostility of the parents toward each other or toward the child) that seems so intense that they fear to express it and may even be unaware of its existence. One patient who spent months claiming she never felt angry or irritated began to have dreams of violence and ultimately expressed her fear that she could not regulate the expression of her angry feelings. "I don't dare," she said, "because the last time I got angry I threw my best friend hard up against a door." To admit that all is not going smoothly for one's child is to acknowledge that some reality needs to be faced.

Denial is a primitive way to deal with conflict, often involving a kind of all-or-nothing approach to emotions. Parents who use denial may be angry with the child for simply being a "problem" or for arousing feelings which, if expressed, might lead them to express other feelings (such as dissatisfaction with or insecurity about their marriage or their parental roles). In such cases individual, couple, or family therapy may be indicated.

Insofar as the denial is based on fear that the child's failure is their (the parents') fault, some reassurance on that score may help. In many cases, the presentation of the child's learning problem may have to be periodically repeated. In addition, special support from the school should be encouraged to help make certain that the desired treatment is in fact being implemented.

A special case of this pattern appears when parents (often middle-class) bring in a child who, they claim, has a learning disability, but who is, in fact, retarded. The parents have frequently been told elsewhere that their child scored in the retarded range on an intellectual test or has acted in ways that suggest retardation, but their fear that the child will not meet the demands of upward social mobility obstructs their acceptance of this situation. Parents who have just learned that their child is retarded have asked "Will he be able to get into a good college?" It is important to explain in some detail the damaging emotional consequences of trying to force a retarded child to perform at an average intellectual level. One must make it clear that such treatment will produce the same terror of failure that anyone would experience if told "You absolutely must do more than you can possibly do."

Other parents deny their child's problem in order not to experience feelings of disappointment and depression. They may feel sad about their child's failure, but they believe that to express sorrow is weak or embarrassing. In such cases a simple sentence or two from the interviewer explaining that many parents feel disappointed, sad, and angry when their child fails can let them know that their feelings are not bizarre or inappropriate.

Other parents intellectualize. This is particularly common if they are well-educated or wish they had been. They quote Ginott and Gordon chapter and verse, and tell you what they said to their children, presenting what sounds like a reasonable case for their excellent handling of the emotional aspects of the child's failure. But their tone of voice may be flat when they tell the interviewer about their behavior, or the interviewer may even observe an emotional distance when they interact with the child. These are often parents who cannot figure out how to implement your simplest recommendations (because doing so would require a closer emotional relationship with the child and greater sensitivity to the child's feelings). At this writing one such father, a very bright professional person, has spent months trying to think of an activity he could share with his son that would have nothing to do with achievement or competition. He comes up with such suggestions as "I could have him read aloud to me. He does that very well." Achievement in school may be so important to such parents that they find it hard to create a home atmosphere in which happiness or closeness, rather than achievement, is the chief aim. This problem is closely related to that of denial, although it is more sophisticated. There is the danger that intellectualizing parents may convince the interviewer they are doing just what the interviewer suggested, when in fact they are not. They may also be unaware of this themselves. Being able to name a wide range of emotions and even to identify them in their child does not necessarily make them able to respond to those emotions in helpful ways. Furthermore, intellectualization, like denial, often serves as the lid to a basket of marital or other dissatisfactions with life. Here again, some form of psychotherapy may be indicated.

INTERPRETING TO CHILDREN
The interpretive interview with the child is at least as important as the discussion with the child in the initial interview. A surprising number of physicians and other professionals concerned with learning problems never have an interpretive talk with the child. They may feel that it is the parents and teacher who will carry out the recommendations or who are best at taking responsibility to see that these recommendations are carried out. But in fact it is much easier to implement a treatment plan if the child feels treated like a person rather than like a test subject or a problem the parents brought to the clinic.

What does one say to the child? The principle here is the same that is most useful when children ask questions about sex, death, divorce, or any difficult subject: Tell the truth, calmly, and do not offer so much information that the child feels overwhelmed. When a child asks where babies come from, one begins by saying they grow in the mother's stomach, rather than beginning with descriptions of the sperm, the egg, and intercourse. Now, it is a bit trickier when the topic is a school problem, because so many children have been shamed and frightened about their troubles that if left to themselves they would never dream of mentioning the subject. So it is up to you to raise the matter.

In deciding exactly what information to give and how to present it, it is important to keep in mind the purpose of talking with the child. A child who understands the recommendations and the reasons for them is more likely to cooperate well and try hard than a child to whom the regime is an external imposition with a mysterious rationale. Another reason is that consideration for the feelings of the child dictates that you and the parents owe the child some explanation. To say nothing is to allow the child's fantasies to run wild; and these fantasies often include feelings of being stupid, of being guilty or sinful regarding school failure, or even of being possessed by the devil. Because of society's emphasis on school performance, and also because children spend so many of their waking hours in school, they often understandably think that poor school performance is synonymous with general worthlessness.

Although we prefer not to have physicians wear imposing white coats when seeing children, this interpretive interview is one time when it helps to point out the physician's position of authority (e.g., "I am the person who knows all about school problems, and I can tell you that your reading trouble does not mean you are a bad person. I can tell you that there are lots of very good, important things about you, and you should remember that this is true, no matter what you have thought and no matter what anyone else might tell you.") In essence, then, you want to give these children information and an attitude with which to arm themselves against peers' or adults' taunts and criticisms.

A third reason for talking with the child is that it can contribute to defusing pathological interactions between the child and the parents. Particularly if the parents are accusatory or secretive about the school problem, laying the cards on the table can help (if you then tell the parents exactly what you have told the child).

We usually tell the child, in simplified form, what we tell the parents. It could go like this: "You have come here so that we can try to find out the best thing for you to do about this trouble you are having with reading (or spelling, or writing, or arithmetic, etc.). The first thing you should know is that no one can tell why it happened, just as no one can tell why some kids can run faster than others or why some have stronger arms than others. You are not sick, you are not naughty because you are not able to read, and God isn't punishing you for anything you have done." (We may include more or fewer things in the last sentence, depending upon what we suspect the child believes is the cause of the trouble.) "We gave you some tests and asked you and your parents and teacher a lot of questions so that we could figure out how to help you."

Next, before going into specifics, we present a general, individualized view of people. "Inside people's heads, they all have brains. One part of the brain has to do with how well or how badly people sing. Another has to do with how well or badly they swim, another with how they speak, another with how they read, another with how they write, another with how they do arithmetic. There are about as many parts of the brain as there are things that people can do. You know that some people grow tall when they are very young. Other people grow tall when they are older. Some people have big feet and little noses, and some people have little feet and big noses. Well, that is how brains are, too. Some people are good at singing and terrible at swimming. Some children are good at drawing and bad at reading. There are lots of examples of this." Here we usually ask the child to think about people in the family and classroom and to name a strength and a weakness of each.

We might continue: "The child you mentioned who cannot sing well but can read well has a singing part of his brain that is growing slowly and doesn't work as well as the reading part of his brain. You have a singing part (or whatever strength the child has) that works well but a reading part that is not growing as fast as some of the other parts of your brain. This doesn't mean that you are dumb or bad. You wouldn't think that someone with a tiny nose or small hands was a particularly bad person. Well, you cannot read very well, but you can do some other things well. I cannot remember how to get to lots of places in this city, but some people can. You wouldn't think there was something wrong with me. You would probably just think that this is one thing I have trouble doing. That is how it is with your reading."

Now, although we want to avoid making the child feel guilty for the school problem once poor motivation has been ruled out as a primary cause, we do not want to go to the other extreme and make the child feel helpless in dealing with the slow-growing part of the brain. So we might say: "You have trouble reading as well as many other kids in your class, but that does not mean that you cannot read at all. It is very important for you to keep trying your best when your teacher works with you on your reading. The other children will get better and better at reading all the time, and so will you. Most kids who have had trouble with reading can read as well as most other people by the time they grow up, and you probably will too. But you won't get any better if you don't keep trying. We are talking to your teacher about the best way for you to work on your reading now. When he works with you, you should try not to worry about how the other children are reading. I'll bet they don't spend much time worrying about whether they can sing (or skip or snap their fingers) as well as you. What I want you to think about is whether each day you learn more about reading than *you* knew the day before. That is the most important thing."

For a child who is particularly sensitive to the taunts of other children, we sometimes add: "So the next time that girl you told me about calls you 'Dummy,' you can tell her that the doctor who knows all about who is dumb and who is smart told you that you are not dumb. You can also tell her that it's more important to try your best than to be the best already."

INTERPRETING TO EDUCATORS

Particularly if good rapport is maintained with the local school authorities, it is often possible to report the outcome of a learning disability evaluation to the relevant school personnel in writing, and to expect that the report will be studied with care and heeded if possible. But there are some occasions where such routine reporting has to be supplemented by a direct meeting with relevant school personnel to safeguard the child's interests. Those are:

1. If the recommendations are unusual for that school system and require question and answer explanations
2. If the recommendations would involve making new arrangements in the school
3. If the recommendations run counter to school policy
4. If the school has a prior commitment to a course of action other than that recommended
5. If the school personnel have a negative image of pediatric or learning clinic intervention
6. If the use of drugs is involved and this causes discomfort among educators
7. If there is friction between teachers and parents that needs to be resolved
8. If there appears to be a risk that recommendations will be understood differently by the parents and the school

The manner in which such an interpretive meeting should be conducted will be made clear by the circumstances. It is good to begin with a restatement of what appear to be the relevant practical issues. These are gone over with reference to their significance for the child's family, in order to ensure a proper distribution of emphasis. The next step is to secure general assent to this statement of the problem and to permit others the opportunity to modify and supplement it. Next, the clinician embarks on a statement of the findings. This should be short and precise, with each outcome explained in plain language. A good effect on morale is secured if data are not only explained but also shown to the group, and if reports are also made available. The manifest openness of this approach is invaluable for securing ultimate compliance and cooperation from all concerned.

When the need is to acquaint and reconcile school personnel with a particular clinical philosophy, this philosophy should be fully explained first and only later defended. Most objections will become irrelevant during the course of the explanation and will never be voiced. The remainder can be handled courteously and will not seem overwhelming.

It is essential not to let visiting specialists in education and other related areas box themselves in with extreme statements early in the discussion. If such are made, retracting them later may involve unacceptable loss of face. Thus, it is preferable for clinicians to present the essence of their interpretation and counsel first. If this is thoughtfully done, the foundations of an atmosphere conducive to exchanging ideas will have been laid, and the subsequent discussion will more likely be of good quality. This strategy is especially valid in situations where parents and educators are squared off against each other in embattled antagonism and resentment. That is because a comprehensive statement from the clinic relatively early in the meeting can shift the focus away from entrenched positions and permit both sides to give ground imperceptibly. Giving both sides full credit for common sense and commitment to the child's well-being helps this process along.

At the conclusion of the discussion it is often possible, without appearing unduly didactic, to have parents and teachers summarize the action to be taken. This assures comprehension and contributes toward a commitment to follow through. Finally, it is always made plain that learning clinic personnel can readily be reached by telephone about issues that do not merit a return visit, or to make a further appointment should this become necessary.

THE IMPORTANCE OF EDUCATING OTHERS IN THE
AFFECTED CHILD'S LIFE

Most of the remedial steps we have suggested involve only the child, or at most the child, the family, and the teachers. But there is an important step that can be taken by anyone who is involved in the life of a child with school failure; that is, to become educated about the nature of the child's problem. In the best of all worlds this should be done by everyone involved—not just by the child but also by the child's classmates, playmates, extended family, neighborhood acquaintances, etc. As noted in the sections about interpreting to the parents and child, a dearth of knowledge and understanding is a potent source of fear and confusion. Anyone who deals with a person who is not typical or "normal" can easily fall into the trap of exaggerating that person's difficulties or ascribing other failures, inabilities, or weirdnesses to the person that are not actually present. This is particularly true of children. Children in a regular public school located near a sheltered workshop for re-tarded people were found to call the retarded people "mental" and to assume that they were insane, uncontrollable, and extremely ag-gressive. That is, the retarded people were considered monsters of some kind. When some of the grade-school students were told straightforwardly that "mental" only meant "referring to the mind," that being retarded just meant learning much more slowly than other people, and that some of the retarded people were likely to be aggressive and others not to be, just like anyone else, their fear diminished. As they came to understand the exact nature of retardation, the associations that they assumed to be constant and inevitable—for example, between aggression and retardation—diminished. They learned that when retarded people are aggressive it is often because they have been mocked and frustrated more than other people. Perhaps most important, they found a way to under-stand the experience of retarded people in terms that were com-prehensible to them and that had no strange or supernatural con-notations.

Learning disabled children are in some ways exposed to even more ridicule than the retarded, because the learning disabled are more likely to remain in regular classrooms, or at least in regular schools. Though this is usually the appropriate course, it also means that they may daily be called stupid, different, and weird. Young children have great trouble, unless an adult or mature child helps them, in regarding others as having strengths and weak-nesses. If one dramatic weakness or unusual attribute is found to exist in a particular child, the other children in the class are not likely to say, "But Mary does have the following strengths, or abil-ities, or desirable qualities." Instead, they are likely to withdraw from, reject, and mock the child.

There is a simple measure that can reduce this fear and rejec-tion. Once considered, it seems obvious and imperative, even for classrooms or families that have no failing child. It is to teach chil-dren about brains and how they work. Consider what the children in your school imagined about the brain. A smart child was said to be "a brain." A child who had trouble learning was said to "have no brain." Children regard brains in a total way: You either have one or you don't; there is little or no sense of the enormous variety of activities centered in the brain or of the extent to which any one person's brain-based abilities may vary. Schools have health classes, nutrition classes, and sex education classes in which children learn about many parts of their bodies. But hardly anyone provides detailed teaching about the workings of the brain, even though this would not rouse the moral conflicts provoked by sex education classes.

What should schools and parents teach children about brains? One can teach children about the exquisite specificity of cerebral function and use that as a concrete basis for encouraging a relativistic view of people. That is, one explains that different parts of the brain help or limit enormous numbers of abilities and that each person's brain has relative strengths and weaknesses. One has to teach the child (and if necessary the teachers and the other children in the classroom and neighborhood) the concept of individual differences. That is done best, of course, if one deeply believes in this concept. It is something people talk about all the time. They say "Aren't ethnic groups marvelous? Isn't variety a wonderful thing?" But when it comes to children, most people expect them all to have good grades. People profess devout belief in the principle of individual differences, but when it is their child who deviates from the norm, when they have to acknowledge that their own child is not typical, it is harder to keep the principle in mind. But that is, of course, the very time when everyone needs most to think about the importance of individual differences.

It is necessary to teach that a learning disabled child, besides being not generally bad or stupid, is also experiencing difficulty with only one part of the brain. It is also important to explain that all people's brains are shaped about the same, and that everyone has brains in which some parts work better than others. It is particularly helpful to include one's own brain in this category. Most children do not realize that their parents or teachers are imperfect until they approach adolescence, but one needs to teach the young child that even adults are not perfect. One of the best ways to make a child's learning disability or hyperactivity less upsetting is to say, "I have the same kind of problem, except mine isn't with reading; mine is with singing, or with finding my way around town."

Another aspect of relativism that is helpful if communicated to the child is the principle that, although reading is important in school and in the world, other things are important elsewhere. A learning disabled child's abilities, for example, may make that child more accomplished in the swimming pool than some of the best readers in the class. Basically, the attitude to create at home and in the school is "This child can do these things, but cannot do some other things so well right now. Parents, siblings, teachers, and classmates also have things they do well and other things they cannot do." By age five most children can stop and think what their best friend can and cannot do well. Once one begins to use this approach, it is surprisingly easy to maintain it. It is a relief for all concerned to drop the pretense that anyone is perfect, or should be perfect, or has to meet unreasonable standards in order to be acceptable. This makes it easier for the child to know what to say to other children; for example, "I'm in the lowest reading group because the reading part of my brain isn't growing very fast." When the child has the support of such simple but specific beliefs, then that child is no longer a "dumb" child; instead, this is a child who is basically normal but who has one area of the brain that is growing slowly. In a relativistic atmosphere, if another child says, "Ha, ha, you're in the lowest reading group," your child will know that the taunter has weak areas too. Most important, the child will know that, whatever happens in academic subjects at home and even in school, people are not judged only by how well they read. The child will know that everyone is judged on a large number of different variables, possible achievements, and personality characteristics. Such a child can then learn because of genuine interest and can feel free to try as hard as possible, instead of being seized by panic when approaching a reading book regarded as the sole standard for measuring self-worth.

TERMINOLOGY USED FOR INTERPRETATION

Diagnostic categories and labels are used as a sort of shorthand to designate some complex but accurately specifiable situation. They are at their most useful in dealing with discontinuous categories that either pertain or do not (measles, pregnancy) and with characteristics about which there is a consensus of agreement. Where the phenomenon to be labeled is better considered a deviation from the norm in degree rather than kind, the label's implication will be ambiguous—unless a metric exists for the deviation in question, and unless people agree on the critical degree of deviation that justifies use of the label. As already discussed, learning problems are deviations in degree, not kind, and no simple metric exists for measuring various critical behavioral or neurological characteristics. Further, the taxonomy of learning problems is highly controversial—so much so that each expert's terminology embodies a wealth of implicit meanings not known or even recognized by others. Thus there are strong arguments against using any of the many available diagnostic labels in this area. To use them is to tell different people different things about the child and to exaggerate, by implication, how much we know about these matters. And by using such facile terms as dyslexia, minimal brain dysfunction, or word blindness, we do violence to the individuality of the child's experience of learning and living.

None of this should be taken to suggest defeat in trying to understand the child's predicament. Such understanding can be accomplished without using any labels. Terms that are not diagnostic categories but that merely designate the area of difficulty are acceptable; the labels "learning problem" (or disability), "hyper-activity/distractibility," and "selective reading unreadiness," are purely descriptive; they neither make neurological assumptions nor imply the coexistence of any specific cluster of behavioral disabilities. Rather, they set forth the challenge: Discover the detailed motive behind the child's learning problem, the nature of the child's restless distractibility, the particular readiness functions that are inadequately developed. Our own categories of cognitive power disorder and cognitive style disorder, though they accurately classify children with brain-based school problems, still refer to subgroups that are heterogeneous; these terms require further analysis and are subject to misinterpretation by others. They do not need to be used in interpretations presented to parents, children, or educators.

It is possible to present a completely adequate interpretation without using any diagnostic terms whatever. One simply describes the child's area of difficulty, indicates which particular mental operation the child seems to find unduly difficult to perform, and explains how the child might be helped to perform that mental operation. The discussion is entirely pragmatic, operational, and directed at an individual predicament. This not only protects the child against adults' preconceptions but also serves to focus adult interest on the child, rather than on contentious abstractions that could elicit self-centered reactions irrelevant to the matter in hand. Terms such as "dyslexia," "brain damage," "hyperactivity," "drugs," "enrichment," and "patterning" have private and highly emotional connotations for many people. While we would not deny the validity of these reactions, they do get in the way of helping children.

At the end of the interpretation it is worthwhile to draw people's attention to the fact that no labels were used. Make it clear that this was deliberate. It makes it impossible to compare the child, by means of a label, with any other. It also makes the responsible adult less likely to accept some dogmatic program for "the dyslexic" or "the brain damaged" without inquiring into what exactly is done. And it helps all concerned to think of the child as a person rather than a case.

6. Prognosis and Prediction

The outcome of a learning disability may be viewed in terms of the brain basis of that disability, in terms of academic status, or in terms of self-realization of the affected individual. These three aspects of prognosis may diverge substantially, particularly in the older individual. The physician should emphasize self-realization, should put reasonable stress on academic outcomes, and should de-emphasize hypothetical or untestable neurophysiological considerations.

The ultimate outcome of a learning disability depends on the nature of the underlying impairment of brain development; the locus, extent, and severity of the cognitive deficit; the age at which the difficulty is recognized; and the age at which effective treatment is instituted.

NATURE OF UNDERLYING BRAIN ABNORMALITY AND
ULTIMATE ACADEMIC STATUS

When learning disabilities result from deviant brain development, this is of early origin. The immature brain has considerable compensatory potential. Only if brain damage is very widespread will there be no available brain areas to compensate for those that are damaged, and only then will general mental retardation supervene. If restricted brain damage, however severe, occurs early, it will always prompt some compensation by the residual intact brain, so that the individual will not be totally and permanently deprived of the affected cognitive skill. Even when a whole cerebral hemisphere is inactivated, as long as this occurs early in life the patient ultimately acquires many, if not all, of the cognitive skills for which the damaged hemisphere would have been specialized (such as language in the case of the left hemisphere or spatial skills in the case of the right), because of compensation by the hemisphere that remains intact.

There is no particular etiology of brain damage which would destroy any hope of at least some cognitive gain with advancing age. Only in the rarest cases do children gain nothing at all, year after year, in the area of their intellectual weakness. Rather, the question is: How will the individual's rate of maturation compare to that of the majority of people? Will the gap between the patient and age-equivalent national norms narrow, widen, or stay the same over the years? Are we dealing with a temporary lag, a fixed relative deficit, or a cumulatively growing inadequacy?

There is, unfortunately, no way of predicting the correct alternative in the individual case. The presumptive nature of the original insult (genetic, anoxic, traumatic, etc.) is no guide, nor do clinical appearances help in prognosis. Naturally, the more severe the deficit at a given age, the more likely it is to be severe subsequently. But differential prognostication is not possible, and actual outcomes are extremely variable.

In retrospect, can one make inferences about whether maturation did or did not catch up with the norm? Even this is not yet possible. That is because academic outcomes are no secure guide to the state of underlying brain maturation. One individual, as a result of exceptional effort or instruction, may gain ground, even though the functional deficit remains. Another, as a result of being ill-taught or poorly motivated, may lag academically even though cognitive maturity has been achieved. Changing social demands and a widening range of social and employment options for the adolescent and adult further blur the future. Thus outcomes with regard to the underlying brain function cannot be inferred from academic outcomes. The reliable measurement of such outcomes awaits the availability of more direct tests of brain function itself. Under these circumstances, physicians should avoid committing themselves to any definite neurophysiological prognostication.

NATURE OF COGNITIVE INSUFFICIENCY

Cognitive insufficiency may vary, both in its locus and in its severity and extent at that locus. Thus, the locus involved may be within the verbal, spatial, or numerical areas of function; and the degree of deficit may vary in its extent—that is, in terms of the number of subskills within the general cognitive mode that are implicated. As a general rule, the greater the extent of the deficit, the earlier in life it becomes apparent and the more severe the subsequent handicap. Thus a verbal deficit may be so selective as to implicate only the relatively sophisticated operations of breaking words up into their constituent speech sounds and reconstituting them from those sounds. Only the challenge of phonics instruction would bring out such a limited deficit. Or a verbal deficit may be so pervasive as to implicate not only reading and writing but also aspects of spoken speech, thus virtually amounting to a general language disability rather than a specific reading disability. Such difficulties may already be apparent in the speech and speech comprehension of a preschool child. A more general deficit also tends to have a less favorable prognosis. For instance, a specific deficit in ability to learn by phonics leaves open alternate methods of reading instruction, whereas a general involvement of reading-related verbal processes does not.

Academic outcome is determined by the child's residual cognitive potential and by the relative value that society attaches to the skills that remain available to the child. Difficulty with spelling and with script both implicate writing, but beyond grade-school poor script is well-tolerated, and the typewriter may effectively compensate. Reading and writing are more valued than art and design, and a visuo-spatial deficit in children with good verbal skills leaves them with a better outlook toward schooling than that of children with the reverse pattern. Not only reading and writing but also many other academic subjects customarily learned from textbooks (history, social science, and even mathematics) remain open to a child whose selective cognitive deficit spares the verbal area; but they are closed to the child whose area of severe impairment prevents reading.

AGE AT DIAGNOSIS

A learning disorder may be diagnosed before it has occurred (prediction), as soon as it takes effect (diagnosis at school entry), after it has become long-standing (the failing child in the classroom, prognosis in adolescence and in the long term) or never.

PREDICTION

Many professionals make strenuous efforts to predict learning difficulties well before the age at which formal instruction customarily begins. They hope that successful prediction will, in the positive cases, permit early intervention, which in turn will avert the problem. Predictions of future learning problems are based either on (1) learning problems actually experienced in preschool, or (2) a defect in supposed precursors or predictors of academic readiness skills.

Learning is not limited to the traditional school setting. It occurs both outside school and before school entry. One need no longer passively await school entry and then infer the risk of school failure from the fact that it has just occurred. Much grade-school failure is heralded by discernible preschool difficulties. An increasing number of preschool educational and custodial programs make it increasingly probable that trained staff will detect relative deficiencies in cognitive areas, such as language, that will be crucial for academic progress. Staff members can also discern weakness in task orientation which, if it persists, could likewise impede a child's education. Nowadays, as never before, the opportunity exists to have the relevant cognitive capabilities and task orientation evaluated by objective observers who have had experience with many children of like ages. Systematic observation of preschool children for existing problems has clear advantages over predictive testing. One is the advantage of observing age-appropriate behavior, rather than performance that one hopes might presage behavior that would be pertinent at a later age. Also, if problems are uncovered (e.g., problems of language development or of attention), then their nature suggests what should be done. Failure on a predictive test does not clarify what to do—except to teach the child the test items failed (which is ridiculous, but which nevertheless sometimes happens). If the result of testing is that the preschool child receives help with an existing problem, this is its own justification, regardless of whether subsequent grade-school status is correctly predicted.

The preschool teacher may observe that one child works intermittently and stops concentrating on each assignment prematurely (unless the teacher provides immediate and instant structure). Another child works steadily but continues concentrating longer than necessary, requiring the teacher's insistence to depart from a no longer relevant train of thought. Such extremes of impulsive and compulsive behavior have ominous implications for a child's ability to succeed in grade-school.

It is clear that superficially valid inferences about future learning power and style can be drawn from present learning power and style, based on "clinical" observation. In contrast, standardized testing is quite ineffective with respect to all but the grossest manifestations involved. So are screening tests that claim validity on the basis of no obvious or proven relationship to school learning, but rather on the basis of unsubstantiated hypotheses or on some empirical validation process. All existing screening tests that do not have obvious surface validity should be considered still in the research and development phase and not yet fit for clinical use. The more remote the behavior tested is from the behavior to be predicted, the less likely it is that one will ever be usefully predicted from the other. This applies particularly to the frequent practice of inferring future reading achievement from observation of gross motor behavior. There is conceivably some statistical relationship between gross motor and specific cognitive deficits, because widespread damage of the central nervous system can cause both. Thus, both general and selective intellectual impairment are particularly common in children with cerebral palsy. But many markedly cerebral palsied children have no learning difficulties whatever, and there is no acceptable evidence of a *causal* connection between motor deficits and deficits in higher mental functions. Clumsiness will of course affect a child's handwriting, and lateral gaze abnormalities may interfere with visual scanning (e.g., across a printed text). But more substantial blocks to learning are central in origin and imply more than sensorimotor immaturity.

In giving mental tests, the younger the child the more it is necessary to rely on sensorimotor accomplishments for indirect information about mental status and prognosis, and the less reliable is the result. In other words, the earlier the mental prognosis is attempted, the more it is subject to error.

For decades people have tried to develop tests that will predict learning problems. These have ranged from the fairly reasonable to the nearly ridiculous. An example of the latter are the so-called infant IQ tests. Their uselessness is due to two factors: One is that the baby's score on the infant IQ test is a poor predictor of that baby's eventual score on a child or adult IQ test. The other is that, as we discussed in the section on psychological testing, a school-age child's IQ test scores do not reveal the presence or absence of cognitive power deficit, and even the subtest scatter gives only the most general information about what kind of deficit a child might have.

There are, of course, a number of measurements that one can make on preschool children which do correlate significantly with grade-school reading progress. Much of this correlation is accounted for by the fact that many children who score well on the predictive tests have higher intelligence than those who score poorly. If intelligence is held constant, some tests show a significant correlation but not a high one. In other words, as far as we know, any combination of existing tests would misclassify an unacceptably large proportion of the screened population.

One reason for this is that most existing tests are "norm-referenced" (see Chap. 4, Educational Tests, pp. 117–124). If they predict at all, they tell how well children will do in relation to each other. This is not what we want to know in predicting school failure. Rather, we need "criterion-referenced" tests, which can tell us whether the child will be capable of *sufficient* reading achievement to function adequately in the classroom. How much better than sufficiently a child will do is irrelevant for our purposes. So, for entering first-graders we need to know what is the minimum level of each readiness skill that will permit the child to benefit from reading instruction. Now, we do not even know which these readiness skills are, let alone how to measure them. So we can hardly expect to predict their presence at school entry given the current state of knowledge. In practice, supposedly predictive preschool screening tests reflect the theoretical biases of the people who designed them, and this by no means guarantees that they are valid. In brief, our knowledge of mental development falls far short of enabling us to predict reading failure.

An alternative approach attempts to define an "at-risk" population on neurological grounds. Taking account primarily of the child's condition at birth, the presence of certain perinatal catastrophies and of minor congenital anomalies, this approach is doomed to failure. Measures of adverse influences on newborns are crude, and their relationship to subsequent mental development is ill-understood. In addition, much learning disability and hyperactivity are genetically determined and cannot be detected by studying potentially damaging events in early life.

Erroneous prediction may take either of two forms: false-positive or false-negative results. In the first case, failure is predicted but does not happen; in the second case, failure is not predicted but occurs. All tests are subject to some such error, but the extent to which either error type can be rightly tolerated without the test being discarded depends on the availability and urgency of effective therapy. If effective therapy exists, is readily available and relatively inexpensive, and works better the sooner it is instituted, then a relatively high incidence of false-positive prediction could be acceptable. But none of these stipulations currently holds for learning disorders.

When a child is cognitively immature, no means are known for accelerating maturation. Pending spontaneous maturation, remedial instruction has to be purely pragmatic; it must equip the child to cope with social challenges and meet social expectations. There is little social pressure on the preschool child. A waiting period may suffice to permit further brain maturation and render individualized teaching unnecessary. That often happens.

The outcome of preventive measures is uncertain; such measures are also costly in terms of time, effort, resources, and money; and there is no evidence that instituting them early confers a significant advantage. Therefore, insufficient benefits accrue from correct prediction to justify the risk of false-positive prediction. Regrettably, all existing instruments suffer from the risk of generating false-positive prediction.

Furthermore, a false-positive prediction of learning failure has potentially serious repercussions. Like a self-fulfilling prophecy, it can so influence parents' and teacher's expectations and attitudes and the child's self-concept as to generate the very failure it is intended to forestall. Children who would have begun to read adequately, if no one had tested them and fretted over them before grade one, may become so anxious about whether they will be ready when they begin grade one that their anxiety interferes with their performance. Perhaps the worst effect of this unnecessary testing is that it encourages parents who are already too achievement-oriented and pushy about their children's intellectual abilities to become even more so. It teaches them that society's representatives—the school system, advising pediatricians, etc.—agree with them that it would be the worst thing in the world if their child could not read at age six. It deprives children of their childhood.

On the above grounds, prediction should be postponed up to a point where action with a reasonable chance of success can be taken; and such prediction should be based, if possible, on the child's actual behavior and performance in a learning situation. The closer the time of testing is to the time of proposed teaching, the better will the test predict the child's response to teaching. This is because the frequent variability in the rate of a child's mental development makes long-range extrapolation an inaccurate way to determine what the child's learning requirements will be.

Oddly enough, the very people who often attack IQ tests as culturally biased and misused tend to be vocal proponents of predictive preschool testing. Some people make a moral issue of this, acting as though predictive testing were "preventive medicine," the virtue of which is taken for granted. If predictive testing really did allow one to prevent learning failures, one would naturally support it. But since it does not, it should be abolished. The time and energy people devote to such testing would be far better used in testing children just before they begin grade one, *but only in cases where there is some reason to suspect a deficit*, and in testing and giving extra help to children who actually do have trouble when they start grade one.

Pending major advances in prediction, the only responsible policy is to defer diagnosis of learning disability and institution of remedial measures until it can be directly demonstrated that the child is immature regarding some skill clearly related to academics.

DIAGNOSIS AT SCHOOL ENTRY

The later one makes a cognitive evaluation, the more accurate that evaluation is likely to be. The shorter the interval between the testing and the scheduled time for deciding on educational placement, the more reliably will the test guide the placement. Thus, when there is no pressing advantage to early initiation of remedial education, it is logical to defer definitive assessment to the last possible moment before the relevant time of decision. In the case of placement at grade-school entry, the summer before the child enters first grade is such a time. School readiness testing in that period will most reliably guide a decision to have a mature child enter first grade, to hold an immature child back a year, to place a mentally dull child in a special education class, and to provide a child with selective unreadiness for first grade with appropriate additional help from the start. In this way, the probability of an initial failure experience is minimized.

If underachievement is defined as a failure to realize academic potential, then children with learning disability do not necessarily underachieve, even if their achievements fall short of age-relevant national norms, because the learning disability reduces academic potential in the area of the disability. That lower potential cannot itself be budged by therapy (though it might rise spontaneously on account of a maturational spurt). But most learning disabled children do not achieve even up to the level of their limited potential. There is an additional component of underachievement contributed by inappropriate teaching. If children are taught in the conventional manner, and if this does not meet their particular learning requirements, then they will fall short of realizing their academic potential. It is the goal of remedial education to close the gap that is due to a teacher-student misfit. The goal for learning disabled children cannot always be that they learn normally. It can always be that they achieve up to their own potential. The sooner an effort is made to determine and implement the type of instruction best-suited to the individual case, the more likely it is that at least this modest but realistic goal will be attained. Diagnosis at school entry is ideal from this point of view.

The Failing Child in the Classroom

The undiagnosed learning disabled child enters grade-school with certain expectations of personal success, and these expectations will be shared by other significant people—parents, teachers, siblings, and peers. Failure to meet these expectations results in a cycle of unfavorable consequences.

The child, bewildered by the failure, is further beset by the reactions of others. Teachers, frustrated in their attempts to teach, may resent the child and suspect idleness or hostility. Parents may vacillate between resenting the teacher for botching the teaching, the child for disappointing and embarrassing them, and themselves for some imagined role in the genesis of the problem. Peers may make derogatory comments, and siblings may resent the spotlight of parental attention being focused on the affected child.

Whereas mild pressure along these lines may pose a salutary challenge for the child that elicits extra effort and superior performance, more severe pressure results in a lowering of the child's self-concept and evokes a hopelessness that leads to virtual suspension of additional effort. Pressure further escalates as a result, and instead of realistically appraising the situation, the child adopts one of three characteristic defenses—by showing anxiety, manifesting alienation, or blandly denying that any problem exists. Insofar as these defenses protect the child from intolerable stresses, they serve a short-term adaptive purpose. In the long term, however, they create an unfavorable climate for the intense effort required by even the most expert remedial education. Eventually, the child is definitely labeled as a "case," and expectations and therefore pressures are relaxed, but only at the price of accepting the "inevitability" of failure (see Fig. 1, p. 16).

The longer the child continues to fail in the regular classroom (be it due to nondiagnosis or to ineffective remediation), the less favorable is the prognosis. For even if the underlying neurophysiological insufficiency should resolve itself spontaneously, a cycle of secondary complications may perpetuate the learning disability.

PROGNOSIS IN ADOLESCENCE

The longer the history of a learning failure, the more likely it is that the failure will continue. This is partly because only the more severe cases last long and partly because of the attendant demoralization. Ultimately, a crucial determination must be made. Have all reasonable educational measures been taken, and to no avail? If so, vocational alternatives must be explored. Whereas the generally retarded person is severely limited in vocational options, the learning disabled individual by definition possesses cognitive strengths upon which nonacademic vocational choices can usually be based.

Insofar as reading and writing disability is the most common, the usual concern is to find rewarding occupations that make minimal demands on literacy. Those children who have well-preserved spatial or numerical skills can often succeed at mechanical and other nonverbal occupations (particularly if arbitrary qualifying requirements involving reading and writing are waived). Children who are clumsy or spatially disoriented as well as illiterate represent a more serious challenge, and they may not achieve anything better than menial vocational placement. Thus the prognosis for social adjustment and personal fulfillment depends on the individual's basic intelligence, the selectivity of the cognitive deficit, and the flexibility of the social setting with respect to both vocational areas and training programs.

If academic advancement is definitely not to be expected, then the sooner a vocational choice is implemented the better. The individual is thereupon released from the grip of insurmountable obstacles, while the family group is released from uncertainty and permitted to adjust to a stable reality.

LONG-TERM PROGNOSIS

Remarkably little systematic information is available on the long-term outlook for children with selective reading disability. Some reports have stressed favorable vocational outcomes, including a surprisingly high percentage of successful graduations from high-school, whereas other reports have stressed persistence of reading and particularly spelling difficulty. It seems likely that the outcome figures are greatly affected by the nature of the sample studied. The larger the influence on reading failure of such nonbiological factors as inadequate exposure to language, bilingualism, low motivation, poor social circumstances, or substandard instruction, the better the long-term prognosis, as such factors are relatively amenable to change. Hence the more carefully chosen the sample of children with sharply selective reading problems, the less satisfactory the outcome figures. Our best information is that the more severely affected children remain substantially behind in their achievements throughout their school careers and as adults. Incidentally, graduation from high-school is a misleading criterion because many children are permitted to graduate despite the fact that they are years behind in reading skills.

It is unclear whether those children whose reading problems persist into adulthood have a deficit in some reading subskills that never corrects itself, or whether their underlying deficits do correct themselves but leave the victims unwilling to learn basics at a relatively late age. Presumably both of these things happen, but one has no idea in what proportion. It seems clear, however, that for the severe cases current remedial education does not provide a complete answer.

THE IMPACT ON PROGNOSIS OF REMEDIAL
INSTRUCTION

There is a glaring discrepancy between remedial teachers' views about the efficacy of their interventions and the results of large-scale controlled studies of remedial outcomes. It is hard to find remedial teachers who are not convinced that they are highly successful in most cases. Fortuitous circumstances or lack of parental cooperation are usually held responsible for the occasional failure. Still more enthusiastic are those who have developed and marketed remedial programs or those who manage schools dedicated to the problems of the learning disabled. Such experts, however, are quite ready to admit that other specialists, using other methods elsewhere, might have less success. In view of this optimism, and noting that in developed communities most older learning disabled children have experienced multiple remedial approaches, it is remarkable how many of them still cannot read. Large-scale studies of remedial versus control pupils paint a bleak picture. If the remedial group shows any advance over the other, this washes out soon after remediation is discontinued.

Remedial instruction is not scientific; objectivity is too much to ask for under these circumstances. The pitfalls are obvious. In children one deals with a shifting baseline of maturation. Whether children are superior, average, or delayed, they do develop, gain skills, and acquire knowledge over time. This does not mean that the gap between the remedial and normal children is closing. But to be aware of this pitfall in interpretation, one has constantly to keep in mind the normative standard of reference; this is a hard thing for the instructor to do. Also, when gains are made it is not clear whether they were contingent on the particular instructor or kind of instruction, or whether they would have occurred with special help of another kind or even without special help. Finally, any instructor necessarily teaches a particular subset of academic material and often succeeds in doing so. But are the children able to generalize what they have learned to other materials, and are gains maintained after therapy is discontinued?

Large-scale studies suffer under different but equally crippling handicaps. Samples are ill-defined, the criteria used being a certain amount of underachievement for the child's current age, or else some controversial neurological diagnosis. Proper account is not taken of the quality, duration, and continuity of the remedial effort; and a proper control group is hard to define, because there are usually relevant reasons why some children are offered therapy and others not that cannot be held constant between groups. When medication is involved things become even worse, because there is typically little record of the type, dose schedule, and duration of medication, and the children's long-term gains are usually assessed after medication is discontinued. This latter is a senseless procedure that makes results unintelligible on account of the state-dependence of learning (see Chap. 9). In addition, large-scale studies appear to include children who are depressed, alienated, and undermotivated. No single approach will do for all these types, and little can be learned from such studies.

WHAT TO DO?
Relying on common sense, children who have difficulty must be helped (though without extravagant expectations of a "cure"). When public resources are limited, help should be preferentially channeled, for pragmatic reasons, to those children whose difficulties are moderate and likely to be overcome with help. Only if additional resources are available should they be expended on children whose deficits are severe. This is because progress toward substantial improvement is usually slow, so that the cost-efficiency of concentrating on these children is low. It makes little sense to support elaborate boarding school programs with high staff-student ratios for a few children, while funds remain unavailable for the

many thousands who could benefit from short but regular periods of individual tutoring, for purposes of which they are withdrawn from the regular classroom.

The lobbying emphasis in the area of learning disabilities runs counter to the above advice. The severe cases are more dramatic, more evocative of rescue fantasies in the minds of concerned adults, and easier prey for the purveyors of useless and expensive crank therapies. Also, citizen pressure groups naturally have a disproportionate attraction for the parents of severely handicapped children, and such parents understandably tend to agitate for the type of help that they consider their own children need. As always in public policy, the appropriate response to such legitimate demands is not to yield in a grudging piece-meal fashion, but rather (as a matter of national, regional, or local policy) to design and cost-account steps to alleviate the problem in all affected children.

7. Remediation

HOW TO CHOOSE A REMEDIAL PROGRAM
In preparing to meet the learning requirements of the learning disabled child (see outline below), decisions about some or all of the following have to be made: (1) type of school, (2) type of classroom, (3) classroom structure, (4) the manner of teacher-student interaction, and (5) the content of teacher-student interaction.

Principles in the Education of Children with Learning Problems
   I. Establish the Child's Learning Requirements
      A. Achievement level (in terms of grade equivalent)
      B. Selective strengths and weaknesses at that level
  II. Establish and Meet Adjunct Needs
      A. Individualization of instruction
      B. Controlled level of surrounding activity
      C. Supportive pharmacotherapy
      D. Supportive psychotherapy
 III. Instruct According to These General Principles
      A. Didactic
         1. Teach at educational (not chronological or mental age) level
         2. Make implicit links in explanation explicit
         3. Check understanding/retention of each point before moving on to the next point
         4. Minimize potentially distracting displays (including irrelevant but salient stimulus dimensions)
         5. Let learning time be self-paced
      B. Motivational
         1. Base motivation on teacher-student relationship (avoid distracting physical motivators)
         2. Compare the child's progress to previous achievement level (not that of other children)
         3. Intersperse difficult tasks with tasks the child can master
 IV. Avoid Speculative Methods*
      A. Enrichment — where it floods the child
      B. Multisensory approach — where it simultaneously bombards rather than successively focuses selective attention
      C. Physical education — when it purports to accelerate brain maturation (as opposed to raising morale)
      D. Laterality manipulations
      E. Nutritional fads
      F. Optometric maneuvers

* These include any procedure that relates hypothetically, rather than logically, to the educational good.

TYPE OF SCHOOL

Although school is usually discussed in terms of a child's acquisition of knowledge, the classroom is much more than a medium of instruction. The school-age child's life is typically divided between home and school, and for 12 years, between the ages of 6 and 18, a substantial part of the child's life is spent in the company of classmates and teachers. Thus the classroom provides a social and intellectual climate. Whether the school environment appears congenial or not makes a big difference in how children feel about their school years and how they remember them later. Diversity in school helps children understand the greater diversity encountered in adult life; but it is important that within the diverse group there be some other children with whom they have much in common. Also, children should have access to their intellectual peers. However profound a selective learning disability may be, if the affected child has otherwise normal or above average intelligence, that child should, if possible, remain where contacts can be made and maintained with other children of comparable intellectual powers. So it is preferable to maintain such children in a normal school (withdrawing them as appropriate for special help in subjects where they have selective difficulties) instead of relegating them to an institution for special education where they might find children who are peers in their area of selective weakness, but who are not their intellectual peers outside that area. Only if children have subnormal or borderline intellect *outside* the area of selective difficulty would placement in a special education facility for slow learners seem an attractive choice. That is because normally intelligent children should be offered the opportunity to interact with intellectual peers at intermissions, mealtimes, and after school, as well as in the classroom when subjects outside their area of selective weakness are being taught.

The third type of institution, the school specializing in the instruction of learning disabled children, should be used most sparingly. There are two ways to use such a facility. One is as a day school for a limited period of time, during which intensive remedial instruction is offered with the intention of boosting the children's achievement levels enough for them to return to regular instruction. The other is as a boarding school, to provide a child with temporary escape from an oppressive overall environment.

The use of a special institution for learning disabled children is reasonable if rational goals are set. These goals are pragmatic; the child may have been lagging in so many subjects for so many years that less intensive management does not offer hope of success. Individualized instruction in the wide areas of weakness plus regular parallel instruction seeking to offer a total educational experience should be continued for a limited period of time. It will only rarely be possible to upgrade the children's achievements to levels matching their chronological ages or those of their mental age peers, unless in the interim they happen to undergo sufficient spontaneous brain maturation to acquire the necessary learning potential. But that should not be the goal. Rather, the goal should be to dispose of the underachievement *relative* to the child's own learning potential, and to have the child acquire academic information at a rate that is appropriate to his or her learning potential in a manner that may be laborious but not oppressive.

When the child then returns to a regular classroom, this calls for circumspection. Usually it is necessary to have such a child in the classroom with somewhat younger children or in a relatively slow stream. Also, for the first few months the teacher and other support personnel must be especially vigilant for signs of strain. Remember that even if the child is now achieving at a level comparable to classmates who never needed remedial instruction, this was only by dint of individual attention and extra effort. It is hard to predict the consequences of stopping that individual instruction and losing the incentive it generated for additional effort. Thus, the class placement should be kept flexible, and further withdrawal opportunities should be offered as the need for them becomes apparent.

Boarding schools for learning disabled children should be reserved for children who have suffered many years of repeated failure — because of exceptionally profound cognitive immaturity, or because sensible steps for individual instruction were not taken, or even because the problem was not recognized. By this time, the affected children have often developed such negative self-images and negative (or ambiguous) relationships with their teachers, classmates, parents, and siblings, that they find themselves in completely oppressive life situations without the mental energy, enthusiasm, or incentive to try any more. This situation is likely to engender progressive psychopathology. In such cases a completely new environment is called for, one in which reasonable optimism is combined with the opportunities and incentives needed to prompt additional effort. Such an environment may be secured in a specialized (and inevitably expensive) institution for the learning disabled adolescent.

TYPE OF CLASSROOM

For reasons just discussed, it is ideal for the learning disabled child to spend as much time as possible in the normal classroom. In addition, at times of economic recession government pressures for "mainstreaming" exceptional children become intense (although these are usually alleged to stem from a primary concern with the child's personal welfare). It has recently become fashionable among educators to speak approvingly of this "mainstreaming" a wide range of exceptional or "special needs" children—which means emphasizing the need to educate them in the "mainstream of society" (the regular classroom).

It was, of course, in the mainstream of society that children with learning disability and hyperactivity were for so long totally neglected. Proponents of mainstreaming, however, would point to some differences in approach. They would assume that the necessary individualization of instruction would take place within the regular classroom, so that children's special educational needs would be met. At the same time, the mainstreaming would overcome the children's feelings of isolation and would permit them to stay with their peers. But how, then, do the children avoid feeling stupid and defeated in the very setting of their most humiliating failure? The answer is that the mainstreaming philosophy is democratic; the children are taught to respect "differences"—and to accept a defeat as just one more way in which human beings differ from each other, rather than as something that is dehumanizing and a proper subject for ridicule. A necessary condition for making this approach work, however, is that the class include not one or two, but a substantial minority of "special needs" children. The diversity serves the instructional process. It also makes the classroom teacher's job effectively impossible.

A teacher who is ideally equipped intellectually and ideally trained could possibly muster the formidable energy and resources needed to individualize instruction for so many different children—and to be adequately conversant with and sensitive to their special characteristics and needs, which may extend to quite technical and medical issues (as with children who are cerebrally palsied or epileptic). Most classroom teachers have not been trained to individualize instruction at all, let alone do so with such sophistication. Thus, enabling teachers to make mainstreaming work for the children would require a revolution in teacher training. While waiting patiently for this revolution, the concerned professional should be wary of eager references to mainstreaming of learning disabled and hyperactive children. Does this turn out in practice to be a euphemism for pretending that the child does not have special needs? Is it a euphemism for a retreat to the harassed classroom teacher, inadequately helped by a willing but untrained aide, trying to deal with assorted learning and behavioral difficulties, some of which would give pause to experts? Finally, is it a euphemism for penny-pinching by administrative authorities seeking to circumvent the need for special expenditures on special resources for children with individual needs?

The recent debate on mainstreaming is helpful because it reminds us that children should not be withdrawn from their regular educational settings and from their peers more than is demanded by their need for individual attention. When learning subjects in which they have no disadvantage they should remain with the general group. Use of special institutions and of measures requiring that children be transported for hours every day should be minimized. But there must be no retreat from the hard-won principle that, above all, children with unusual learning requirements must have these requirements met on an individual basis. Unless the learning disability is very mild, or the teacher in the regular classroom is exceptionally skilled and energetic, mainstreaming such a child without any individual instruction only perpetuates the problem and, indeed, makes the identification of the child as "learning disabled" a meaningless exercise.

Another approach, which is still consistent with maintaining these children in a regular school, relies upon flexibility with respect to the levels at which they are taught. Thus they might be taught at a third-grade level in mathematics and a second-grade level in reading, or vice versa. This approach is of course applicable only to children who are not too far behind. Therefore, it generally applies effectively only to the younger, earlier-identified learning disabled children. Also, it is cumbersome to apply if it implies shuttling a child between different classrooms, a procedure that can highlight the child's difficulty and produce humiliation. However, the approach is very useful if the school can provide mixed-grade situations (where within a single classroom children are working in different streams for different subjects—that is, in "ability groupings").

This approach makes sense in terms of mental development. After all, the uncomplicated learning disabled child may not differ qualitatively from the younger, normal child who happens to be at the same achievement level in a particular subject. Therefore, the learning disabled child should be able to partake of the same level of instruction within such a group (e.g., a normal second-grader and a reading disabled third-grader might both be taught in the traditional way from a second-grade reading book). However, this is not necessarily true for all learning disabled children. It is more true for those younger ones who have what are later revealed as transitory immaturities of a fairly general type; it is less true for those with very specific *selective* and profound deficits in cognitive power, and also for those whose difficulties have become compounded by the effects of unsuccessful instruction. The mixed-grade device is a rational first step, attempting to accommodate the level of instruction to the child's individual needs, and it may succeed. If it fails, however, it highlights the absolute necessity of providing the child with a more individualized program than can be provided within the regular classroom situation, however flexible that situation might be.

Should the child shuttle between ability groups for different subjects or be withdrawn from the regular classroom for individual instruction in particular subjects? This is a practical decision that depends as much on available resources as upon the initial appraisal of the child's disability. A key factor, however, is severity. The more severely underachieving children, and those who also have serious conduct disorders, cannot be accommodated conveniently without doing injustice to the other children in the class; the latter will be deprived of their teacher's attention because of the inexorable demands emanating from their cognitively or emotionally needy classmates. In such cases, there is the temptation to transfer the disabled child from the regular classroom to a special resource classroom for the learning disabled, within which special groupings and appropriate methodologies are supposedly used.

Attractive as this device sounds, it entails a serious risk. This is that some dogmatic remedial methodology may be imposed on the children, because it is judged appropriate for "the learning disabled," without reference to the specific difficulties of each individual child. In fact, if there are 8 or 10 such children in a learning disability class, the teacher, in effect, will have 8 or 10 classes to teach; for it is highly likely that each child will have different problems that require different explanations, and each will require what is in effect an individualized program. Most teachers do not have the energy and resourcefulness to achieve this, and it is understandable that they often retreat into a single arbitrary methodology which can be imposed conveniently on all children in the group. Unfortunately, all too often these methodologies do not have the desired effect of helping the children learn, as we shall discuss later.

We thus advise that relatively large groups of learning disabled children not be taught communally, but rather that no class include a greater number of children than a teacher can instruct individually by shifting attention from child to child. How large that number is will depend not only on the skill, experience, and energy of the teacher, but also on the diversity of the problems existing among the children. The teaching may be itinerant (by a teacher who serves more than one school) or done in a "noncategorical" resource way, in which the child's difficulties are not labeled (i.e., diagnosed) and the remedial method is not prejudged.

CLASSROOM STRUCTURE

Within contemporary school systems there is a wide range of

classroom structures. Classrooms vary in the degree of control exerted by the teacher, and also in the extent to which a child's activities are self-directed or are structured by the teacher. In addition, there is a wide range of physical classroom variation, from the traditional rows of seating to the "open classroom's" fragmented grouping of children into various clusters in larger spaces. (Contrary to general impressions, the physical arrangement of the open classroom does not necessarily imply a permissive and unstructured educational approach.)

The degree of structure provided the child is important with respect to instruction of the learning disabled. It cannot be discussed in terms of open versus closed classrooms, but rather is a parameter that may vary within either type of instructional setting.

In general, the more gifted and motivated that children are, the more it is appropriate to permit them to be self-directed in their choice of activities, and the more justifiable are expectations that the self-direction will result in optimal academic and personal growth. Thus, unstructured situations are particularly useful for those children who have better than average intelligence. The less able that children are in a given academic area, the less is self-direction appropriate, as it tends to leave them floundering. Learning disability is an extreme case in which a high degree of structure is essential for several reasons.

When children engage in self-directed activity they rarely choose to do things that they find exceptionally difficult, let alone ones personally threatening to their conceptions of themselves. Learning disabled children have sensitive areas of looming educational failure. They will not engage in activities in those areas without some external incentive. When they do explore such areas, much more than the customary control needs to be exercised over how materials are assimilated. Furthermore, children who are failing in the classroom may manifest, in a manner either primarily or secondarily related to their failure, an approach that is impatient, impulsive, or overcautious. Impulsive children need a superimposed structure to keep their activity within useful limits, so that learning may proceed. Overcautious children need a structure that provides for appropriate pacing, so that they do not fritter away study time on inessential detail and thereby go without important educational experience. (Overcautious children need direction as much as do the impulsive and distractible children who continually switch away from the task.) Thus, in general, children who have learning problems should be in highly structured environments. This does not mean, of course, that discipline should be unduly rigorous. On the contrary, a warm and supportive attitude is essential to the emotional welfare of these children.

Manner of the Teacher-Student Interaction

Teachers of learning disabled children, in order to be effective, require more than average sensitivity to the children's feelings about what is being done. They must be constantly aware that the children are attempting something considered exceptionally hard that is fraught with the threat of impending failure and social condemnation. Thus, these children depend heavily on steady encouragement. The encouragement must be realistic rather than exaggerated, because children are sensitive to deceit and exaggeration. If a child has handed in a clearly imperfect piece of work and knows it, there is no point in responding with extravagant praise, which ultimately undermines the student-teacher relationship. It is usually possible, however, to make some encouraging comment with complete honesty by appropriately distributing emphasis. If the child's work is sloppy but handed in on time, one might comment "Thank you for letting me have this on time. It helps me a lot." Conversely, a slow but meticulous worker will be encouraged if criticism of the time taken is tempered by approval of the care invested. Or the teacher can focus on some part of the assignment and point out truthfully that this is something the child could not have done a week or a month ago. Appreciative comments about the amount of effort the child has put into the work can be made regardless of whether that work was done correctly. The focus of the interaction should be on the child as that child is, was, and will be. Comparisons with other children who have more, less, or the same degree of handicap are to be avoided. So are cheery exhortations of the "We'll make it" or "We shall overcome" type. It is not necessary to "motivate" children, or to remind them how important reading is for their happiness and success, or to tell them how pleased mother and father would be. Children are already aware of this to the point of nausea. The most helpful comments teachers can make are the ones most clearly and specifically related to the academic task. Teachers should openly praise every successful step the child makes. Furthermore, they should permit the child to continue working on the crest of a wave of success, even if that takes longer than usual. Conversely, if the child keeps failing, it is useful to switch to another task in which the teacher knows the child is able or even gifted, so that the child can find some relief in exercising a skill, and the teacher can legitimately give praise for successful performance.

For many learning disabled children, particularly the older ones, the teacher's ability to set up a positive and active student interaction is so crucial that it outweighs the importance of the teacher's specific training or extensive background experience (as long as a commonsense individual approach is used). No one teacher can possibly have a personality that will elicit enthusiastic cooperation from every learning disabled child. The need, therefore, is not for a small number of highly trained professionals, whose contribution would be but a drop in the ocean. Rather, it is for more numerous, less intensively and formally trained, but intellectually flexible people who are willing to attend to children's personal as well as educational needs.

Learning disability instructors can be drawn not only from qualified educators but also from teachers-in-training, and even from intelligent high-school girls and boys. Such flexibility in accepting human resources for teaching purposes is justified in principle and essential in practice. Relatively few school systems have sufficient staff to meet the individualized needs of all these children, and the numbers of staff tend to fluctuate with the prosperity of the school system, which in turn fluctuates with the economy. It may thus be some time before the individualized needs of all learning disabled children will be met through formally allocated resources made available by the government. In the meantime, those who can afford it may have to pay for private tuition.

An alternative course would be for cooperative organizations of parents of learning disabled children to teach not their own but each other's children. The one person who should rarely, if ever, teach a learning disabled child is the child's own parent, even if the parent is perfectly capable of giving the necessary type of instruction or is even a qualified teacher. That is because the relationship between the teacher and the learning disabled student is sensitive, emotionally charged, and full of the continuous threat of failure. Such students have already found it hard to avoid feeling that they have disappointed their parents because of their academic difficulty. It would be a particularly heavy imposition were a parent to become the teacher, because this would further confront them with their learning failure in the most personal possible fashion. Yet parents of learning disabled children are usually intensely interested in these problems and often well-informed about them. Many of them are potentially excellent teachers for learning disabled children coming from families other than their own.

Teaching the learning disabled may require longer and either more or less frequent sessions than those dictated by the usual routine of the school workweek. The teacher of learning disabled children must be flexible in the disposition of teaching time, so as to be able to adjust the time interval between practice sessions; this enables children to build up cumulative understanding and memory of a body of knowledge. The teacher must not practice with them so frequently as to bore them, or so infrequently as to extinguish all memory of the previous session—making it necessary for the children to learn as if for the first time.

One-to-one interaction is an essential feature of the individualized instruction necessary for the learning disabled child. This interaction is not practicable in the regular classroom and is not necessarily practicable even in the special classroom for variously handicapped children. During this one-to-one interaction the instructor will not practice some predetermined methodology, but rather will attend to the child's individual understanding and existing fund of knowledge. The extent to which the school week must be devoted to such one-to-one interaction, and the period of time for which this will be necessary, depends on the severity and scope of the child's cognitive power disability. In milder cases, brief but regular withdrawal from the regular classroom for one-to-one sessions may suffice. Such withdrawal not only guarantees these children relevant instruction, but also protects them from the humiliation of stagnating mentally while their classmates interact and learn. For the more severe cases, the withdrawal might effectively cover most of the working week and might thus have to be managed in a separate classroom. But we have already mentioned the danger that if a number of learning disabled children are thrown together in a special classroom without recognizing their different education requirements, their needs will not be met any better than in the regular classroom. The group within which a learning disabled child should be taught must be small enough to allow the teacher to interact individually with each child for as long as necessary. This, of course, depends upon the teacher's personality and energy even more than on the teacher's specific training and background; it also depends on the diversity of difficulties experienced by the children, and upon any conduct or behavior problems that might consume the teacher's attention, time, and energy. Thus, whether the child should be in the regular class, in a special class, or with an individual part-time or full-time tutor is a pragmatic question. The answer to it must be based not on general principles but on the nature of the child's difficulty and the teaching resources that are available.

The Content of the Teacher-Student Interaction
Principles
Children's failure to learn at a rate customary for their chronological and mental age, due to a problem of cognitive power, does not imply that they are unteachable. It merely indicates that the teaching methods used did not meet their learning requirements. Whatever the children's selective cognitive immaturity or deficit, at some stage they must have been unable to understand ex-

planations or to remember information the way it was presented. Since grade-school instruction is progressive, failure to understand and remember renders the child unable to follow the further course of instruction. The transaction in the classroom becomes increasingly unintelligible, and the child falls farther and farther behind. The rational step here is to determine what the child does understand and know. One can then infer what were the earliest explanations not understood or the earliest information not retained; it is then possible to present the explanations better or to make the information more memorable. How to do this can be deduced from a knowledge of children's mental development (see Chap. 3). When something is unusually hard to explain to a learning disabled child, this is best compared to the difficulty that might be experienced in explaining the same point to a younger normal child. The younger child will be unable to provide the necessary cognitive structure; the teacher has to provide it. While the specific information to be conveyed and the specific manner for doing this will vary from child to child, one can set out in general terms three properties of a "better explanation" and of the manner in which information can be made "more memorable." These are as follows:

1) MAKE EXPLANATIONS COMPLETE. A person who explains something to another consciously or unconsciously takes account of what the listener presumably already knows or understands. Teachers usually fill in only those segments of the explanation that they feel the listener might not spontaneously grasp. The effectiveness of the explanation thus depends largely on the teacher's insight into the fund of knowledge that the student brings to the learning situation. That insight is likely to be accurate if the student resembles the teacher in age, sex, social and ethnic background, state of physical and mental health, and cognitive development. To the extent that the student and teacher differ in one or any combination of these attributes, to that extent is the teacher increasingly likely to misconceive what the student already knows. The risk that arises from such misconceptions is that the teacher may omit from the explanation some crucial step in the sequential logic which the student is not in fact able to fill in. The student then fails to understand the explanation. Teachers who are accustomed to teaching normal children at a certain grade level have a feeling for what these children already know. They will not remind them unduly of this information for fear of boring them and losing their attention. Such teachers would not necessarily have a feeling for what a learning disabled child does or does not know. Therefore, when teaching such a child, the teacher has to spell out explanations in

full detail, leaving out no logical step, however trivial and obvious it might appear to an adult or a normal child. In this context a better explanation is always a more complete explanation, and a fully complete explanation cannot, in principle, be misunderstood. Hence the first task in better explaining is to make all implicit steps in the argument explicit.

As an example, consider explaining to children which letter is lowercase *b* and which is lowercase *d*. For normal first-graders it might be sufficient to point to each letter in turn and say its name or sound. For unmotivated children it might be necessary to construct some game or gimmick that would stimulate their curiosity. For learning disabled children, however, such devices are merely distractors and make the task of learning more difficult; their motivation, after all, is not the problem. Let us look at the usual method for teaching learning disabled children, which is also generally thought to be the simplest. It is usually assumed that the easiest way to teach a child the difference between *b* and *d* is to point to one and say "That is a *b*," and then to point to the other and say, "That is a *d*." What typically passes for an additional explanation for learning disabled children can be judged from the three following examples of a conventional remedial approach to letter reversals. (See Hammill and Bartel, 1975).

1. Have the child trace, then write, each of the two letters.
2. Use pictures illustrating words that begin with the letters the child reverses. For example, for letters *b* and *d* use a picture of a boat and a duck. Place the duck to the left of the *d*. Place the picture of the boat next to the lower part of the *b* and to the right of it.
3. Tell stories about the letters; for example, "This is *b*, *b* is on the line, *b* is tall as a building, *b* looks to the right."

It is easy to see how—what with boats and ducks and such paraphernalia—a child has little chance of happening upon the critical distinction between *b* and *d*. The child may not even know right from left. Is *b* really as tall as a building? Is *d* less so? The confusion of concepts dragged into a straightforward issue should suffice to keep the child in the remedial classroom for some time.

If we look at this usual way of teaching those two letters, we see that to show a child the two shapes while saying "This is a *b*, and this is a *d*" actually requires the child to infer all of the following information:

1. Here is one shape.
2. Here is another shape.

3. This shape has a stick that goes up and down.
4. This other shape has a stick that goes up and down, too.
5. This shape has a bump.
6. The other shape has a bump.
7. The bump on this shape is at the bottom of the stick.
8. The bump on that shape is at the bottom of that stick, too.
9. The bump on this shape points this way.
10. But the bump on that shape points that other way.
11. This shape sounds like *b*.
12. That shape sounds like *d*.
13. The name of this shape is *bee*.
14. The name of that shape is *dee*.

So, in the simple sentence, "This is a *b*, and this is a *d*," we are actually giving the child 14 items of information to learn and remember. For a learning disabled child, this takes too much for granted. Depending on the specific kind of disability, the child may have trouble with any type or any combination of the types of information presented in items 1 through 14. That includes both visual and auditory information (how the letters look and what sounds are associated with them), as well as subcategories of information (such as orientation of letter parts or the names of letters) knowledge of the latter being in fact totally unnecessary to being able to read.

Hence, with those learning disabled children who find it difficult to deal with orientation, one proceeds stepwise, in something like the following manner:

1. Look at this piece of paper.
2. There is a shape on it.
3. See how the stick part goes up and down.
4. Notice that there is a bump at the bottom.
5. Notice that the bump is pointing this way.
6. Now look at that other shape.
7. See how its stick part also goes up and down.
8. See how it also has a bump at the bottom.
9. But see how the bump points the other way.
10. (Showing the child a third figure) "Which one of the two is this one like?" etc.

One doesn't proceed to any step until it is certain that the child understands the one before it. Once steps 1 through 10 are completed, the child's attention has been securely focused on the relevant perceptual dimension (orientation) and the critical event in that dimension (mirror-image reversal) that permits *b* and *d* to be distinguished. Next, the child is taken into the auditory modality with all visual material removed. Step 11 will be to acquaint the child with the phoneme (i.e., the sound) *b*, first as it appears at the beginning of common words and then in isolation; and step 12 will be to introduce the phoneme *d* and make sure that the two are properly distinguished. Only when the distinction is secure in the child's mind should one reintroduce the visual material and then affix the appropriate label to the appropriate shape ("This shape is called "bee").

This laborious manner of instruction is unnecessary for most children but is necessary for those children whose cognitive immaturity includes a tendency to make letter reversals. In fact, even the number of steps outlined here may be insufficient. It is usually correct, when attempting to focus a child's attention on either the visual or the auditory dimension, to begin with a major contrast in that dimension. Only when the child has switched attention to that dimension should one allude to more subtle differences within it. In orientation, a 90-degree rotation of the figure is the most salient, and inversion of the critical feature is more salient than mirror-image rotation. Thus a child should be taught inversions, like *b* with *q*, before mirror-images, like *b* with *d*. Similarly, when teaching the differences between phonemes it is preferable to start with phonemes that contrast the ways that the lips and tongue are arranged in sound production — such as *b* and *r*. Only after the child has learned the trick of listening to an individual speech sound should one introduce subtle differences culminating in the difference between *b* and *p*, which involves only one distinctive feature (voicing).

Naturally, when a child is led through elaborate, exhaustive, and potentially very boring explanations, the teacher must maintain the child's morale and interest in the process. This will call for personal characteristics and insights from the teacher that harmonize with the personality of the child. Such appropriate teacher-student matching in terms of personality is essential to the arduous process of remedial teaching in learning disability. Boats and ducks won't do the job.

2) GIVE INFORMATION BIT BY BIT. The second relevant aspect of explanation deals with the rate at which the information is imparted. Again, teachers will have some feeling, conscious or unconscious, about the rate at which the listener can take in and mentally process information. They must not make overambitious assumptions about the learning disabled child. On the contrary they must, after presenting every item of information, secure feedback from the child about whether the information has been understood. At no point should they risk overloading the child with several items of

information that build on each other unless they have made sure that the early ones have been understood. That is, the teacher must never be more than one logical step ahead of the student. So only when the teacher has established, by explicit questioning, that the first step is understood is it appropriate to proceed to the second step; and only when that has been understood is it right to proceed to the third, and so forth. This means that the pace of teaching must be adapted to the individual child, and this implies that the customary classroom time schedules should not necessarily be followed.

3) MAKE IT MEMORABLE. The method for making an item of information memorable is not qualitatively different from that of making an explanation comprehensible. It is important not to take a mystical view of memory (regarding it as an imaginary box that varies in size within people's heads in a manner inaccessible to intervention). Remembering depends on the ability to shut out the here and now, and the ability to reconstruct the previous experience. Previous experience is easiest to reconstruct if ingredients (called "cues") of that experience are still (or again) present at the time one recalls it, and if a maximal amount of relevant information was gathered during the initial experience.

The teacher can make information available to a child by focusing the child's attention on those aspects of the information that distinguish it from alternative information with which it might be confused. The teacher may also supply associations or otherwise fit the item of information into what the child already knows, rather than leaving it as an arbitrary fragment that defies ready recall. When trying to have a child recall something that is not spontaneously remembered, the teacher feeds in cues one by one until remembering occurs. It is hoped that at the next rehearsal fewer cues will suffice, and fewer still at the next, until remembering becomes as fluent and automatic as it must be for skills like reading and writing. Thus, poor remembering indicates that there may have been deficiencies when the item was first taught. These deficiencies can be ameliorated if the teacher guides the child's initial exposure to the information and fills in gaps at the time of recollection.

Practice
When they come for help, most learning disabled readers will already have had some reading instruction. This can have important repercussions on the way they perform during the assessment (usually making it more difficult to understand the problem). If a child fails to use phonics, for example, is this because of mental immaturity, or is it simply because that approach is new? If the

child has a very restricted sight vocabulary, is this due to poor visual memory or to slavish adherence to a phonics approach? It is often difficult to obtain a clear account from the teacher of what reading instruction method was used. Therefore, one must often draw one's conclusions from the way children perform.

If children make frequent "careless" mistakes, guessing their way through text on the basis of either context or words' initial letters, this could be due to pressure by the teacher to "read for meaning." Such pressure is premature for children who cannot yet recognize many of the words in a passage. If children read each word literally, even those with irregular spellings, they are using an otherwise helpful phonics approach. If children apply phonics to virtually every word and do so each time the same word appears, they are failing to obtain an overview of the word after decoding it bit by bit. If they read a text correctly verbatim but cannot then answer questions about it, they have been so preoccupied with the labor of decoding that they have had no attention to spare for understanding.

These are examples of maladaptive strategies. They can be corrected simply by proper spacing of rehearsal and by slowing children down when they read sloppily or speeding them up when they decode slavishly. By use of flash cards bearing word fragments that progressively increase in length, a correctly decoded word can be added to a child's sight vocabulary so that sequential decoding becomes unnecessary over successive encounters.

To pursue discussion of such techniques further would be to engage in details of remedial reading instruction beyond the scope of this volume. But it is worth making the general point that when progress in learning is arrested primarily by biological unreadiness, the problem may be further aggravated by an imbalance in how the child learns to use various strategies. Regardless of whether the basic difficulty can be overcome, such secondary complications can always be resolved by insightful individualized instruction. Interestingly, such instruction can be individualized not only by tutors, but also by teaching machines.

The role of programmed learning methods in the instruction of reading disabled children is equivocal. They do offer at least a degree of individualized instruction. Their overriding merit is that they produce information in a graduated fashion, at a rate directly under the child's control. Thus they avoid the danger, so real in the large classroom, of flooding a child with unintelligible information. For many children this approach alone may make the difference between learning success and failure.

On the other hand, a programmed text will be effective only to the extent that the content of the program allows for, or is aimed at, the specific types of difficulties different children might have. No one knows to what extent existing programmed texts respond to the particular difficulties experienced by various children with selective reading disability. Ultimately any program must have self-defined limits, of a sort that a teacher need not and should not have. Furthermore, the program's effect on morale may be either good or bad, depending on the child's personality and emotional needs. Some children might find it a relief to escape from the scrutiny of a teacher into a more neutral interaction with a machine; with a sigh of relief they may get down to the task unobserved. Other children will miss the personal interactions and supports that they need to impel them to further efforts; for these children, the need of a relationship supporting their efforts to do something they find hard may be paramount.

Programmed texts have the obvious advantage of saving the time of skilled personnel; and where they are available, it is quite reasonable to try them to see if they work for a given child. However, the possibility that they might not work should be kept firmly in mind, and not much time should be wasted if a failure is observed before the child is shifted to a more personalized instructional process.

On reviewing the principles of individualizing instruction, one may wonder which teachers are qualified to teach in this manner. Clearly, regular teacher training is not directed along this line. But it is unclear that various courses in special education are either, for the usual emphasis on materials and on motivation of classroom groups completely misses the point. What is needed is a problem-solving approach to the challenge of generating successful explanations.

First and most important, the ability to construct effective explanations calls for a thorough understanding of the material being taught. Few teachers obtain such fine-grained understanding during the brief teacher training process. Specific instruction in task analysis, especially in the basic subjects, would have to be offered in order to inculcate an analytic and flexible approach to individualization.

Second, teachers would have to be taught to be more alert to signs that a child has failed to comprehend. Allowing children to answer on a volunteer basis can cloak profound individual ignorance which accumulates if permitted to persist uncorrected.

Third, teachers need to become acquainted with a range of pertinent information outside the boundaries of conventional education. The greatest need is for understanding principles of children's mental development (as studied in developmental psychology), but a variety of medical matters should also be drawn to their attention.

Finally, teachers should be made aware of a wide range of instructional approaches to reading, writing, and arithmetic, not because they would necessarily wish to apply these approaches formally and in detail, but because such approaches are a rich source of ideas and devices for conveying the better explanations that teachers should always be seeking to provide.

The excellent teacher constantly recognizes new challenges and constantly learns on the job. The greatest single contribution to generating large numbers of excellent teachers would be creation of a model for teachers—by members of education faculties—that embodies a logical, analytical, and intellectually questioning approach.

REVIEW OF SOME WELL-KNOWN REMEDIATION TECHNIQUES

We have discussed our general approach to techniques of remediation. There is an ever-growing number of such techniques, developed by workers in many fields and for various purposes. One is bombarded by advertisements offering them for sale, journal articles assessing their reliability and usefulness (usually by the technique's proponents), and claims by special groups or clinics to have found *the* effective method. It would be impossible to discuss all of these techniques here in comprehensive detail. Therefore, we have chosen to illustrate the commonsense approach we advocate for evaluation of specific techniques, in the hope that readers will thereby acquire a sense of how to apply our approach in evaluating any technique suggested for use with an individual child.

In general, there is never any excuse for spending outlandish amounts of money and time on remediation; no remedial technique is appropriate for all learning disabled children; and no child can learn equally well with all techniques, or even with all of those that are highly regarded.

Also, as learning disabled children develop, they may outgrow some of their cognitive limitations but display new ones as they approach more difficult material; therefore, one must always be prepared to switch techniques as the child grows older.

Alternative Approaches to Reading Instruction

There are many different programs for teaching children to read, of which the two best-known are the whole-word or "look-say" method and the phonics method. These two methods have held alternating sway over successive generations of teachers and children. But superordinate to this dichotomy is the one between the proponents of an analytic or subskill approach to reading instruction and those who favor acquiring reading skills in a "natural" way, somewhat similar to the acquisition of natural spoken language.

The "natural" method
Proponents of the natural approaches point to what they regard as the remarkable ease with which children learn spoken language without specific instruction. They feel that children could learn written language in just the same way if given the opportunity. Extreme theorists of this type would use reading teachers merely to provide materials, incentives, and praise and would allow the children to do their intellectual work unaided. Others would not be quite so passive with regard to specific instruction, but would nevertheless (from the beginning) have the child read not individual words but phrases, sentences, and meaningful passages. They would place little emphasis on the niceties of spelling and would permit children to maneuver through printed material by having them supplement the actual reading skill brought to the task with guesswork based on knowledge of the general characteristics of the language and the sense of the passage. In this method the child's misreadings are not corrected; rather, the child is encouraged to read copiously in the expectation that, with increased reading speed and larger amounts of material read, the accuracy and fluency of the reading skill will by some not totally obvious mechanism spontaneously improve.

Natural methods of reading instruction may work for certain children, probably those who are highly gifted and curious, or else those who, like "hyperlexics," focus a pathologically intense attention on the printed word. But highly gifted children will learn with or despite any teaching method, and they are not our present concern.

Children who experience more than the usual amount of difficulty in learning to read certainly cannot be taught by such sloppy means. If they are, they learn to guess their ways through a passage, so that by the end of each reading session they have learned some compensatory trickery but nothing much about reading as a perfected skill. Just as in complex athletics and gymnastics it is best to teach first the component movements and then how they might be put together, so in reading instruction it is essential to teach the children first to read a sufficient though limited vocabulary of individual words. Only when they can do this with effortless facility is it time to string the words together in short phrases and let them acquire fluency by hastening their eyes across the printed line. If connected passages are introduced prematurely the children will not identify the words, because that is hard for them; instead they will take the easy way out and guess their way through the passage, not learning anything more about the reading process.

The analytic methods

Among the more analytic approaches to the teaching of reading, the correct choice among the whole-word, phonics, linguistic, or syllabic methods of instruction will depend on the child's particular pattern of strengths and weaknesses rather than upon any general consideration. When a child is well able to use the phonics approach, this is a powerful tool by which to acquire initial acquaintance with a word. Beyond that point, with repeated exposure the word should become automatically available. But many children do not have the phonic analysis and phonic synthesis skills needed to provide this preliminary acquaintance with words when they enter the first grade. Undoubtedly, carefully graduated logical instruction in phonics can maximize what a given child can do by this route. But even then there will be some children to whom phonics will not be readily accessible for another year or two. Such children can often be taught at least a limited vocabulary quite effectively by the whole-word method. Conversely, some children with immature visual abilities might do better with a greater early emphasis on phonics.

Critics of analytic reading instruction remark that the fluent reader seems to bypass the stage of transforming the printed word to the word that is covertly sounded out. Instead, the fluent reader seems to deduce meaning directly from the printed page. Even if that is so, however, it occurs as the product of many years of practice. It does not follow that what fluent readers do, beginning readers should begin to do. It is inescapably necessary in beginning reading instruction to have children first sound out each printed word (using only spoken words already in their vocabulary) before extracting meaning from phrases and sentences.

When beginning reading is taught to a child who has failed, the approach is not fundamentally different from that which is customary with normal learners. The differences are in the instructional emphasis, which depends upon what particulars the child finds difficult and also upon the teacher's attitude, which is geared to a child with a history of failure and fear of more failure.

The section that follows deals with commonly used ways of improving instruction for those who find learning difficult.

READING PROGRAMS FOR THE LEARNING DISABLED

Rational forms of the basic analytic approach to reading that offer additional help to the child with a selective reading difficulty are all individualized. The discussion that follows focuses on such individualized programs.

The many commonly used programs attempt to provide additional help for the problem reader in one or more of these ways:

1. By providing a simple *intermediary* step which, when learned, serves as a foundation for reading conventional scripts. The intermediary steps are phonetic renderings of the language (as in Pitman's Initial Teaching Alphabet, where 42 symbols represent the distinctive English phonemes) or a set of picture words (as in The Peabody Rebus). These intermediary steps are used to inculcate systematic reading habits and to defer the more difficult real orthography until the children have overcome much of their fear of the reading process.
2. By reinforcing a whole-word approach through *multimodal* activities. Thus in the Fernald (VAKT — visual, auditory, tactile, and kinesthetic) approach the child is committed to learning each word as a whole but begins by looking at, tracing, and simultaneously saying the word in syllables. Tracing is discontinued in successive stages, and the child then writes from memory. Finally, merely looking at the word and saying it is considered sufficient. Thus the overload imposed by the whole-word approach is mitigated by a highly systematic rote approach to learning.
3. By using a *phonic* approach and deferring the acquisition of irregularly spelled words. The rationale for this procedure is that students who experience difficulty require a reliable and comprehensive mechanical approach. They cannot afford to guess, as is done so often in whole-word reading. Furthermore, the whole-word approach, even when successful for reading, is often inefficient for spelling.

Specific individual programs have different merits and problems. Two systems that attempt to highlight phonemic similarities and differences make use of arbitrary color cues to do so. These systems are Words in Color (Gattegno) and the Color Phonics System (Bannatyne). In both the phonemes are identified by color. It is questionable, however, whether the irrelevant color cue helps more than it distracts. The methods that follow do not make use of such artificialities are preferable.

The *Gillingham* technique professes adherence to Samuel Orton's now outdated ideas on the relation between reading acquisition and cerebral dominance; but in fact it is a rigidly systematic phonics approach which also takes advantage of multimodal drilling similar to that of the Fernald method. Phoneme sequences are pronounced with increasing speed for blending, and words are pronounced with decreasing speed for analysis. The phonogram (a basic vowel-consonant unit for building up words) and syllables are used for word construction from smaller units. Consistent left-to-right reading is maintained and made practical by finger-tracing.

The *Progressive Choice Reading Method* (Woolman) offers a systematic and graduated approach to both auditory and visual aspects of reading. Letter discrimination is taught by matching, and letter writing is taught first by tracing and then from memory. When the pronounciation of the letter has been learned, one proceeds to letter-sound correspondences, first on the basis of meaningless letter pairings (to minimize guessing based either on general configuration or context). One then progresses to regularly spelled words. Lowercase is introduced after uppercase, and irregular words come into the program later. The system is based on the excellent principle that concrete evidence of mastery at every level must precede moving to a more difficult level.

The *Integral Phonics Reading Program* (Stevenson) is another systematic phonics program. The initial focus is on the first vowel in the one-syllable long-vowel word. The first consonant is then blended in. Short vowels, being more difficult to analyze auditorally, are used later. Again, an automatic response is obtained at each step before moving on. This program has the special feature of being designed so that it can be used by parents and other untrained instructors.

An instructional method applicable to language and arithmetic as well as reading, and which incorporates many sound principles, is DISTAR (The Direct Instructional System for Teaching Arithmetic and Reading). This method, designed for small group instruction, makes provision for observing the responses of individual children. The method is analytical and attempts to spell out the successive links in each argument. Provision is made for a graduated exposure to information at a pace that minimizes overload, and for repetition of explanations when mistakes occur. The emphasis is on conceptual rather than rote learning. The approach to reading is phonic, is highly structured, and deals with decoding prior to comprehension of words.

Followup studies have credited DISTAR with impressive success in work with disadvantaged children. Ingredients that contribute to this success are emphasis on stimuli stripped of irrelevant attributes so that children can focus on what is universal rather than accidental about the examples used to illustrate a concept. Also, no relevant knowledge is taken for granted, so that the children are not left floundering in incomprehension because they are too shy or disorganized to ask for the specific information they lack. Besides being helpful for disadvantaged children, these features are very important for learning disabled children.

Remedial Handwriting

When handwriting is a major problem, legibility and speed should be considered separately. A variety of exercises in the actual movements used in writing are available. These should emphasize the commonest sources of illegibility—failure to close letters (which accounts for about half the errors) and looping letters that should not be looped or not looping ones that should be (which accounts for about a quarter). Readiness exercises in supposed prewriting skills—such as eye-hand coordination, copying of shapes, and eye movement training—are of dubious relevance and are not recommended.

Arithmetic Programs for the Learning Disabled

Programs for teaching arithmetic to children who experience difficulty in this area include the following:

The Montessori Approach. This relies on materials designed to be self-teaching. They are concrete and include geometric shapes, counting boxes, sandpaper numerals, arithmetic frames, counting frames, and bead chains. These materials are used to demonstrate the readiness operations discussed in Chapter 3. The main merit of the approach resides in the use of concrete materials to exemplify abstract principles. The instruction system is rigid, and children are severely constrained with respect to how they may use the materials they are given. This approach makes the method unpopular with those who value giving young children the opportunity to express individuality.

The Cuisenaire-Gattegno Approach. This system uses 291 rods varying in length and color. The children discover principles by using the rods, and the teacher observes and asks questions about what the child is discovering. That is, the child first explores the rods independently and then undertakes directed activities with them, in the course of which a set of basic principles is discovered. Mathematical notation is then introduced, and only subsequently are number values assigned to the rods. This approach has the merit of enlisting the student's active participation and enthusiasm. The concrete nature of the materials helps those children with whom the more abstract traditional approach has not succeeded.

Seeing Through Arithmetic. This approach uses an illustrated workbook in which each concept is well practiced before the next is introduced. The systematic clarification of concepts is useful for the slow arithmetic learner.

Mathematics in Action. This method has minimal verbal content and is suitable for the student whose mathematics progress is impaired by a language or reading disability.

Programmed Math. Given a student who already has mastered mathematical concepts, this is useful for developing facility in computation by means of feedback and self-correction.

Structural Arithmetic and the *Developmental Program of Quantitative Behavior for Handicapped Children.* These are comprehensive programs which combine the merits of the approaches described above.

DISTAR Arithmetic. This has been covered in the previous section.

IRRATIONAL METHODS FOR REMEDIATION OF LEARNING DISABILITY

Irrational training programs may involve perceptual activities, such as matching stimuli or pointing to specified stimuli; perceptual-motor activities, such as copying two- and three-dimensional patterns; motor activities, such as chalkboard and directional training; fine motor activities, such as work with pegboards; and gross motor activities, such as work involving the walking board, trampoline, and use of tools.

PRINCIPLES

Rational methods of remediation all meet the unusual learning requirements of the learning disabled child by some individualized instructional program. Irrational methods share the goal of "helping learning disabled children's brains to develop" by training them in activities that have no self-evident relationship to reading, writing, or arithmetic readiness, but which are alleged to be prerequisites for readiness to acquire those skills.

Any skill can be taught to the developing child when the relevant mental operations have come under the control of the maturing brain. Inability to perform in an age-appropriate manner indicates deficient control by those brain structures that would normally have matured by that time (given that the child was motivated and the environment supportive). But it does not follow that development of a given level of behavioral control is contingent on prior development at some other "more primitive" level.

For instance, a child may be pathologically clumsy and yet very intelligent. Nor can it be assumed that practice within an area of academic failure can exert a maturing effect on the relevant part of the brain, let alone on other parts of the nervous system.

Methods that purport to accelerate brain development can be divided into those that claim to have a general maturing effect on relevant areas of the brain and those that claim to modify the way in which the brain-based cognitive function is organized (it being implied that this organization has an important effect on the efficiency with which the mind functions).

A variety of physical exercise programs, so-called perceptual and perceptual-motor training practices, and various stimulation and enrichment techniques are all guided by the simplistic assumption that if some is good, more is better. Undeniably, if children are deprived of sensorimotor opportunities to an extreme degree, their ability to realize their potential for action will be handicapped, sometimes grossly. But even after extreme deprivation it is striking how soon children will catch up when placed in a normal environment, provided their mental health receives careful attention. But such encouraging experiences are no guide for the management of a child who, in the context of a normal environment, fails to acquire abilities. There is no physiological evidence for the view that supplying such a child with a superabundance of normal experiences will accelerate brain development. This hard fact undermines the theoretical basis of enrichment and stimulation techniques.

The theoretical basis of multisensory approaches is similarly invalid. Again, this depends on a simplistic notion: If one sensory channel is "closed," information fed into another channel that is open will circumvent the barrier; and in some unspecified fashion the closed modality will then become available for learning. Again, our knowledge of how the nervous system works does not justify this belief. The same reservation holds for recapitulation methodology. Some have claimed that children may fail to develop an appropriate high stage of central nervous function because, for unknown reasons, they did not pass through lower stages. This is not only invalid in theory but also lacks validation in practice. Proponents of the theory prescribe exercises that take the child through creeping, crawling, and all the physical stages of infancy and early childhood. Exercising such children has not been shown to materially improve their functioning at the sensorimotor level of behavioral control, let alone at higher levels of cerebral organization. In short, no way of accelerating cognitive development is known when that development is delayed for biological reasons (for instance, when there have been flaws in genetic programming or early brain damage).

Irrational methods of remediation include:

1. Manipulations intended to foster brain development
2. Manipulations intended to accelerate hemispheric lateralization of cognitive function
3. Exercises intended to foster sensorimotor capabilities assumed to be prerequisites for the development of reading and writing skills.

ATTEMPTS TO FOSTER BRAIN DEVELOPMENT

Enrichment techniques that surround children with stimulation in the modality and category deemed relevant to their disability have not been shown to have any effect on brain development. Insofar as this stimulation (be it visual, verbal, or other) is intense and rapidly changing in form and content, it can only serve to overload and confuse the learning disabled child. As has been explained, such a child is already experiencing undue difficulty in picking out the critical features of messages from a host of irrelevant features. That is not to say that during the interaction between the therapist who "stimulates" and the child, useful information may not be imparted and learning may not in fact occur. But if this happens it is not for reasons envisaged by the theoretical basis of the methodology. And since any benefit that occurs is unplanned and incidental, the method falls far short of optimal efficiency.

Attempts to enhance a particular level of nervous system development by recapitulating developmental stages that occurred before the customary time when the cognitive skills in question should have appeared are equally ineffective and irrelevant. Effectively reducing children to a lower developmental level not only fails to promote their neurological development but infantilizes them in their own eyes and in those of their parents and other helpers. Insofar as the manipulations that make up such programs are quite unrelated to anything called for in the classroom, it is hard to find even incidental merit in these actions.

ATTEMPTS TO FOSTER LATERALIZATION OF FUNCTION

Various forms of pressure have been exerted on lefthanded and ambidextrous children for many years. These range from mild inducements to use the right rather than the left hand for specific activities, to forceable restraint of the left hand, to a variety of other physical manipulations that are supposed to change the way functions lateralize in the brain. These approaches are subject to the general criticism that peripheral manipulations do not have the desired effect (or any effect) on cerebral maturation, which is biologically preprogrammed. Also, the process that these approaches supposedly accelerate does not exist [2]. For while it is true that some nonrighthanded people have right rather than left hemispheric (or even bilateral) language representation, there is no acceptable evidence that this prejudices their language or learning abilities. The excellence of a developing cognitive function will depend on the development of its neural substrate, regardless of where that substrate is located in the brain. Thus, even if one could modify cerebral organization by peripheral manipulations, it would still be a pointless thing to do.

The numerous theorists whose methodologies purport to foster lateralization lack a sound theoretical basis for their methods. This may or may not invalidate their methods, depending on what actually goes on between therapist and child. For instance, the now quite unacceptable neurological theorizing of Samuel Orton relies heavily on a supposed relationship between nonrighthandedness and failed left lateralization of language. Yet Orton's two guiding principles — namely (1) simultaneously attending to the visual, auditory, and kinesthetic attributes of letters and words and (2) directing the training towards fusing smaller units of information that the child can handle into larger, more complex wholes — are completely acceptable, the first for some children, the second for all.

PHYSICAL EXERCISE AND PRESUMED PHYSICAL DEFECTS
Various theorists have regarded the abilities to control movement and posture in space, perform feats of figure-ground discrimination, and acquire a variety of eye movement coordinations that make for fluent scanning of the visual environment as prerequisites to learning to read and write [1]. Hence, children with reading and writing problems have been subjected to intensive exercise programs emphasizing the maintenance of balance and the coordination of whole-body movements, to perceptual training that focuses on discriminating shapes unrelated to the written word, and to optometric exercises that train children in shifting their gaze (when they cannot read short words or even individual letters, let alone worry about fluent refixating) across a printed text like a fluent reader. All such programs lack a theoretical basis and have failed to find support from objective experimental studies. With respect to optometric approaches, a recent statement by the American Academy of Pediatrics, the American Academy of Ophthalmology and Otolaryngology, and the American Academy of Ophthalmology asserts that eye care should never be instituted in isolation when a patient has a reading problem. The statement points out that children with learning disabilities have no greater incidence of ocular abnormalities such as refractive errors and

muscle imbalance than do children who are achieving normally. Whereas such abnormalities should be corrected, this holds true equally for children with and without reading problems, and the correction should not be expected to correct the reading problem. The statement notes that there is no peripheral eye defect which produces a dyslexia and associated learning disabilities, and eye defects do not cause reversals of letters, words or numbers. The statement finds no evidence for claims that children with learning disabilities learn better subsequent to (1) visual training (employing muscle exercises, ocular pursuit, and glasses) or (2) neurological organizational training (laterality, balance board, and perceptual training). The statement warns that maneuvers such as unnecessarily prescribing glasses may create a false sense of security that might delay needed treatment.

The above does not imply that all such programs are useless. But whether they are useful depends upon the specific nature of the skill that the child is expected to acquire. If the skill itself is of some use in everyday life or could serve as a morale-booster, and if the program succeeds in inculcating the skill, then the exercise does have merit. But it has to be kept clearly in mind that the benefit achieved will not generalize beyond the specific skill acquired. It is true, of course, that unintended or nonspecific benefits may accrue. When a child is desperately in need of certain explanations and information, the therapist may deviate from a pointless methodology to offer the child the help that is really needed. From this help and from the growing affiliation between the therapist and child there may derive much benefit of a type not foreseen in the methodology. This is all for the good, but that kind of benefit could have been more simply and straightforwardly achieved without the theoretical clutter of an irrational remediation technique.

In explaining why many parents who have gone in for expensive and time-consuming irrational methodologies do believe that this helped the child, we must keep two further principles in mind. One is "cognitive dissonance." This refers to the fact that when people have invested a lot of physical, financial, and emotional effort in anything, they are emotionally biased toward seeing some merit in it. It would be emotionally devastating were they to believe the effort had been completely sterile. The other principle relates to cerebral maturation. Children's mental maturation proceeds by fits and starts, but in all but the most severe cases it does proceed. If the irrational methodology in question is continued for long enough, then spontaneous cerebral maturation might occur coincidentally, and the child might acquire additional mental skills regardless of—or even in spite of—the training procedures. In such a case the parents will be inclined to attribute the gains to the method, and in this they will be encouraged by the practitioner involved.

TALKING TO PARENTS ABOUT IRRATIONAL METHODS
Having referred to the irrational remediation methods' lack of theoretical basis or empirical validation, we must now consider the important practical question: Since it is unlikely that the child would benefit from such methods, can we nevertheless in good conscience advise a child's parents against resorting to them when "other methods have failed?" And if we try to do so, how can we make our arguments convincing? It is necessary to challenge two assumptions. One is that "the usual methods have not worked." The methodologies resorted to first rarely fully and logically satisfy the criteria for thoroughly individualized instruction. We cannot accept failure until we have satisfied ourselves that sensitive and carefully planned individualization has been tried for an adequate period of time and has failed. That will rarely have happened. The second assumption is that "nothing is lost by trying the specified irrational method." This is simply not true. The parents' time, effort, emotional energy, and money are lost. And far more serious, in case after case the child's physical and emotional effort, prolonged concentration, hopes to avoid failure, and prospects for living a normal life are lost as well. In this manner a lengthy, elaborate, and emotionally charged program that is later revealed to be a time-consuming sham may destroy the child's last hope for success and last incentive ever to try again with real effort and enthusiasm. These risks are too great. However severe, however long-lasting, and however hard accepting the child's disability may be, a more mundane and plodding but rational approach is much preferred.

HOW TO DISCONTINUE REMEDIATION
One remediation goal that has widespread support is to reintroduce the child into the mainstream of age-appropriate scholastic endeavor. This goal is based on the implicit assumption that a "cure" is possible. In some cases of spontaneous brain maturation, or when attention is the problem and medication is fully effective, this mainstreaming is indeed practical. But in many serious cases of learning disability, unqualified reinsertion of the child into the mainstream causes disaster, regardless of how much the child has benefitted from the remedial help.

Typically, the remedial situation offers children a more sympathetic setting with more individual attention and, accordingly, elicits more effort than does the regular classroom. Only if the children keep up this effort will they continue to hold their own. It is unreasonable to expect such effort to continue without supports and while the child can see the ease with which other children master the academic material. It is essential to work out a transitional program in which remedial supports are continued (or their equivalent substituted) on a part-time basis, and to observe the child's progress with exceptional care. For it will take at least several months before one can be assured that the child's confidence and internally directed motivation are equal to the challenge of the regular classroom.

EMOTIONAL SUPPORTS DURING REMEDIATION

The child's innate intellectual ability is the major determinant of the potential for success. But personality variables, which are modified by the child's life experience, strongly influence the extent to which that potential is realized. Effective remedial teaching entails more than the delivery of academic information. It needs to be supported by attitudes toward the child on the part of the teacher, family, and others that take account of the child's predicament and of the personality characteristics required to meet it.

A strong desire for personal accomplishment (called competence motivation) is innate in human beings and strikingly evident in young infants. Approval and praise from others do not sufficiently account for the efforts young children make to master their environment. They find satisfaction in the doing itself, in the ability to perform. Time and again, children try to do themselves what a parent is perfectly ready, willing, or even determined to do for them more quickly, smoothly, and efficiently. This competence motivation, which is such an attractive feature of young children, is relatively resistant to adverse pressure. But a crushing repetition of failure will finally dispel the pleasure of performing effective action for its own sake. Then the disabled learner, no longer self-motivated, becomes dependent on necessity and external rewards.

In managing such cases, necessities have to be emphasized and external rewards given, but the main goal is to restore that inner pressure to achieve so that it becomes autonomous and impels children on—regardless of the desires and demands of others. This cannot be accomplished by sympathy and praise alone. It can be accomplished only by showing children that they can achieve by their own efforts. Naturally, this is not always possible within a child's area of maximum academic difficulty. But the insightful teacher will note areas where the difficulties are less or absent and will point out good performances in those areas, thereby restoring the child's feeling of general personal competence.

Whereas, at least initially, competence motivation is universal, children vary with respect to other personality factors. Of these, anxiety and compulsiveness are important to the learning process. It has been shown that children who are very compulsive, very anxious, or both benefit most from being taught in a highly structured environment. Anxious children, in particular, fare poorly in an unstructured situation, presumably because they do not dare to take the initiative—which is exactly what the situation demands. Instead of orienting to the task, these children will often remain intensely dependent on social approval and will constantly observe the teacher for cues about what to do next, instead of attending to the problem itself. Here the environment interacts especially strongly with the basic personality. Children who have been deprived of social approval in their younger years (e.g., institutionalized children) will show this concern about the teacher's behavior rather than about the specifics of the task.

Naturally, the dynamics of the family both affect and are affected by children who fail in school. For their part, failing children may be so resentful of their parents that they will make less effort to succeed the more parents desire their success. Or they may be so cautious that they will not risk attempting anything unless they are completely sure of success. They then wear the trappings of a spurious stupidity that does less than justice to what they can in fact achieve.

For their part, the other family members may derive some secondary gain from the failures of the failing child. The self-esteem of other children in the family may be based on comparing themselves favorably with the child in question; and an unexpected performance improvement on the part of that child may precipitate disturbed behavior in a previously undisturbed sibling. In a more general sense, family members may find the failing child's problems to be a convenient repository for more deeply seated fears, anxieties, hostilities, and resentments that, as the child improves, become evident and then reveal that they are primarily directed against other family members. Clearly, the potential risks to the mental health of the family are complex and greatly variable, but by no means negligible. The teacher cannot be expected to handle this situation. The pediatrician might wish not to do so either, but must in any case be alert for distress signals with respect to the mental health of the family and must make arrangements for family therapy forthwith if they occur.

REFERENCES
1. Cratty, B. J. *Physical Expressions of Intelligence.* Englewood Cliffs: Prentice-Hall, 1972.
2. Kinsbourne, M., and Hiscock, M. Does Cerebral Dominance Develop? In S. Segalowitz and F. A. Gruber (Eds.), *Language Development and Neurological Theory.* New York: Academic Press, 1977.

3. Wynne, S., Ulfeder, L. S., and Dakof, G.   Mainstreaming and Early Childhood Education for Handicapped Children: Review and Implications of Research. Final Report. Bethesda, Md.: Bureau of Education for the Handicapped, 1975.

SUGGESTED READING
Hammill, D. D., and Bartel, N. R.   *Teaching Children with Learning and Behavior Problems.* Boston: Allyn & Bacon, 1975.

Haring, N. G., and Bateman, B.   *Teaching the Learning Disabled Child.* Englewood Cliffs, N.J.: Prentice-Hall, 1977.

III. Cognitive Style Disorders

8. Temperament

When people are faced with a problem or with an unexpected or unexplained event, they must do two things: they must think about the problem in an appropriate way, and they must continue to keep their attention on it until they can come up with a sufficiently accurate response. The first part of the process is called "adopting the correct mental set" or "task orientation." A person who is uninterested, undermotivated, or preoccupied might fail to do that. The second part of the process involves what we will call the "concentration span"—the length of time a person concentrates on a problem before venturing to make a decision. A normal person can concentrate on a task, even in the face of distraction, until the task, for practical purposes, has been completed. But however purposefully a problem is tackled, if the effort is abandoned before enough of the surrounding uncertainties have been resolved, then the solution will be premature and subject to error. On the other hand, if a person continues to concentrate on a problem even after enough uncertainties have been resolved to permit a reasonably accurate solution, then diminishing returns will be derived from the additional time spent. Such a person will be using time inefficiently and will lack understanding of how to respond to varying situations. We call those who habitually concentrate for an excessively long time "overfocused" and those who concentrate too briefly "underfocused."

People who reduce uncertainty insufficiently have an *impulsive* cognitive style; because they hastily abandon one task for another; they also appear distractible to observers. People who reduce uncertainty excessively by continuing to work too long on a problem have a *compulsive* cognitive style; their continued preoccupation with the same matter will make them seem withdrawn from other elements in their environment. Both of these cognitive styles are stable "temperaments" of the individuals involved.

Of course, not all problems that a person encounters require the same depth of problem-solving. Some situations are easily analyzed, and further thought about them is unproductive. Others require concentrated and well-maintained attention. Within the normal population are individuals who vary greatly in temperament— some are relatively impulsive, others relatively compulsive. The former will feel more at home in situations that call for quick and relatively superficial decision-making. They will function best in occupations (journalism, public relations, commercial travelling, etc.) that suit this temperament. However, impulsive people acting within normal limits have the flexibility to modify their impulsiveness when the situation clearly demands it. Other normal people function best when more complex issues are presented that have no strict time limitations. Such people also tend to do best at particular occupations (library work, certain kinds of research, etc.). But again, compulsive people who are within normal limits have control over their attention and can function in a more impulsive way if necessary, even though they may not prefer it.

A temperament is a stable personality trait that may be inherited and that is already present in early childhood. No one knows how many temperaments contribute to individual differences among human beings, and it can be quite difficult to disentangle behavioral styles that are inherited from those that result from life experiences. The customary way to accomplish this is to compare identical and fraternal twins with respect to the characteristic in question. Although there are some methodological difficulties to guard against, it is generally true that an inheritable personality trait is more likely to make a parallel appearance in identical twins than in fraternal twins, whereas an environmentally imposed trait will not lead to any such difference. On the basis of this criterion we can at present define at least four general categories of temperament: Impulsive versus compulsive; active versus inactive; sociable versus unsociable; and placid versus emotional. The extremes at either end of each of these continua usually represent maladaptive (and therefore psychopathological) behavior. The extreme form of activity, for example, can be mania. It is also possible that particular interactions of two or more personality traits within an individual child can affect the child's ability to adapt. For instance, an impulsive child with a very active temperament might face greater problems and be noticed sooner than one with a relatively inactive temperament. Indeed, interactions such as these might go far to account for the widely varying behaviors among those children who are properly labeled hyperactive in the sense of being unduly impulsive and distractible. In this vein, a particular backward style may represent either an adaptation to a particular stress or an innately determined strategic preference (temperament). In other words, adaptation to stress may involve a behavioral style that differs from that style the person would naturally have favored, all things being equal. When impulsive or withdrawn behavior is most manifest during stress, and is less striking in neutral circumstances, it represents a situation-determined adaptation. But when such behavior is most evident in neutral circumstances and is, if anything, less evident under stress, it then is a feature of the individual's temperament.

When an *extreme* temperament (e.g., impulsive or compulsive) coincides with lack of a flexible style, a social misfit occurs and clinical problems arise. Children with this problem, who are locked into their style, react appropriately to only a minority of life situations. They fail to modify their preferred style to suit the situation, and thus they behave in a maladaptive fashion. The extent to which they make a successful social and vocational adjustment will be affected by many circumstances, including the attitudes of others in the social group. But when the situation is extreme, there may be no occupation and no life-style that can accommodate the affected person. The impulsive temperament, when extreme, has achieved the most notoriety under the labels "hyperactivity" and "hyperkinetic syndrome." (Other equivalent diagnostic labels include "overactivity," "organic drivenness," and "hyperkinetic disorder of childhood.") When clinicians describe a child as suffering from "minimal brain dysfunction" (MBD) they are often thinking primarily of the child's impulsive style.

The wide range of temperament differences within a normal population is probably neither accidental nor due to lax genetic engineering. It is quite logical for beings like ourselves, who live in complex situations that call for different coping styles at different times. Consider sociability, for example. Insofar as a group or community affects the lives of its individual members, sociability is adaptive. Sociable individuals tend to apprise themselves relatively quickly of group feelings and decisions. This helps them ingratiate themselves with the group, influence decisions in their favor, and perhaps even achieve group leadership. But not everything that makes for survival in our society depends on the group. Individual skills and commitments are also adaptive, and much can be achieved by the individual without reference to the group. If everyone were highly sociable and spent much time socializing, then the exceptional, unsociable individual would derive a massive advantage from committing time to individual achievements that would be all the more effective for being so rare. Genetic patterns leading to unsociability would then tend to increase until the competition for individual achievement opportunities became sufficient to neutralize any further advantage.

If, conversely, most people were unsociable, then the occasional sociable person would reap overwhelming benefits. Genetic patterns producing sociability would increase, and roughly the same ultimate equilibrium would be achieved. This theory of an equilibrium — known as a stable evolutionary state — serves to explain the perpetuation of diversity in Darwinian terms.

We can apply the same logic to the genetic determinants of impulsive and compulsive temperaments. In an environment with diverse sources of reward and diverse hazards, some situations favor hasty decision-making that sacrifices certainty for speed. Other situations favor reflection that will produce some required degree of accuracy. Thus one would expect a stable evolutionary state to emerge in which a diversity of decision-making would be represented in the population — as is in fact the case.

This line of reasoning might lead one to suppose that there should be a niche for everyone, regardless of cognitive style preference, in our society. However, the current genetic mix represents a response to selective pressures active a long time ago, and is by no means necessarily adaptive to the contemporary situation. In fact, technological change and the increasing complexity of modern life are rapidly invalidating the impulsive response style. Few threats are overt, immediate, and best faced with rapid unthinking action. Many threats are covert, subtle, and call for protracted analysis before making a decision. Thus, the more developed a society the more of a social liability is the impulsive style, whereas the opposite (compulsive or overfocused) style, in its milder forms of expression, meets an increasing need.

A final variable that is as yet little understood is flexibility. To what extent and at what cost can individuals deviate from their preferred styles if the situation demands it? The issue could be addressed experimentally by observing a person's choice of tactics under various conditions. This is clearly a critical variable but requires detailed, extensive investigation.

SUGGESTED READING
Buss, A., and Plomin, R. *A Temperament Theory of Personality Development.* New York: Wiley-Interscience, 1975.
Eysenck, H. J. *The Biological Basis of Personality.* Springfield, Ill.: Charles C. Thomas, 1967.

9. Impulsive Extremes

The impulsive and distractible behavior of the hyperactive child is a well-known factor making for underachievement in the classroom, but it also has a serious impact on many other real-life situations. The manifestations of impulsiveness can be classified under four headings: motor behavior, problem-solving, social interactions, and emotional style. Hyperactive children often have deviant motor behavior (as the label implies), are more deviant in problem-solving (as their attention problems indicate), and are often still more deviant in their social interactions and emotional style. Unless all of these four facets are considered, it is not possible to get a proper picture of what one is up against in trying to help these children. These four aspects of hyperactive behavior are not equally important at every age. The motor abnormality is more prominent early and less important as the child becomes older; the attention problem is least important at the beginning, very important during the school years, and less important later; and the social and emotional problems increase in importance as the child grows older. Anyone who does not look beyond activity levels may be deluded into thinking that because a hyperactive child is not moving excessively any more, that child has recovered. This bad mistake is often made. While each hyperactive child manifests impulsive temperament in a somewhat individual fashion, it is possible to put together a composite case history which illustrates the natural progress of the condition, although of course no one child should be expected to exhibit all the manifestations cited.

DESCRIPTION

MOTOR BEHAVIOR

The restless and at times exuberant motor behavior of hyperactive children was what first attracted attention and led them to be labeled according to the motor manifestations of their cognitive problem. This motor element in impulsive behavior has in fact been overemphasized. In the account that follows, the limitations on the use of motor manifestations as diagnostic criteria should be carefully noted.

Most hyperactive children show a relatively high level of motor activity, and in most cases this obviously comes early in their lives. It has frequently been noted that even very young infants who are later identified as hyperactive were restless and achieved motor milestones early. This restlessness could be associated with feeding problems. Such an infant typically gobbles food, perhaps swallows air, and manifests signs of "colic" (by stiffening and screaming). Some such children behave in this tense fashion even at times when genuine colic would be an unlikely cause.

Unduly short periods of sleep are also noted in many cases. The child awakens after a few hours, not hungry, wet, or upset, but alert and ready to play; the parents are the ones who are unhappy to be awake at that hour. So they will complain that their child sleeps rather little. It may not be clear whether more sleep is needed, since the child will sometimes seem fully energetic even after a few hours of sleep and will sometimes seem sleepy but on the go. This situation, which needs to be sorted out, may perhaps differ from child to child; typically, however, there is a sleep pattern which disrupts the parents more than the child. This sleep pattern reflects the hyperactive's great responsiveness to external change as well as a possible need to generate change. In their intense form, these manifestations make for a very hard-to-manage infant at this stage, but parents and their advisers usually choose to blame the mother for some hypothetical "error" in child-rearing rather than seek medical help.

Intense responsiveness to stimulation, and even stimulus-seeking (in the form of an unbridled exploratory urge) is striking in the toddler. But even more than is usual at that stage, the hyperactive toddler explores all available situations, even at considerable physical risk. Such a child dives into everything, explores the various crevices in the house, finds and eats poisons or medicines, and then shows up in a hospital emergency room with poisoning or a broken limb. These emergency room visits for assorted injuries occur several times as frequently among hyperactive children as among average children. In particular, hyperactive children are very apt to ingest poisons, especially the tranquillizing pills that their parents so often keep close at hand. Stewart et al. [30] estimate that one out of four boys brought in for accidental poisoning shows hyperactive behavior in grade-school.

Whether this intense exploration is seen as a problem, and even an unmanageable one, depends on the social situation. In an extended family, the impact may be absorbed by several family members and thereby lightened for the individual; and in poverty-stricken families a child is frequently released into the environment in the morning and gathered in again much later, having used up a great deal of energy without detriment to the household. In contrast, the perfectionistic middle-class parent, living in a home that contains valued and fragile objects, is a ready victim for this type of child.

A hyperactive youngster's excessive movement tendencies are conspicuous during preschool and kindergarten. In the more formal academic setting of the customary grade-school classroom, such a child's constant shifting of position, interference with others, and tendency to rush out of the classroom attracts the teacher's unfavorable notice. At this stage, it becomes difficult to document excess amounts of movement. It may rather be the type and timing of movement that makes the hyperactive child differ from the rest; the constant repositioning of the body may betray reorientation of the child's thoughts. On the playground, however, where a high level of activity is acceptable, the movements of hyperactive children are hard to distinguish from those of the rest.

In general, children's activity levels progressively decline over the first decade of life. Hyperactives' excessive movement tendencies are less marked by the end of the first decade and usually disappear completely around the time of puberty. A high energy level may remain, but this is no longer manifested by inappropriate and intrusive movement tendencies. Bedwetting tendencies, though unduly prolonged in many hyperactive children, have also usually been resolved by then.

PROBLEM-SOLVING

Not all impulsive and distractible children show the above-mentioned motor characteristics. However, they all show a characteristically curtailed problem-solving style. The difficulty is not in initial focusing of attention but rather in maintaining focus. How this affects their schoolwork and other intellectual achievements depends on their general intellectual level. These children do begin tasks; they are constantly beginning tasks; but they abandon them prematurely and leave them uncompleted unless the task takes little time or the child is very bright. If the child is very bright, even brief concentration on a task may be sufficient. So a bright hyperactive child may not have a learning problem. In other words, the child may not be underachieving, because much of what happens in a classroom is repetitious, and a bright individual can pick up the gist of it with brief bursts of concentration. However, the average hyperactive child abandons that concentration without having adequately understood or rehearsed the material; and the next time this material is approached the same thing happens again. Cumulatively, then, the hyperactive child of average intelligence falls behind academically, because this concentration difficulty excessively prolongs learning time. Such children tend to fall behind not just in one or two subjects, but rather in whatever requires focused concentration for any appreciable length of time; thus they only seem to pick up those things not requiring focused concentration, such as learning language. These children therefore have normal language development and a reasonable vocabulary. Their real problem is that they are not so much unwilling as unable, or able only with extreme effort, to exclude competing possibilities. They focus on a task but have to break off to look at who is coming to the door, check on what jacket the child next to them is wearing, or wonder what is happening out the window. These are tendencies that these children can overcome, but only with tremendous effort. They may make such effort in a doctor's office, and the doctor may say "The child kept perfectly still for me, "implying that if only the parents had the doctor's personality and character they would have no problem. But that is not true, because once that supreme effort has been made for a few minutes, the child leaves the intimidating situation and goes wild with pent-up energy. So such observations as "The child can watch a favorite television program" or "The child sits still in the office" do not invalidate what parents tell. In this case what parents and teachers report is crucial; it is more important than what occurs in a physician's or psychologist's office.

Impulsive children will usually make immediate and overtly observable decisions. Sometimes, if they are more introverted, they will merely let their minds drift, and then return to the task of signaling their decision in plenty of time. Thus their work will be impetuous and sloppy. It will also fluctuate in quality. Impulsive children who underachieve academically are very difficult to place according to their true academic level. On repeated achievement testing, they may show quite different achievement levels at different times. If the testing situation is made interesting and relevant for them, they may reveal an academic competence unsuspected by their teachers (who are more impressed by repeated failure to pay attention and complete assignments). "Careless" errors abound. The child jumps to conclusions, focuses on the most obvious rather than the most critical aspects of the situation, and volunteers incorrect information. In most cases the extent to which this happens is by no means constant. It is well-known that, given intense personal attention, hyperactive children may surprise their teachers and themselves with the quality of their performance. The snag is that this effect does not outlast the presence of the adult. As soon as the adult turns away, the child reverts to the inefficient, impulsive style.

This maladaptive impulsiveness is most apparent in a structured situation that calls for sustained thought. Thus, it often becomes evident first to the experienced preschool teacher, generally becomes more obvious in grade-school, and often remains a problem in high-school and even in adult life. Where the impulsive temperament persists, an adult who has not been fortunate enough to select an impulsive occupation will often be fired because of irregular performance.

INTERACTIONAL STYLE

The way impulsive children deal with their peers may be seriously inappropriate. Impulsive individuals tend to impose their needs on others. They come on too strong, approach too briskly, and do not go through the customary pattern of hesitation and tentative courtship when meeting a new person or joining a new group. Quite often the group lets out a blast and the child comes crying back again. This kind of impulsive advance, met by rejection, followed by the same advance, again met by rejection, is a typical hyperactive pattern that reveals more about the basic difficulty involved. That difficulty is one of learning to modify behavior on the basis of negative experience. Hyperactive children are not oblivious to negative experience; they do not like being rejected or hurt any more than anyone else; but somehow they do not seem to be as able as others to change their behavior on the basis of such experience. So they continue to do the thing for which they are punished. When permitted to do so hyperactive children will take over and shape social situations according to their exclusive personal needs, and will control the situation through either domination or manipulative behavior. Although such children are often intensely sociable (at least at first), their friendships tend to be short-lived. They have a low frustration tolerance, squabble endlessly with their siblings, and are unpopular with classmates because they so constantly demand (and gain) the teacher's attention, and have a high rate of absence from school. We typically hear that such a child is quite capable of learning if the teacher stands close by, but does nothing in a group or else messes about, so that the teacher must constantly leave the group to attend the child. This evokes resentment from both the teacher and the other children. As compared to relationships with peers, a hyperactive child typically has an easier time forming relationships with much older children, who can handle the impulsiveness, or with much younger children, who are willing to accept domination. Relationships with parents become an endless struggle centering on disciplinary issues. Failing to do what they are asked, or to restrain their immediate impulses, hyperactive children respond to restraint with physical outbursts, to physical punishment with spiraling temper tantrums, to deprivation of privileges with heedlessness, and to isolation with persistence of the initial impulse. The more passive hyperactive children use whining manipulation to gain their ends.

As all these cases demonstrate, regardless of the particular personal interaction involved, there is no evidence that the child has given the interaction the amount of problem-solving thought that it deserves. Accordingly, interactions between hyperactive children and others tend to be superficial, dealing with external matters, and not reflecting understanding or empathy appropriate to the age levels involved.

In adolescence, this impetuous and inept social style may become a severe handicap. Unable to attract friendship in the customary manner, the impulsive individual may either react by withdrawing from the group or by commencing attention-seeking delinquent behavior. Impulsive reaching for short-term advantage, particularly if this is associated with a low anxiety level, will generate behavior customarily termed "psychopathic:" the reckless, guiltless, and self-centered striving for immediate personal advantage that characterizes the psychological deficit labeled "primary psychopathy." It is unclear whether the increased prominence of antisocial tendencies in older hyperactive children arises from activities of an increasingly conspicuous subgroup of hyperactive children, or whether hyperactive children in general become more antisocial as they grow older. It is clear that early aggressive tendencies predispose a child to later antisocial behavior, and perhaps a distinction can be made between hyperactive children who are primarily distractible and immature and those who are primarily aggressive.

EMOTIONAL STYLE
Hyperactive children tend to communicate in a shallow and defensive fashion. In the face of obvious realities, hyperactive children will deny that there is any school problem or any problem in relationships with parents, peers, or others. Nevertheless, they are often depressed and hold themselves in low esteem. They will fail to account for their actions or even to stop and think about the reasons they do things. Many hyperactives lie easily and convincingly. A child so little given to problem-solving and thoughtfulness will understandably exhibit scant empathy for the feelings of others. The hyperactive's existence is egocentric, not deliberately but by default. The lack of empathy and warmth is least obtrusive when relationships are casual, but most handicapping when relationships are long-lasting and need to be close, as in marriage.

DIFFERENTIAL DIAGNOSIS
In the differential diagnosis of both motor and cognitive impulsiveness, distinctions must be made between behaviors that result

from the impulsive personality trait and similar behaviors that have other causes.

HYPERMOTILITY

Not every child who moves a lot is hyperactive. Some children are genetically endowed with a high activity level; their movements differ from those of hyperactive children in being adaptive, goal-directed, and generally effective in securing goals. Other children squirm, wiggle, fidget, and twitch because of anxiety. These motor manifestations differ from the impulsive ones in that they are intensely situation-specific (most obvious in the classroom, the doctor's office, and other irksome situations). Also, they have a different quality. Whereas the motor rearrangements of impulsive behavior have constantly varying and unpredictable patterns (and large amplitude), excess movement from anxiety is a repetitive low-amplitude fidgetiness restricted to certain parts of the body; anxious movements are typical for the individual and highly stereotyped in nature. Also, anxious movements increase under stress, but impulsive movements often decrease. So whereas gross measurement could confuse these three patterns of excess movement, detailed observation should sort them out.

Superfluous movements may also occur in classroom situations if children are out of their depth intellectually and cannot follow the material that is being taught. This fidgeting is an expression of boredom and discomfort. Conversely, a child whose accomplishments happen to be well above the level of the transactions in the classroom may fidget or undertake extraneous activity on account of boredom due to familiarity. These, of course, are problems not of the child but of the teacher-student interaction.

IMPULSIVENESS

Impulsiveness as a biological manifestation (a character trait) must be distinguished from the impulsive behavior of people driven by intense emotions. The latter differ in that their impulsiveness centers on identifiable goals, whereas the hyperactive's impulsiveness ranges across all life situations. Also, some people, usually from deprived and culturally alienated settings, act impulsively because this is their social norm, and they lack the experience provided by a reflective model.

DISTRACTIBILITY AND SHORT ATTENTION SPAN

Attention may lapse or wander. It may lapse into inactivity in very passive and undermotivated people, or into unconsciousness in cases of minor epilepsy. It may wander to the general environment, not only in hyperactive people, but also in people who are bored because they find their task too easy, too hard, or for some reason unacceptable. And it may wander to internal thoughts or feelings in people who are anxious, obsessed, or thought-disordered.

Temper Tantrums

The tantrum of the foiled impulsive child must be distinguished from the unsocialized aggression of the child who lacks effective parental control, the anger of the paranoid personality, and the admittedly rare outbursts of the temporal lobe epileptic.

Manipulative and Attention-Seeking Behavior

A distinction must be made between behavior due to hyperactivity and that due to faulty child-rearing of the so-called permissive kind, in which parents yield because that is the easy way out. Children reared in this way learn to exert control by manipulation, and in this respect resemble constitutionally impulsive people.

In the classroom, hyperactive children typically make endless demands on the teacher for personal attention. This is also true of two other kinds of children—those who come from broken or depersonalized homes and have been deprived of attention, and those who experience intense anxiety about their accomplishments and classroom situation and feel a continual need to be reassured that they are performing satisfactorily.

Disorganized and Chaotic Behavior

Stemming from insufficient reflection, this style of behavior can result from lack of an organized role model, as well as from preoccupation with anxious or psychotic thoughts. On rare occasions epileptic and degenerative brain conditions can surface in this way. Finally, disorganization may represent passive-aggressive intent toward the nominal authority figure—a kind of inert negativism.

Self-destructive Behavior

The hyperactive's tendency toward injury, ranging from the trivial to the catastrophic, must be differentiated from the deliberate self-destruction of the depressive, the untutored accident-proneness of the neglected child, and the injuries suffered by the abused child.

Social Ineptitude

The hyperactive child blunders into social situations without either adequate preparation or empathy with the feelings of others.

This thoughtless ineptitude is in sharp contrast to the tentative shyness of the overfocused child. Other children are socially ill at ease on account of inadequate parental guidance and deficient role modeling. Peers may shun the company of children who act in bizarre ways on account of thought disorder.

EMOTIONAL SHALLOWNESS

Hyperactives rarely act as if they were in touch with their own feelings or could empathize with those of others. This pattern must be distinguished from schizophrenic detachment and flatness of affect, as well as from the defensiveness of the child with deep emotional disturbance. Overfocused children, though capable of displaying considerable emotional depth, may reserve such displays for a few select individuals and confront the clinician with cold formality.

Finally, a diagnostic consideration that relates to all six of these categories relates to the timing of the behavior involved. As the hyperactive child lingers in the same situation, or repeatedly encounters it, the child's behavior deviates increasingly from the norm. Normal children and hyperactive children may be quite hard to distinguish in many respects at first viewing, but the difference becomes immensely more obvious over time. Observers who only catch brief glimpses of these children are free to theorize about the myth of the hyperactive child. Observers who stay with the child are soon compelled to acknowledge the harsh reality of the problem.

RESEARCH ON HALLMARKS OF HYPERACTIVITY

The abnormal behavior ascribed to hyperactive children seems so general that one might expect considerable overlap between them and normal children, hypoactive children, and children with other forms of psychopathology. But as we have seen, this overlap is more apparent than real. Hyperactive children do have clear-cut characteristics that differentiate them from these other groups. However, one obtains a much more precise appreciation of the nature of the hyperactive child's difficulty from observing how stimulant medication helps many hyperactive children behave more normally. Properly administered, stimulant drugs normalize a hyperactive child's behavior. So by assessing children on and off medication, one can get a precise idea of the type of improvement that is to be expected when the therapy is appropriately used.

A major drawback to accepting unreservedly the evidence of interested observers such as parents and teachers, supplied either directly or in the form of questionnaire responses, is the fact that virtually any individual becomes more tractable on stimulants. Not only do favorable responders become more heedful of instruction and more susceptible to social pressure, but even adverse responders (insofar as their attention turns more inward) may appear to cause less trouble. It therefore becomes easy to keep children on levels of medication that may make them less of a discipline problem, but that seriously impairs their ability to perform tasks. It is thus highly desirable to seek corroboration of observers' subjective impressions from objective tests of the child's actual performance. Only if the child's performance is unquestionably improved by the given drug at the given level is it justifiable to prescribe that drug for long-term use.

We have sharpened our understanding of hyperactive behavior through a series of experimental studies comparing children's performance of a number of tasks done the same day on and off drugs in a double-blind fashion. The children were given pills before breakfast and pills before lunch; at one of these times the pills were the active drug, and at the other they were dummy (placebo) tablets that looked and tasted identical. The children were tested after both administrations, but no one was told when the active and when the placebo tablets were given until all the testing had been completed. The following eleven experiments were done in this fashion.

LEARNING
We designed a learning task in an attempt to approximate the classroom learning situation in a rigorous way. Children were shown color slides of animals, one at a time, and were told in which of four zoos ("North, South, East, West") each animal lived. Each child was asked to go through a list of animal-zoo pairings over and over, until each animal could be placed in the correct zoo. Each child did this both on the drug and on the placebo (using different animals on the two occasions). The results showed that a hyperactive child on the placebo typically had much more difficulty learning this information than when on an adequate dose of medication. This difference was found consistently on repeated testing.

RELEARNING AND MEMORY
We asked each child to relearn the animal-zoo material on a subsequent day, having learned half of it on the drug and half on the placebo [31]. The relearning was arranged so that some of the relearned material had been learned in the same state (i.e., material learned on the drug had been relearned on the drug; material learned

on the placebo was relearned on the placebo), whereas some of it was relearned in the alternate state (i.e., material learned on the drug was relearned on the placebo, and material learned on the placebo was relearned on the drug).

The design can be summarized as follows:

	Drug	Placebo
Day 1	learned animal-zoo pairings 1–16	learned animal-zoo pairings 17–32
Day 2	relearned animal-zoo pairings 1–8 and 17–24	relearned animal-zoo pairings 9–16 and 25–32

What was the result of holding the "state" (medicated or non-medicated) constant, as opposed to alternating states?

Results: The advantages of holding the state constant were substantial. Not only did hyperactive children learn best in the drug state as opposed to the placebo state, but it was also an advantage to them to learn and relearn in the same state. Their learning was "state-dependent."

If this result turns out to apply in the classroom and other situations in which children learn, then it would suggest that stimulant therapy should be maintained at as uniform a level as possible, rather than being limited to mornings and afternoons of weekdays during school semesters, as is commonly done. If off the drug in the evening, can a child relate a homework assignment to what was learned during the day? If asked outside school hours about something learned at school, can the child remember? This issue has not yet been studied over the long run or outside the laboratory, but the experimental findings suggest that it would be a useful precaution to minimize fluctuations in the drug state as much as possible.

CONCENTRATION SPAN

What is the nature of the difficulty that hyperactive children experience in a learning task like the zoo animals test? As we see it, this difficulty is best expressed in terms of limited "concentration span"—the length of time a child will concentrate on any one item of information. Concentration is not something that can be measured directly. The fact that a child is looking at an item of information is no guarantee that thought is being devoted to it. Conversely, a child who looks away may be visualizing, associating with, or otherwise elaborating upon what was seen. Nevertheless, the following method does give an indirect measure of concentration time: Vary the length of time that each of a series of items is offered for inspection, and determine the point of diminishing returns. At what critical point does further inspection time produce no further improvement in performance?

Psychologists who specialize in verbal learning are familiar with the "total time principle." This asserts that the amount of material learned depends on total study time. It does not matter how often each item is shown, or for what duration, as long as the total study time is held constant. Thus, if one wants to learn a vocabulary of 60 words in a foreign language and has half an hour available, one could inspect each word once for thirty seconds, or twice for fifteen seconds, or six times for five seconds. According to the total time principle, the course chosen would make no difference. The same amount of vocabulary would be remembered regardless of the frequency and duration with which the individual words were presented. However, there is an underlying assumption here that is critical for our purposes. This is that the individual will concentrate effectively throughout the study period. This includes the presumption that the individual will work on each item for the length of time it is presented. But if a child's concentration span is limited, this is unlikely to be the case under conditions where a few long-lasting presentations are made (as opposed to many very short presentations). So if a word is held in front of an impulsive child for eight seconds rather than four, the last four seconds may be wasted because the child will concentrate for only four seconds anyway. So we predict that for hyperactive children on a placebo, the total time principle will not hold for the longer inspection periods, but will regain validity when these children are on an effective dose of stimulant.

We tested this prediction using the animal learning test that has already been described [6]. Children were shown the materials in each of three different ways: Individual items were shown for 4 seconds, for 8 seconds, and for 12 seconds. Naturally the number of times each item was shown varied inversely with the exposure duration, so that total learning time was held constant.

Results: Hyperactive children on the placebo learned best under the shortest exposure condition, a little less well under the intermediate condition, and much less well under the longest exposure condition. For this task, the average concentration span was no better than 8 seconds, and the total time hypothesis did not hold; the hyperactives only concentrated on each picture for at most 8 seconds, even if it was available to them for 12 seconds. When the same children were on the drug, not only did they learn better in an absolute sense under all these conditions, but the improvement was most marked for the longest inspection period. The concentration span became 12 seconds plus, and the total time principle applied.

Clearly, when hyperactive children have trouble learning, this is partly due to their impaired concentration span. Such children learn best when there is a rapid change of materials. But even more effective than that is the appropriate use of a stimulant agent, which not only improves performance but actually normalizes it in the sense of restoring the applicability of a general law of learning, the total time principle.

DISTRIBUTION OF ATTENTION

If hyperactive children shift attention away from the designated task, what do they do with that attention? Do they simply go blank and stop thinking? Do they become self-engrossed like anxious children? Or do they keep on attending, but to items declared irrelevant by the teacher? The latter of these possibilities seemed most probable to us, and we tested this experimentally.

Children were given material to learn in a setting where other features of the display were declared irrelevant [33]. Nevertheless, when retention of information was then tested, the test asked not only about what was remembered of the designated materials ("intentional" learning) but also about what was remembered of the irrelevant items ("incidental" learning).

Results: As expected, hyperactive children on the placebo actually remembered more irrelevant items than when they were on the drug. They had paid attention to them despite instructions.

We can thus infer that at the expiration of their concentration span, hyperactive children shift their attention to other information instead of that which was designated for learning. It follows that they would gain educational benefit from being surrounded by educational displays, so that wherever they look they learn something. More simply, this diffusion of attention to irrelevancies could also be overcome by taking an appropriate dose of stimulant.

THE EFFECT OF THE NATURE OF THE
TASK ON CONCENTRATION

The concentration span concept does not incorporate the view that this span is of constant duration. Rather, our model indicates that hyperactive children would concentrate longer on relatively complex and engrossing materials. We tested this by providing them the same material two ways—in a plain form and in a manner involving variations in color and location [1].

Results: Under the latter more complex circumstances, the hyperactive children did better. But they did best of all on the drug, and on the drug it did not matter whether the materials were presented in a plain or fancy manner.

MAINTAINING CONCENTRATION

Another experiment involved having children perform a "tracking" task [15]. By manipulating a lever they attempted to hold a dot at the intersection of a horizontal and a vertical line—an intersection that moved unpredictably across an oscilloscope screen. As subjects spend minute after minute doing a task of this kind, they normally increase their time off-target; that is, as time passes their performance worsens.

Results: We found that hyperactive children on the placebo showed this decrease in performance much more quickly than either normal children or they themselves when on the drug. This was thus another instance of their inability to maintain concentration. Incidentally, we also found that both hyperactive and normal children's manual skill in holding the dot at the intersection of the lines was greater under the stimulant. This direct effect of the stimulant on motor skills is relevant to the previously reported finding that treated hyperactive children perform better on motor skill tests, such as the Lincoln-Oseretsky Scale, than they do when untreated. It is possible that stimulants do have a limited role to play in the control of clumsiness where this exists.

PLANNING

Each child's ability to plan a route through a maze was examined by means of the Porteus Mazes Test, which has alternate forms for use in repeated testing to minimize practice effects [13].

Results: We found that the hyperactive children scored higher on this test when on the drug than when on the placebo. On the drug they could think ahead and not commit themselves impulsively to blind alleys—from which they would then have to retreat, losing time, credits, and points on the test. It has long been known that the Porteus Mazes Test is sensitive to hyperactivity and its correction by stimulants. The present finding is important in that it makes this test available for diagnostic use in documenting children's behavior on a single dose of drug as compared to placebo.

CAUTION ON A MATCHING TASK

It has been theorized that the basic ingredient of the impulsive style is the tendency to maximize speed to the detriment of accuracy. A test specifically designed to assess this type of decision-making is the Matching Familiar Figures Test (MFF). This consists of a number of displays of line drawings. On each display there is a test figure and an array of other figures; all the other figures closely resemble the test figure, but only one is completely identical. The subject is asked to find the correct match for the test drawing. If this is done hastily, mistakes will result. Only laborious checking off of component features one by one will permit a completely accurate MFF performance. Among normal people there are those who tend to respond quickly but make mistakes on the MFF — the "impulsives." Others — the "reflectives" — tend to respond slowly but accurately. There is some evidence that children classified as impulsive on the MFF are also impulsive in other contexts — for instance, in the classroom. And conversely, MFF reflectives tend to make more deliberate decisions in such real-life situations.

Based on this line of reasoning, one would predict that hyperactive children should exhibit short latencies (response times) and high error scores on the MFF, and if favorably influenced by stimulants, should increase their latencies and decrease their error scores. In fact, one of these predictions was borne out but not the other [22]. On medication, children's error scores dropped precipitously, but their average latency did not change.

Our analysis of this unexpected outcome led us to a behavioral dichotomization of favorable responders into the impulsives, who make hasty decisions, and the distractibles, who spend no more time on a task than the impulsives but who wander off the task, and who thus are unduly slow to respond. We then classified hyperactive children into "fundamentally impulsive" and "predominantly distractible" categories on clinical grounds and gave them the MFF. We found the impulsives had short latencies that lengthened on the drug, while the "distractibles" had long latencies that shortened on the drug.

We therefore had to modify our initial expectations with respect to hyperactive children's MFF performance. If we look only for children classified "impulsive" by MFF, we miss a sizeable number of stimulant-responsive hyperactives. These are the children who internalize rather than act out their flitting attention, and who leave decisions in abeyance rather than hastily getting them made. Those distractible children do not conform to the popular stereotype of the wildly rambunctious hyperactive. But they need help anyway. This experiment reminds us of them and suggests a possible diagnostic test.

COOPERATING

We also employed the widely distributed toy known as Etch-a-Sketch ® [18]. To use this toy the child draws a line on a surface by manipulating two knobs simultaneously, one with each hand. One knob draws a vertical line, the other a horizontal line. Turning the knobs simultaneously produces oblique lines. The child was asked to draw a line inside predetermined outlined paths which were placed over the maze. The number of infringements of the limits was scored. We then asked the child and the mother to cooperate on this task. Each of them manipulated one of the two knobs. We also recorded the amount and nature of what each person said to the other.

Results: The hyperactive child alone made far fewer infringements when on the drug than when on the placebo. The mother-child pair also performed better when the child was on the drug than when the child was on the placebo. On placebo, the mother gave many directions and the child gave few, and what was said by both was generally negative in affect. When the child was on the drug, the mother gave the child fewer instructions and they were more positive; the child gave the mother more information and instructions, and these were more positive. In sum, the interaction and cooperation between the two were far superior in quality when the child was medicated. This result offers the parent a vivid demonstration of what to look for in a favorable stimulant response. It also demonstrates how ready mothers usually are to interact pleasantly with their child if the child's behavior makes that possible.

RESPONSE TO DISCIPLINE
The child was asked to discover a predetermined route through a maze developed by Lykken [9]. This maze has twenty choice points represented by rows of buttons. At each choice point there are four alternatives; one is correct, two are incorrect, and the remaining one is both incorrect and "punishing." The "punishment" in our study was the sounding of an extremely unpleasant tone.

Results: Normal children, while learning to make the correct decisions, also learned to avoid the "punishing" incorrect buttons. Hyperactive children on medication did likewise. But the same hyperactive children, when on placebo, showed no signs whatever of learning to avoid the punishing locations. This difficulty in "avoidance" learning can be directly related to the difficulty parents experience in trying to enforce limits on their children. It is noteworthy that many adolescent psychopaths fail to learn to avoid "punishing" locations on the Lykken maze, just as hyperactive children do while on the placebo.

SELF-IMAGE
Another study of ours examined the responses children on and off medication made on a self-image questionnaire [17].

Results: As judged from these self-reports, hyperactive children were much more realistic about their school and personal situations when on medication than when on placebo. This could reflect the tendency of the untreated hyperactive child to deny difficulties even when they are quite obvious.

RISK-TAKING

Do hyperactive children take more risks than others, and what types of risks might those be? There are many accounts of hyperactive children climbing onto, over, or into dangerous places and being hurt. Indeed, the chances of a hyperactive child being seen in hospital accident clinics because of injuries have been estimated four times as great as those of other children. However, no controlled demonstrations of this effect exist. We designed a study to evaluate hyperactive children's risk-taking in the following way [9]. A gadget dispenses one marble each time a lever is pressed. The child is told that the lever can be pressed as many times as desired, and each marble obtained can be traded later for two cents. We also tell the child that if the lever is pressed often enough, the next time all the marbles acquired will be lost. Alternatively, we tell the child roughly the same thing, but instead of saying the winnings will be lost we warn that if the lever is pressed too often a nasty electric shock will be delivered. We then observe how many times children who are favorably responsive to stimuli and children who are adversely responsive to stimuli press the lever when on the drug and when on the placebo. Naturally we never actually had a trial in which all the marbles were lost or in which any electric shock was actually delivered.

Results: With regard to the risk of losing all their winnings, there was no difference between groups or across drug conditions. Both groups of children hazarded about 12 to 15 lever presses on the average, and they did so whether they were on the drug or on the placebo. It was quite different with respect to the risk of sustaining an unpleasant electric shock. The children who were adversely responsive to stimuli limited their efforts both on and off the drug to about five trials. In contrast, those responding favorably to stimuli hazarded an average of about 11 trials before desisting when on the placebo. But when on the drug these same children reduced the number of lever presses down to an average as low as 3.5.

It becomes clear that hyperactive children differ from others in terms of certain kinds of risks only: not risk of material loss but rather risk of physical discomfort or pain. They take these risks not for their own sake, but in pursuit of novel and exciting situations and stimulation. This is consistent with their increased incidence of "self-destructive" behavior, an accident-proneness involving everything from trivial mishaps to devastating calamities [30]. Their intractibility to physical punishment as a disciplinary measure also becomes understandable. On medication, these children's disregard of physical discomfort and of bodily risk was completely corrected, lining them up with other children in this respect.

MECHANISM OF IMPULSIVE EXTREMES

It is clear that much hyperactivity is inheritable (though probably polygenic), not only because it runs in families [23], but also because the biological parents of hyperactive children have been shown to be more than usually subject to three other disorders, each of which has features in common with hyperactivity: psychopathy, alcoholism, and hysteria [2]. Further, it is clear that impulsive and distractible behavior does not define a condition that is completely distinct from the normal state. Most normal people behave impulsively at times, and most are at least occasionally distractible. The difference between them and those whose impulsiveness amounts to psychopathology is one of degrees, albeit at times extreme degrees. In other words, the intensely hyperactive individual is virtually always impulsive, whereas most people are impulsive only in circumstances that are conducive to that style. Both the normal brain and the brain of the hyperactive are capable of implementing both reflective and impulsive behavior. The difference is in the relative prevalence of these two behavior forms in various real-life situations. One could easily suppose that one part of the brain programs an obvious, rough-and-ready decision almost as soon as the problem attracts attention, while another part of the brain effectively holds implementation in abeyance until the decision has been thoroughly checked for detailed applicability. In hyperactive individuals, that second mechanism would appear to play less than its desirable role in behavior, being underactivated for some reason.

Another way of looking at the same issue is to conceive of a selector system. This system is responsible for determining what type of thinking the person will undertake: Will it be verbal, spatial, numerical, etc.? The selector activates the relevant mental processor. Once active, this processor analyzes the available information until enough is known to give an answer with a satisfactory likelihood of being correct. As the initial uncertainty inherent in the situation is progressively resolved by the gathering of relevant information, the ability of the selector to keep that processor in play diminishes, until at some stage the activity of the selector falls below a criterial level; then the processor is switched off, and another train of thought commences. This model would suggest that in hyperactive individuals the selector cuts out prematurely, leaving a residue of substantial uncertainty about the problem at hand. Again the model implies that a particular part of the brain, though available to hyperactives as it is to normal people, intervenes more briefly in the case of hyperactive individuals, presumably because its activation level is lower.

Individual variation of the level of activation of this hypothetical selector mechanism could range from a curtailed role in the impulsive individual through the normal state to an unduly persevering role in the individual who is anxious, withdrawn, or even autistic. The hyperactive individual, then, would be on the same continuum as the normal person, and the point on that continuum at which the transition from normality to psychopathology is attributed would be a matter of judgment.

PREVALENCE OF IMPULSIVE EXTREMES

In the opinion of classroom teachers (as distinct from questionnaire data), the incidence of hyperactivity among grade-school children exceeds five percent. Mental health professionals offer estimates varying from 3 to 10 percent of elementary-age children. Despite propaganda to the contrary, systematic study has shown a rather low incidence of stimulant therapy in terms of the above estimates of the prevalence of hyperactive behavior. For instance, a Minneapolis study showed that a mere 0.36 percent of all children were on stimulant therapy for their classroom behavior, and that no racial or ethnic imbalance was concealed within this figure.

There is clearly a normal range of appropriate reflection, and there clearly exists a group of children so wildly impulsive that no social structure could comfortably accommodate them. How intermediate cases are classified is much more dependent on their life situations and social settings. Certain societies, certain cultures, and certain ethnic groups demand more thoughtfulness from their members than others. A person who might appear impulsive in mainland China might not appear so in the southern United States. A person who might appear impulsive in an academic family might not appear so in an impoverished urban setting. The clinician does well to define the degree of impulsiveness which is abnormal as being that which sets up intolerable social strains within the child's family, classroom, and larger societal group. These strains, after all, will usually have precipitated the child's referral to the clinic.

Not only is a particular degree of impulsiveness viewed differently in the various perspectives of different human groups, but a particular individual will also be more or less impulsive depending on the given situation. Faced with a monotonous task, like waiting interminably for a bus or friend, or driving long distances at night, most normal people will show impulsive tendencies. Given a novel and enthralling situation, even hyperactive individuals will apply themselves quite thoroughly for a time. Thus, the degree of impulsiveness of a given individual varies with the degree of uncertainty associated with the immediate situation. The greater the uncertainty (i.e., the more interesting and challenging the situation), the more the problem-solving apparatus of the brain will be engaged. The more predictable or monotonous the situation, the more an impulsive or distractible tendency will emerge.

Systematic data are unavailable regarding the relative incidence of hyperactivity among adopted children, but it seems to us that an unduly high proportion of hyperactive children are adopted. Suspicions about parental attitudes toward their adopted children come to mind, but these are probably unjustified. Rather, consider the circumstances that often culminate in a child being put up for adoption: an impulsive mating without adequate contraception, or a pregnancy permitted to reach term without the mother being sufficiently committed to take on the baby. This sequence is consistent with parental impulsiveness, which we believe to be inheritable and therefore likely to be passed on to the child. At any rate, it is our practice at some point while interviewing the parents to ask: "Which one of you is like your (hyperactive) child?" Generally one pair of eyes looks sideways (toward the parent felt to be like the child) and one looks down. When the couple does not readily identify either parent's personality with the child's, then the odds are that the child was adopted.

POSSIBLE PRECIPITATING FACTORS OF IMPULSIVE EXTREMES

While the bulk of the evidence suggests that the hyperactive (impulsive-distractible) temperament is a personality trait that characterizes the individual—at least during infancy and childhood and often indefinitely—it has been claimed that hyperactive behavior is sometimes precipitated by postnatal diseases of the brain, psychological stress, and allergic or toxic response to substances in the diet.

The fact that certain forms of brain damage induce an impulsive temperament in a previously nonimpulsive individual is undeniable. There are numerous classical case descriptions of children who suffered severe encephalitis and then became hyperactive to an extreme degree. Retrospective studies dividing children into those with and without evidence of early brain damage ("organic" and "nonorganic" groups) on the basis of histories, physical examinations, EEG tests, and other criteria have produced results that disagree about whether hyperactive behavior is more common in the "organic" than in the "nonorganic" group. Whatever the relative probabilities of the syndrome turn out to be in damaged and apparently undamaged individuals, it seems clear that hyperactivity can result either from inheritance or from brain damage, and that knowing which does not help in determining the degree of hyperactivity involved or in making a prognosis.

Whether psychological stresses can precipitate hyperactive behavior is not known. In the majority of affected children, evidence of hyperactivity can be obtained retrospectively, even back to the first year of life, thus supporting the theory of an organic etiology. But in a minority of cases no such evidence can be obtained retrospectively with regard to the early years. Furthermore, in some cases a plausible psychological stress—like family conflict, or loss, or separation from a parent by divorce—coincided with the onset of complaints about such behavior. Behaviorally, however, children having experienced such stress are indistinguishable from those with problems of a clearly constitutional nature, and the same applies to the probability and degree of completeness of their response to stimulants. It is hard to know whether the unrevealing early history of such cases is genuine or reflects forgetfulness or even denial on the part of the parents. It is also notoriously difficult to evaluate psychological stresses as causes of behavioral disorders, not only because such stresses are frequent and often do not seem to cause any specific disorder, but also because of parents' and other witnesses' natural tendency to associate the two matters in their imaginative reconstruction of long-past events. A conservative view is to regard psychological stresses as potentially exacerbating preexisting impulsiveness or precipitating frank impulsiveness where it had previously been latent.

At any rate, the question of the psychogenic contribution to hyperactivity is irrelevant to the use of stimulant therapy. Stimulants should be tried during the time when behavior is disorganized, and if they are effective their use should be continued while all available psychological avenues are explored for relieving distresses that could have contributed to the genesis of the disorder.

Can impulsive behavior be modeled? If children see little or no reflective behavior by parents and other adults, will they learn an impulsive style by default? Certainly chaotic behavior can result from chaotic child-rearing, but it is unclear to what extent this simulates impulsive behavior of a constitutional origin. Nor is it clear what would be the effect of stimulant therapy in such a case. At any rate, when hasty decision-making is caused by faulty modeling, this should be amenable to correction by appropriate instruction. Programs suitable for this purpose and applicable, for instance, to inner-city children have been published. But there is no reason to suppose that modeled impulsiveness is confused with the constitutional syndrome in many cases.

One can model not only people but also images—for instance, on television. Hence the possibility is sometimes raised that watching television might foster impulsive ways of acting. It is true that many television programs seem geared to the impulsive style, in that the succession of images and events is so varied but one could hardly think deeply about them even if one wished to do so. This perhaps explains why one so often hears it said of hyperactive children that they keep still when watching television and may stay glued to the set for hours. So rapid is the succession of events on the screen that they need not themselves shift mental focus to generate new trains of thought. The program does it for them. But television merely fills time for hyperactive children. It neither helps nor hurts them. There is no reason to suppose that it generates an impulsive style.

Numerous chemical substances have been suspected of precipitating hyperactive behavior in children. The best-verified effect is that of barbiturates in exacerbating impulsive and distractible behavior. This usually comes to notice when a child who is coincidentally epileptic is treated with the otherwise excellent anticonvulsant phenobarbitone. The epilepsy might well improve over time, but with some children the parents will return with a new complaint of impulsive and distractible behavior.

It is generally agreed that barbiturates, which are commonly used in the control of epilepsy will aggravate any coexisting tendency to hyperactive or impulsive behavior. Unfortunately, the two other drugs most generally useful for epilepsy control, Mysoline and Dilantin, can have the same effects. This can confront the physician treating a hyperactive epileptic child with a serious dilemma. Furthermore, simply introducing a stimulant to counteract hyperactivity may not have the desired effect. In certain hard-to-control child epilepsy cases stimulants have the effect of making the fits completely intractable to treatment. Thus, when prescribing stimulants for an epileptic child, one must be alert to the possibility that the seizure state could be aggravated and must withdraw the stimulant therapy if this happens.

Maternal smoking during pregnancy appears to cause stimulant-sensitive hyperactivity [7]. A study of hyperactive children and suitable control groups showed that the mothers of the hyperactives smoked considerably more during pregnancy and at other times than did the mothers of the control children. Incidentally, there was no difference in the pattern of smoking by fathers in the two groups. A possible mechanism involved here could be the increased incidence of obstetric complications associated with heavy cigarette smoking. This could produce fetal anoxia and brain damage. Or carbon monoxide could accumulate in the bloodstream and cause fetal anoxia. The absence of a smoking difference among fathers weakens the alternative explanation, that there is a genetic linkage between the tendency to produce hyperactive children and the tendency to smoke heavily.

A less well-founded suggestion is that hyperactive behavior is due to "malillumination"—too much x-radiation and deprivation of that part of the visible spectrum that is lacking in standard artificial light sources. Substituting full-spectrum bulbs and screening out x-rays from fluorescent light sources was said to reduce the incidence of hyperactive behavior in the classroom. This type of finding is, of course, uninterpretable. The so-called Hawthorne Effect could be involved: It is well-known that any environmental manipulation can change behavior for quite nonspecific reasons. Dummy manipulations are needed as a control procedure for studies of this kind. It is, however, salutary to reflect on how readily even the most preliminary and inconclusive experimental findings in this area burst into public prominence through the newspapers. This occurs as consequence of intense public interest. Unfortunately, it is not something which serves that interest.

Dietary excesses and imbalances have frequently been suggested as etiological agents for some or all cases of learning disability and hyperactivity (as they have for countless other disorders). None of this theorizing is based on definitive evidence. The proposition that comes closest to plausibility is related to lead. Some evidence has been presented to indicate that children with relatively elevated but subtoxic lead levels in their blood or hair, children showing no signs of clinical lead toxicity, might be more than usually subject to aggressive and restless behavior [24]. Claims have been made for the efficacy of chelating agents in reducing hyperactive behavior among children with serum lead levels that were relatively high in the "normal" range. An animal model, a lead-poisoned mouse that is said to be hyperactive, has been produced; this hyperactive state is said to be exacerbated by barbiturates and corrected by amphetamines, thus simulating the drug responses of hyperactive children [29]. The megavitamin (formerly called the "orthomolecular") school of thought attributes a variety of nutritional imbalances to children with learning disability. Therapy with vitamins B_1, B_2, B_3, B_6, B_{12}, B_{15}, and folic acid has been advocated. The claimed benefits of orthomolecular therapy seem nebulous, however, and although the approach has been advocated for many years, its proponents have still not accomplished a methodologically sound validation. Incidentally, blood sugar levels are supposedly low in many learning disabled children—another claim unsupported by controlled experimentation.

Intolerance to certain foods has long been incriminated as a cause of colicky restlessness in babies and jittery irritability in older children [11]. Whether these manifestations are identical with those of impulsiveness and distractibility, as previously discussed, is doubtful. Exposure to such untolerated foods can strikingly impair children's group relationships, particularly with parents, but in a way perhaps more suggestive of some intense, overfocused, hostile adverse responders than of the slap-happy impulsiveness of the stimulant-responsive hyperactive. The foods that have most frequently been held responsible are milk, corn, wheat, and eggs. The subject needs systematic study. Pending this, it would certainly be good practice to take a careful history with respect to food intolerance in every case. But if there is no evidence whatever of symptoms referable to food intolerance other than hyperactivity, then the hyperactivity is unlikely to be explicable on this basis.

A great deal of recent notoriety has been given to the suggestion that a wide range of natural and added substances in the diet are responsible for some or all of the hyperactivity of many hyperactive children. Popular suspects include the red and yellow food colorings and salicylates. Some preservatives have also been mentioned, and suspicion has also been cast on a wide range of other colorings and flavors [8].

Whereas many dramatic case reports have been publicized, systematic studies have so far failed to verify the proposition that any substantial amount of hyperactivity is attributable to toxic or allergic effects of such added substances. These studies have followed the customary double-blind crossover pattern and have used a diet including suspect substances versus a control diet [5] or several control diets; or they have used alternate versions of an identical diet, into one of which the suspect substances are introduced.

When the diet and stimulants have been incorporated into the same design, it has become clear that any dietary effect is much less marked than the effect produced by stimulant therapy. Thus, these studies offer no justification for imposing on children and their families an arduous and highly restrictive diet to which the whole family must conform and which imposes domestic drudgery on at least one parent. However, these studies do not rule out the possibility that a few hyperactive children do experience exacerbation of hyperactivity on account of one or more of these substances. Because of inherent weaknesses in their designs, such studies could have masked positive effects. In particular, enormous placebo effects occur with the dummy diets. Such effects might be expected from the additional amount of attention that necessarily devolves upon the child (a situation in which hyperactive children thrive). Also, in these studies it has been the interested parties (parents and teachers) rather than objective observers who have recorded the behavioral evidence, and by virtue of both their emotional involvement and their lack of training in observational techniques one would expect these observers to be exceptionally liable to extraneous and subjective influences. Finally, it is notoriously difficult to ensure absolute conformity to a rigorous diet by anyone, particularly a child; and if we are to believe, as we are told, that even a very minor infraction might precipitate up to 72 hours of hyperactivity, then it is clear that double-blind crossover studies in the field based on questionnaire responses cannot provide a definite answer. Such an answer can only be obtained from strict hospital control of inpatient diets and the measurement, on a continuous basis, of behavioral response to acute challenge with each suspect substance. We have now developed a methodology suitable for such a detailed study, and our preliminary work indicates that colorings in *high doses* do impair learning. But pending confirmation, however, a reasonable practice would be to assiduously seek out potential precipitating factors by the customary means and to remove them from the child's environment if possible, but not to limit the intake of substances whose adverse effects have not been verified.

DIAGNOSIS OF IMPULSIVE EXTREMES

The Teacher's Role in Referral

There has been much public discussion of pressures supposedly put on parents by "school systems" to employ stimulant medication. Any school authorities that do this exceed their prerogatives, because prescription of drugs is strictly a medical matter. More often, however, the truth is that the parents are informed that the child's inattentive, disruptive, and aggressive conduct nullifies any opportunity the child has of benefitting from the regular classroom and neutralizes the teacher's efforts to educate the other children. Teachers are then perfectly entitled, if their experience justifies it, to point out that they have seen or heard of similar children who were helped to overcome their impulsiveness by means of a particular medication regime. This free expression of opinion cannot be construed as an ultimatum. The school may make it clear that unless the parents take steps to help the child overcome the disordered and disruptive conduct, that child can no longer be retained in the regular school system. What particular help to seek, and from whom, is a matter for the parents to decide. The teacher's role is to alert parents to the realities of the classroom situation. The same considerations apply to other education and mental health personnel, such as social workers and child-care workers. Their role is informative and advisory. Inflammatory statements about pressures emanating from the school system are usually based upon the less-publicized reality that the parents sometimes obstinately refuse to attend to the mental health issues at stake, deny a manifest disorder in their child, and insist that the child be retained in the regular classroom against the advice of school authorities.

INTERVIEWING THE PARENTS*

When a failing child seems to display an impulsive style, the physician should be prepared to probe an unusually wide range of domestic and interpersonal situations. It is undesirable to base the diagnosis on classroom performance and conduct alone. That is because many factors determine how children act in the classroom, and it is often difficult to disentangle determinants inherent in the child from determinants more related to teacher attitudes and competence and the spirit in which the class is taught. The teacher's complaint could reflect a repressive system rather than a deviant child. It is, therefore, crucial to establish whether the impulsive style in the classroom reflects a more general impulsive style in many major life situations. If it does, then arguments concerning the school system lose force, and attention is better focused on helping the child to develop a more thoughtful life-style. The physician will have noted the facts concerning the child's shortcomings in school performance and should be particularly alert to striking fluctuations in performance. Does the child try to do assignments and fail, or not try at all? Will a test from time to time reveal that the child knows much more than the teacher suspected? Is the child's performance greatly affected by the particular teacher with whom the child works? Hyperactive children vary notoriously in the quality of their performance, a fact that is disconcerting for them as well as for others. They work far better under direct supervision. Teachers may prefer to complain of poor achievement and be reticent about criticizing a child's behavior.

When parents complain of restlessness and inattention in the home, how does this reflect upon discipline and the setting of limits? How do the parents handle the child's behavior toward other children in the family? Which parent does the handling? How do the parents evaluate each other's role in child-rearing? The interview may reveal strains within family relationships that go far be-

---

* In addition to the material in this section and the next, much of the material presented on interviewing and history-taking in Chapter 4 is also relevant.

yond those directly involving the child. It is often appropriate to ask whether the parents (either one) regard themselves as being or having been similar in temperament to the child. Beyond the interesting matter of inheritance, this may open a Pandora's box of parental feelings that must be addressed if the care is to be managed adequately.

When the child's history is obtained from a parent whose child has been on an effective level of stimulant medication for some time, then there may be a confusing intermingling of descriptions of underfocused, properly focused, and overfocused behavior derived from experiences occurring in different drug states. Some of the things the parents describe may have taken place while the child was effectively off medication (as, for instance, at times when drug levels were minimal). Still other episodes may have occurred during moments when the drug, at its time of peak activity, in fact induced a temporary overdose.

INTERVIEWING THE CHILD
Sometimes hyperactive behavior is grossly apparent either immediately after a child enters the office or after a child has become somewhat accustomed to the situation there. More often it is not. Most hyperactive children are not totally incapable of impulse control and, particularly in the intimidating circumstances of a visit to a doctor's office, exert an uncharacteristic self-control that veils the deviant nature of their usual behavior. Under such circumstances, it is sometimes difficult to gather evidence. Straightforward questions to the child about the areas of difficulty are apt to be met with denial of any significant difficulties. Nevertheless, questions about the child's favorite and least favorite school subjects (and reasons for these preferences), friends (if any), frequency of fights, and feelings of loneliness, of being teased, or of being picked on may reveal a situation involving feelings of considerable loneliness and isolation. Sudden preoccupations may emerge, sometimes with violence or aggression. In the course of the interview, the silent child may suddenly become remarkably talkative and the reserved child remarkably confiding and self-revealing, if the clinician sets the stage for a friendly interaction.

PHYSICAL, LABORATORY, AND PSYCHOMETRIC EXAMINATIONS
Although many hyperactive children have minor neurological abnormalities (and also minor congenital abnormalities outside the nervous system†), these are all nonspecific. The most common are

---

† These may include head circumference > 1.5 S.D. from the mean, epicanthus, hypertelorism, malformed earlobes, high palate, curved fifth finger, transverse palmar crease, gap between first and second toe, and syndactyly at second and third toe.

clumsiness, restless movements, and EEG dysrhythmias. But a positive diagnosis can neither be based on the presence of these abnormalities nor precluded by their absence. As already mentioned, hyperactive children very often do *not* exhibit hyperactive behavior in the doctor's or tester's office. Reliance on the results of examinations and observations in such settings, however skilled, leads to gross underestimation of the number of affected children. The mainstay of the diagnosis is evidence provided by the parents, teachers, and others. This evidence may be gathered by means of a goal-directed interview or by the use of several behavioral checklists.

Useful behavior rating scales are Conners' Parents' Symptom Questionnaires (PSQ) [3] and Conners' Teacher Questionnaire (TQ) [4]. The PSQ requires parents to relate their child's behavior to a variety of symptoms common among children with behavior disorders on a four-point scale ("not at all," "just a little," "pretty much," or "very much"). The responses have numerical ratings of 0, 1, 2, and 3, respectively. A "total symptom score" is obtained by adding up the score for a total of 93 weighted items. Scores can then be derived for the following eight factors: conduct problems, anxiety, impulsive hyperactivity, learning problems, psychosomatic problems, perfectionism, antisocial behavior, and muscular tension.

The TQ requires the teachers to rate, again on a four-point scale, behavior grouped under the headings of "classroom behavior," "group participation," and "attitude towards authority." There are 39 items here, and the resulting total symptom score gives information about the following factors: aggressive conduct, daydreaming, inattention, anxious-fearful behavior, hyperactivity, and sociable-cooperative behavior. The higher the score, the more "hyperactive" the child is considered to be.

Ten items which occur in both the parents and the teacher questionnaires are the more sensitive for the diagnosis of hyperactivity; they constitute a short form, the Conners' Abbreviated Symptom Questionnaire. The items are:

1. Restless or overactive, excitable, impulsive
2. Disturbs other children
3. Fails to finish things started
4. Short attention span
5. Constantly fidgeting
6. Inattentive, easily distracted
7. Demands must be met immediately — easily frustrated
8. Cries often and easily
9. Mood changes quickly and drastically

10. Temper outbursts, explosive and unpredictable behavior

This is indeed a useful summary of the most common behavior patterns that distinguish these children.

We find that children who receive positive scores (15 or above) on this latter test from both teachers and parents are almost always favorably responsive to stimulants. Children who are scored positively only by the teachers or only by the parents could be either favorable or adverse responders. Parents and teachers who rate the behavior of a favorably responding child when the child has and has not had stimulant medication describe the former (unmedicated) behavior as disruptive, troublemaking, and generally impulsive, and describe the behavior under medication as more nearly normal. Although neither parents nor teachers can be totally objective in answering these questions (even if they do not know whether the child has taken the pill), their answers have proven useful as general indicators. In addition, the procedure of asking both of the parents and the teacher or teachers to make ratings serves as a kind of double-check. The clinician will find the ratings particularly useful when keeping in mind the personalities and responsibilities of the teachers and parents (the teacher's responsibility being to teach a room full of children, at least one of whom is hyperactive, and the parents' being to raise a child who is happy and does not unduly intrude on the interactions or bodies of other people). Parents and teachers may have quite different standards of conduct for children and may be unrealistic—either by expecting too much self-control or by being excessively permissive.

The customary psychometric instruments are not designed to detect an impulsive problem-solving style, and no one of them does so reliably. However, performance on such tests can be affected radically by an impulsive approach. The questions require sequences of logical thinking and remembering, for instance. Therefore, if it is thought that a child may be extremely impulsive, one must be cautious in interpreting the intellectual and achievement test results of that child. Children who are being impulsive will be unlikely to answer questions by guessing correctly if they do not know the answers, but they will be very likely to give wrong answers to questions that they are intelligent enough to answer correctly; their impulsive test-taking style will give them lower scores than their intelligence or even achievement is likely to warrant. Therefore, if one takes any notice at all of IQ or achievement test scores of possibly hyperactive children, they should be considered a minimal estimate of the child's potential and knowledge. These tests are best given under circumstances where the impulsiveness is under control, when the child is on an optimal level of stimulant medication. Then they can be given their medication so that its effect lasts through the testing session. In many cases children were sent to us after IQ and achievement testing had been done without giving medication. Later retesting of those who turned out to be organically impulsive often produced dramatic increases in scores on those subtests that require careful, reflective thinking (increases clearly beyond the amount of improvement one would simply expect from the practice effect inherent in any retest situation).

For example, a substantial improvement on the Block Design subtest of the WISC is not unusual; this task requires careful, systematic analysis of a pattern and then a step-by-step construction of a copy of that pattern which must be entirely accurate. Another example is the Porteus Mazes Test, in which the child draws a line to show the correct path through a printed maze. This calls for planning the route before responding. The impulsive individual will draw a path into blind alleys and will then have to retreat. Because the time taken to complete each maze contributes to the final score, Porteus Maze performance is sensitive to impulsiveness.

Tests which ask for responses, that simply sample the child's fund of knowledge but do not call for consecutive thought at the time of asking (such as the WISC Information or Vocabulary subtests), are not very sensitive to an impulsive disorder of behavioral control.

The relative impact of hyperactive behavior on various intelligence scale subtests can be well-formulated in terms of factor analysis. This is a method for determining how subtest results interrelate. In factor-analyzing the Wechsler Intelligence Scale for Children, three main factors emerge. These have been labeled "verbal comprehension," "perceptual organization," and "freedom from distractibility." In hyperactive children we find relatively low scores on the freedom from distractibility factor. This contrasts with the findings for children with selective reading disability, which show the verbal comprehension factor most affected [6].

The manner in which a test is performed may be very revealing to the experienced observer. An impulsive child will often give quick and casual responses, display fleeting attention, and show a wide discrepancy between correct performance on relatively hard items and careless errors on easier ones. Often enough, as the testing continues, the child's performance becomes increasingly impulsive and distractible, even to the point of refusing to continue before all the subtests have been completed.

As already noted, the impulsive temperament is modifiable by use of appropriate amounts of stimulant drugs. Thus, a favorable stimulant response consolidates the diagnosis. This is important for two reasons: First, even meticulous history-taking will define a population up to one-third of whose members are not favorably responsive to stimulants (i.e., are of a different type from the rest). A history of restlessness, an impulsive and distractible style, failure to respond to discipline, etc., does not guarantee that the child will benefit from stimulant therapy. Indeed, in a substantial minority of cases such treatment actually makes the child worse. Second, the only usefulness of a diagnosis in the field of school failure is that it indicates a possibly effective therapy. Unless the diagnosis of hyperactivity suggests some specific means (e.g., pharmacological) to help the child, it is of no value. The reason why the nature and direction of drug response are so integral to the definition of hyperactivity becomes apparent when we consider the nature and mechanism of the impulsive temperament.

MANAGEMENT OF IMPULSIVE AND DISTRACTIBLE BEHAVIOR
STIMULANT THERAPY

The use of psychoactive agents arouses intense feelings, and angry accusations have been hurled not only at those who indiscriminately use stimulant medication but also in wholesale fashion at anyone who ever uses these methods on behalf of hyperactive children. If the debate were at the level of the care and specificity with which these agents should be used, it could be constructive. But instead it occurs largely at a more general philosophical level which presupposes that any use of psychoactive drugs in some way does violence to human dignity and freedom. On the contrary, stimulants are properly used in hyperactivity to permit children to better meet their own goals, not to prescribe those goals for them. To deny them this help, on the premise that the beliefs, biases, or susceptibilities of certain adults should have priority over the welfare of children, would be unethical in the extreme.

Naturally, rather than treat symptomatically, one would prefer to remove the cause of a disorder and effect a cure. If one could resolve a child's impulsiveness problem by removing the precipitating agent from the environment without detriment to the child's motivation or social circumstances, thereby avoiding the use of drugs, this would be ideal. Or if some form of behavioral training could induce the child to be more thoughtful in learning and living, one would gladly discard stimulant therapy. At some time in the future this may become possible, but at present there is simply no reason to suppose that the available alternatives to stimulant therapy can by themselves help children to the extent stimulants do. Thus the practical approach today is to use stimulants in conjunction with other therapies. The child should be denied no possible means of assistance, and the various treatment options should be regarded not as alternatives to choose among but rather as resources to be used in a combination that will best meet the needs of the individual child.

It is also true that although stimulants basically have much to offer many hyperactive children, this is so only if they are used with meticulous care. Because the guidelines for properly used stimulant therapy are so detailed, and because misuse of stimulants is potentially so wasteful and even damaging, we will address this issue in some detail.

It used to be thought that stimulant drugs had a "paradoxical" effect on hyperactive children. This view was based on a dual misunderstanding. First, the title "stimulant" was taken too literally, to suggest that these agents caused people to act as if stimulated into action. That is not so, at least not at the dose levels in question. At those levels such medications are better described as agents that self-maintain the child's focus of attention. Second, it was supposed that stimulants had a "calming effect" (rather than a stimulating effect) on hyperactive children. That also is not so. Hyperactive children are not exactly uncalm. The stimulant renders them neither more nor less calm but instead prolongs concentration, as it also does in anyone else. Thus there is no paradox.

It follows that we need not suspect hyperactive children of some neurochemical novelty in their makeup that leads them to respond to certain drugs paradoxically — that is, with the opposite of the anticipated effect. Rather, we can turn to models of quantitative rather than qualitative difference — in the amount of available aminergic transmitter substance, for instance, or synaptic sensitivity to catecholamines. Such models, in turn, begin to make sense out of the nature of the favorable effect of certain doses of stimulants on hyperactive children — and of the adverse effect of higher doses (i.e., overdoses) on the same children.

Principle

The degree of *any* individual's impulsiveness is predictably and even impressively modified by certain pharmacological agents. Normal people often use caffeine (in coffee and tea) to restrain impulsive tendencies and restore concentration on their task. They often use alcohol to curtail unduly overfocused trains of thought, opening themselves up to a more rapidly fluent social or conversational interchange. The stimulant drugs (amphetamine, methylphenidate, pemoline) are powerful focusing agents. Given to anyone, they will tend to prolong the time attention is devoted to a single issue, regardless of the customary length of that attention

[16]. In other words, given to people who are basically impulsive, a certain amount of stimulant might make them normally thoughtful. But the same amount of stimulant given to normally thoughtful people may make them unduly reflective; and the same amount given to unduly reflective people may cause them to become pathologically withdrawn. By the same logic, a heavier dose might transport an impulsive person through normality into an unduly focused state (thus producing what is in fact a common overdose effect of stimulant medication for hyperactive children). That same heavy dose given to an already overfocused individual may put that person into a clearly drugged withdrawn state.

The opposite rules hold for barbiturates. The same amount of barbiturate that beneficially unlocks the attention of the overfocused individual will totally disorganize a person who already tends to be impulsive. The "favorable responder" to stimulants will also become impulsive beyond all bounds when given a barbiturate (e.g., for anticonvulsant purposes). Alcohol has similar effects, and the minor tranquilizers probably do as well.

These drug effects must reflect aspects of the brain basis of impulsive behavior, but the details of the mechanisms involved are as yet uncertain. Stimulants are known to have both dopaminergic and norepinephrinergic actions, so presumably some parts of the brain that utilize either or both of these neurotransmitters are underactive in impulsive individuals. These brain areas exert better control on behavior when the patient is given the additional pharmacological stimulants. Conversely, the sedatives appear to suppress the action of either or both of these neurotransmitters in crucial parts of the brain. The further clarification of the exact locus of these drugs' effective action in hyperactivity is an urgent research priority. Is the relevant action norepinephrinergic, involving the ascending reticular activating system, or dopaminergic, mediated by either the mesolimbic or striatonigral projections? Or is there some critical balance between these neurotransmitter systems that must be maintained for effective behavioral control? The use of agents that are specifically selective for one neurotransmitter system at a time is needed to elucidate these relationships. In the meantime, however, stimulant therapy, although symptomatic, is the most direct and effective way, in a favorable case, to normalize the deviant behavior.

Stimulant therapy is symptomatic treatment. A legitimate concern about symptomatic treatment, whenever it is used, is that it perhaps covers up, removes from attention, and therefore precludes treatment of underlying pathology. In the case of stimulant correction of impulsive and distractible behavior, does this obscure psychopathology that underlies this behavior, and that otherwise would be amenable to treatment? If one accepts the evidence that hyperactive behavior amenable to stimulant treatment is a personality trait, or temperament, then the concern about masking psychopathology falls away. But even if we suspend final acceptance of this proposition, we can still discuss the issue on other grounds. Compare stimulant therapy to use of antidepressants or tranquilizers. Antidepressants and tranquilizers change a subjective state, a mood, regardless of what caused that mood in the first place. Stimulant therapy, as we have seen, does not change any mood. It changes a style of decision-making.

Now consider symptom removal—as in treating phobias, tics, and the like. If the underlying cause of the symptom remains uncorrected, one would expect that very soon a new symptom would substitute for the one that had been selectively suppressed. But we have no reason to suppose that impulsive children rendered more thoughtful substitute some other deviation for their impulsiveness.

What treatable psychopathology might the correction of hyperactivity leave unattended? Impulse disorders are acknowledged to be resistant to psychotherapy. This does not imply that impulsive individuals are exempt from disordered psychodynamics. But it is precisely when their impulsiveness is corrected that they become capable of functioning with the degree of thoughtfulness and consequent capacity for insight that is needed to make psychotherapy a worthwhile treatment option.

Stimulant therapy does not mask underlying psychopathology; on the contrary, it assists the clinician in searching for associated emotional problems. Where such problems exist, they are managed with advantage against the background of a capacity to be introspective, empathize, and solve problems that is made available to the patient by the proper stimulant regime.

Stimulant response as a diagnostic test
Various studies have indicated some systematic differences between the majority of hyperactive children who respond favorably to stimulants, and the minority who do not. The favorable responders show electroencephalographic and pupillographic indications of underarousal. Our own findings suggest that favorable responders tend on the average to score higher on the Conners' rating scales. Reliable behavioral criteria for distinguishing between these two physiologically quite different classes of children will presumably become available. But for the time being, there is no justifiable substitute for a brief stimulant trial, which serves a diagnostic purpose. Used in this way, stimulant trials classify children into favorable responders, possibly a homogeneous group,

and adverse responders, who are clearly heterogeneous among themselves.

Prescribing a drug to see whether it works, and continuing it only if it does, is standard practice in psychoactive drug treatment. No one can be sure that a particular depressed patient will respond to a particular antidepressant; there are no sure ways, before treatment, to predict the response. When a psychoactive agent is slow in starting to modify behavior, acute trials such as we use with stimulants are not practicable. But if the drugs are fast-acting, acute trials using behavior dependent measures would serve to improve the quality of current therapeutic treatment with all such drugs, as such measures are already doing with regard to stimulants used to help hyperactive children.

Current treatment practices with stimulants
In view of the hit-or-miss nature of stimulant therapy as currently practiced, only a certain proportion of the children treated are likely to be receiving an optimal dose. The rest include:

1. Children favorably responsive but given ineffective doses
2. Children favorably responsive but given overdoses
3. Children adversely responsive given adversely effective doses
4. Children adversely responsive given ineffective doses

Note that in all these cases the treatment given is incorrect. Some children who are placed on treatment and then manifest adverse effects should never have been managed with stimulants. Others who should have received proper doses are denied this help and instead suffer toxic effects on account of overtreatment. Other children who could benefit are denied the benefit through underdosage. Yet, other children who do not need the treatment are nevertheless given it, but in amounts too small to cause behavioral change. Despite this lack of change, they are still taking the stimulant unnecessarily. One further misuse might be mentioned. Finally, some children who would have benefitted from stimulant medication are denied even a trial period on these agents.

The only rational way to correct these mistakes is to determine accurately and objectively in the laboratory what need, if any, a particular child has for stimulants, and what is the optimal dose. The results can be then checked out in the field and rechecked in the laboratory if information from the outside seems to conflict with the laboratory verdict. No prejudgments as to the type of child who should be tried on the medication are admissible. Any child who shows inattentive, distractible, and probably also aggressive behavior should be given the benefit of a laboratory test. No child should be left on the medication unless a striking beneficial effect can be objectively demonstrated. Pending systematically acquired information showing such a beneficial effect, it is pointless to debate hyperactivity incidence figures or to evaluate the prevalence of its management by drugs. For in fact, we have no real knowledge of how many children are involved and how many of them should be on drugs. Similarly, it is pointless to draw conclusions about different reported incidences of hyperactivity or about different needs of hyperactive children on the basis of actual differences in the rates at which they are diagnosed and the manner in which they are treated in different localities, countries, or continents. For until uniform diagnostic and therapeutic standards are implemented, the simple explanation that these differences are due to varying clinical practices cannot be rejected.

How to select the best stimulant regime

The therapeutic goal is to normalize behavior by enabling the child to hold the impulsiveness in check, in a continuously effective fashion throughout the waking day. Insofar as impulsive behavior can adversely affect a child's adaptation in the classroom, in the home, and in the community at large, there is no justification for limiting that effort to any particular time of day, day of the week, or season of the year.

Our research makes clear some of the reasons for keeping extremely impulsive children on medication continuously rather than intermittently. There are basically three kinds of reasons—cognitive, interpersonal, and intrapersonal—and their rationales are as follows:

COGNITIVE. Very impulsive, stimulant-responsive children learn better on medication than off. To allow them to do work at school, but not homework, on medication does two destructive things. First, it worsens their performance on the work that they bring home; and second, it makes them less likely to remember in school the next morning whatever they did manage to learn the night before (see Learning and Relearning and Memory, pp. 220–221).

INTERPERSONAL. From the standpoint of interpersonal relationships, continuous medication is extremely important. Although not everyone would agree that school achievement is important, one would be hard put to argue that good relationships with other people—both in and out of school and in and out of the family—are not at least as essential. Impulsive children antagonize and alienate their siblings and peers, irritate adults, and inevitably suf-

fer from the adverse attitudes that their impulsiveness has generated. Should a child be helped, by medication, to have good relationships with teachers and peers during school hours but not
after school or on weekends? Should a child be helped, by medication, to have good relationships with school-related people but not
with family members? These disparities result from intermittent
medication.

INTRAPERSONAL. Reasons involving the child's intrapersonal state
may be the most important of all. Because hyperactive children are
capable of forming closer, deeper relationships, empathizing more
with others, and being more positive and confident about themselves when on medication, children on intermittent medication
will seem—to other people and to themselves—to be unpredictable, undependable, and unstable. They will have no chance to
develop a positive, stable self-image based on a continuity of style
in relationships with other people. Children find it frightening
when adults or other children around them seem to flip-flop in
their behavior and attitudes. They find it even more terrifying
when they themselves experience repeated flip-flops in their ability to control their own behavior, have the freedom to choose how
to act, be able to select what to pay attention to, etc. But it is precisely this flip-flopping that intermittent medication produces, and
it is thus a destructive, externally imposed influence on the child's
emotional development and stability.

Available agents for the pharmacological treatment of hyperactivity
By far the most commonly used agents are methylphenidate (Ritalin) and dextroamphetamine (Dexedrine). The first agent documented as effective was the racemic form of amphetamine (Benzedrine). Another agent recently shown to be effective is
methamphetamine (Desoxyn). These substances are all closely related and are classified as stimulants (though when used in the
manner and at the dose levels required for hyperactivity management, behavioral stimulation is not encountered). All of them are
known to increase the activity of catecholaminergic synapses in
the brain. The effects divide up into those involving two catecholamines—norepinephrine and dopamine—each of which is
concerned with a separate brainstem system. Norepinephrine is
mainly associated with the reticular formation of the brain and,
therefore, with the system that determines the level of general activation of the nervous system and behavior arousal. Some have attributed feelings of tension or anxiety or even guilt to high levels
of action in this system. Dopaminergic transmission is characteristic of at least two relevant systems, the mesolimbic system

(which some have thought related to a person's expression of emotion and affect) and the striatonigral system (regarded as related to movement and perhaps to attention control). There is some preliminary evidence that through norepinephrinergic action stimulant medications control aggressive, unsocialized, and psychopathic behavior, whereas by their dopaminergic effect they help to maintain the focus of attention. It should be possible to sort this out further by using agents with differential effectiveness in influencing one or the other of these two systems, but no systematic studies of this kind have yet been done. The foregoing considerations do, however, raise the possiblity that at least two groups are among the "favorable responders" to stimulants. One would consist of those classically inattentive hyperactives who respond favorably on account of the medications' dopaminergic effects. The other would be comprised of those aggressive, unsocialized hyperactives whose behavior merges into conduct that could be termed psychopathic, and who respond more on account of the norepinephrinergic effect. This is an issue for further investigation.

Among other agents frequently used for the control of hyperactive behavior, three are noteworthy. One is imipramine, which has similarities with the stimulants and possibly acts in the same way. Another is pemoline (Cylert), which though chemically quite different appears to have actions virtually indistinguishable from those of the customary amphetamine-like medications; pemoline is supposed to have a mainly dopaminergic effect. Yet another frequently used agent, the effect of which is particularly ill-understood, is diphenhydramine (Benadryl). The efficacy of this agent is attested to solely by clinical anecdotes. Being safe and relatively inexpensive, it clearly deserves further study.

The availability of alternate means of treating hyperactive children is potentially important for two practical reasons. One is that it permits the empirical use of a second agent, should the first one used fail to confer benefit or generate idiosyncratic side effects in an apparently typical hyperactive child. The second relates to the possibility that some children who are specifically adverse responders to a customary agent (Ritalin, Dexedrine) might respond favorably to some of the other agents.

Embedded in the folklore of the therapeutics of hyperactivity is the notion that some children inexplicably respond to one stimulant, having failed to respond to another. This is no doubt a possibility but one based purely on clinical impressions, and in no case does a simple alternative possibility appear to have been excluded. This other possibility is that the optimal dose was inadvertently missed because the first agent was not applied throughout its range of subtoxic doses. The equivalent optimal dose might equally inadvertently have been achieved by using the second agent. This does not imply that a second agent should not be used if the first one has failed. But it should only be used if the effects of the first one have been systematically explored throughout its effective dose range, subject only to the absence of troublesome side effects or clear overdose effects.

Of more general potential interest is the utility of some of the less commonly used drugs for patients who fall into that quarter or third of so-called hyperactive children who respond adversely to the customary stimulants. It may be that some of these children are in fact not underfocused at all, but rather that their motor hyperactivity relates to anxiety and overfocusing (see Chap. 5). It may also be that some of the agents supposedly effective in some hyperactive children act specifically on this group. Diphenhydramine, imipramine, and the cholinergic agent deanol may provide examples of this kind. Again, it may be that secondary anxieties are generated in some hyperactive children by their predicament, and that these overlie and complicate the problem. It may be that some other agents, such as the ones mentioned, could with benefit be added to the stimulant regime to help control that secondary anxiety, pending resolution of the child's behavioral predicament.

Studies have tended to show methylphenidate as being slightly less likely to cause side effects than dextroamphetamine. A drawback of methylphenidate, not shared by dextroamphetamine, is its vulnerability to destruction in an alkaline medium. For this reason, methylphenidate should be given at least half an hour before a meal, and not during or soon after eating. This is for fear of its decomposition by alkaline digestive juices. No such restriction attends the use of dextroamphetamine or pemoline.

Might caffeine, as contained in coffee, be an acceptable alternative to stimulant drugs? Formal studies of this possibility have come up with disappointing results, showing caffeine to be less effective than methylphenidate and dextroamphetamine [12]. Perhaps the dosage of caffeine given was inadequate. However, in doses great enough to have significant effect, caffeine could produce gastric and other side effects. There is, in principle, no reason to think of caffeine as more benign than the stimulant drugs. Indeed, because its spectrum of action in the body is wider than that of the conventional stimulants, it quite likely would have more unwanted accompanying effects than an equally therapeutic dose of dextroamphetamine or methylphenidate. Furthermore, when giving whole coffee the dose is hard to control accurately. All in all, the only advantage that caffeine could conceivably offer is that it is socially sanctioned. That might make it a worthwhile alternative for people who reject psychoactive drugs.

A less commonly used stimulant which, however, was the one originally involved in the discovery of stimulants' effect on hyperactivity, is Benzedrine. This is much like Dexedrine. Its merits relative to those of the much more commonly used dextroamphetamine and methylphenidate have not been definitely established.

Dexedrine and methylphenidate are very short-acting. The behavioral effect begins within 30 minutes and is virtually over four hours after administration. Dexedrine and methylphenidate spansules appear to be longer-acting (about eight hours), and it has been claimed that pemoline is longer-acting still; but our studies have shown that its behavioral effect lasts about eight hours.

The proper use of a short-acting stimulant depends upon recognition of its quick, transitory, and noncumulative effect and upon an understanding of the need for as smooth a daily coverage as possible. There is wide variation in the dose levels of a given stimulant required by different children, these levels ranging in the case of methylphenidate from 5 to 30 mg per administration. It is not known whether this variation is due to differences in central synapses or to vagaries in the absorption of the drugs. Certainly there is no known relationship between the effective dose and the child's body weight or surface area. Indeed, adolescents who are normalized by stimulants seem to require smaller doses than they did when they were younger.

We have plotted time-response curves for the behavioral effects of individual stimulant administrations [32] in the following manner: At the time of administration, and at half-hourly intervals thereafter, we sample the child's behavior by presenting alternate versions of the animals test. In the case of a favorable responder there is no placebo effect; without the stimulant test performance remains unchanged or gradually deteriorates. At an effective stimulant dose level, performance steadily improves, reaching maximum improvement between two and three hours after administration; but by four hours the beneficial effect has largely worn off. At less than effective doses little change is noted. At greater than effective doses the effect becomes adverse, but with identical time characteristics—the maximum adverse effect coming at two to three hours, followed by reversion to the base state after four hours. By following this procedure we can therefore individualize the correct dose for each patient.

For a short-acting stimulant to yield even a semblance of all-day coverage, it has to be given at least three times a day (customarily half an hour before each of the three main meals). Even so, there will be marked fluctuations in drug levels—and therefore marked fluctuations in the degree of behavioral effect in many children. If variable behavior is a problem, various adjustments in the dose and timing can be made; in this regard an additional administration is often needed, particularly in the evening if the child is going to bed late. The physician should attempt to minimize these fluctuations in stimulant state. It is confusing for the child and others for the child's degree of impulsiveness to vary sharply within the same day. Also, as noted in the reports of our research, learning on stimulants is state-dependent. This means material that the child learns in a given state (e.g., at the height of the stimulant effect) is not equally well recalled at all times. Rather, it is recalled best when the child is in the same state as at the time of acquisition. This disadvantage of stimulant therapy is minimal if the child's behavioral style is held as constant as possible throughout the day by an appropriate stimulant schedule.

Because laboratory tests of learning and performance to gauge the proper level of stimulant administration are not yet available for general use, the clinician has to rely on evidence from parents and teachers. Fortunately, the initial effects of stimulants are very similar to the effects they will have much later in the treatment. Thus one can determine which dose will have a beneficial effect. One should begin with a small dose, say 5 mg of methylphenidate (three times a day). About every three days this should be increased by 5 mg per administration, until satisfactory improvement is reported, but not to the extent that the child becomes withdrawn, tearful, suspicious, or dulled in interactions with others. These latter patterns indicate overdosage, and scaling down of the dose is then required. Fortunately, as the agent is very short-acting, a single mild overdose lasts so brief a time that it does no harm. Thus, it is necessary in each case to titrate the dose level against the behavioral consequence. Incidentally, the optimum doses for the morning, afternoon, and evening administrations are not necessarily the same.

The degree of hyperactivity that a child manifests is not necessarily constant throughout the day. Some children are more hyperactive in the morning and, correspondingly, require a higher stimulant dose before breakfast than before lunch. In a more uniform manner, children tend to require a smaller evening dose. Nevertheless, the initial prescription can be for the same dose three times a day. The parents are then alerted to the possible need for minor dose modification and are asked to look out for signs of overdosage and underdosage at particular times of the day. Specifically, parents record relevant behavior throughout the day, noting the times involved. This will make unevenness in stimulant coverage evident.

Hyperactive children may object to taking medication in public, because this subjects them to derision from other children. They are accused of being different because they need pills, and they do not want to be regarded as different. This problem centers around the midday dose, which is taken under the supervision of a teacher. If the teacher is tactful and unobtrusive about the matter and does not make a public ceremony of it, then the effect on the child's standing with peers can be minimized, and the child's objections to the medication can be met.

Possible adverse effects
In order of reported frequency, adverse effects of stimulant therapy include: insomnia, decreased appetite, weight loss, irritability, abdominal pain, headaches, drowsiness, sadness, anxiety, tearfulness, lethargy, isolation, tics, psychosis, and others. Some of these are true side effects and occur at therapeutic dose levels. Examples are appetite depression, weight loss, abdominal pain, and headaches. Others are overdose effects that indicate optimum dose levels have been exceeded. They include irritability, anxiety, depression, and detachment from the environment.

Stimulants are appetite depressants, and frequently when stimulant therapy begins the child's appetite decreases, often considerably. There may be some weight loss, though this soon flattens out. However, the subsequent rate of weight gain may follow a percentile curve lower than that previously observed. Certainly there has been no report of any child developing significant nutritional problems on account of stimulant therapy, but the change in eating habits may disturb some parents, particularly those who have an emotional investment in their children's food intake. Counseling should rectify any misconceptions and should reconcile the parents to this phenomenon, which in any case is usually short-lived.

It has also been suggested that stimulant therapy may compromise the height gain of hyperactive children. This claim has achieved wide notoriety and has caused understandable alarm. As compared to untreated controls, hyperactive children on stimulant therapy—specifically Dexedrine and relatively high doses of methylphenidate—were claimed to increase in height more slowly over time. When the children were taken off the medications for periods of months, this relative deficiency in growth was said to be made up [28]. Following this report, many institutions examined their records and performed prospective studies of the same kind. These actions uniformly failed to find corroborative evidence of even the slight effects reported [26]. In sum, reports of significant potential height losses were not substantiated; hence these reports do not contraindicate treatment where it is clearly called for by a significant personal and social problem and where the medication is clearly effective in ameliorating that problem.

Some hyperactive children experience difficulty with (or more precisely exhibit reluctance toward) going to sleep. A few tend to waken during the night or unnecessarily early in the morning. These complaints often emerge first upon institution of stimulant therapy or, if already present, are exacerbated at that time. On account of this so-called insomnia, the *Physicians' Desk Reference* recommends that short-acting stimulants (Dexedrine, Ritalin) be given no later than noon, so that the effect will have worn off before bedtime. It is, however, this very practice which tends to generate or exacerbate insomnia.

The effect of short-acting stimulants given in the morning and at noon has fully worn off by late afternoon [32]. Some have even suspected that the effect is followed by an overshooting of impulsive behavior. We have not been able to confirm overshooting, but it is clear that if stimulants are last given at noon, hyperactive children are not effectively controlled in the late afternoon or evening, and their impulsive behavior is reinstated. It thus comes as no surprise that they should show reluctance to go to sleep and that this should be hard to control by setting limits. The obvious remedy is a third dose given around dinnertime (one-half hour before the meal if the agent is Ritalin) and timed so that the four-hour duration of the agent's effectiveness includes the child's customary bedtime. Children then retain control of their impulses, and the sleep problem is minimized.

One precaution, however, must be taken. Children's requirements for stimulant medication vary in the course of the day. A dose which is sufficient and not excessive during the day is often excessive in the evening, causing the child to become withdrawn, overfocused, ruminative, and for this very different reason also unable to get to sleep. It is a matter of trial and error to determine the precise evening dose that will suffice to control impulsive insomnia without merely replacing it with an overfocused insomnia. However, with suitable adjustment of the medication level, based on reports from the parents, it is possible to overcome this problem.

The smaller number of hyperactive children who awaken during the night present a more difficult problem. They may wake in response to minor stimulation and stay awake on account of impulsive overactivity or depression due to their problems at home and in school. These children may then lie awake for long periods of time; during this time, when they are necessarily completely off the medication, they may secretly break rules set by the parents (for instance, they may raid the refrigerator or make a shambles of their room). Later they become sleepy and overtired, and they function poorly the next day.

Short-acting stimulants offer no solution for this problem, because of the brief period of their effectiveness. The newer, longer-acting stimulants may provide an answer. In the meantime, one available resource is imipramine. This tricyclic antidepressant resembles the more conventional stimulant medications in much of its chemical structure and some of its effects. It is effective in many hyperactive children, and because of its longer action is particularly useful when given in the evening if sleep problems are troublesome. Thus, one might combine a Ritalin regime during the day with administration of imipramine (typically 10 mg) at night before the child goes to sleep.

This last point leads naturally into a consideration of enuresis. Persistent bed-wetting during sleep is common, and although it has often been attributed to functional (emotional) causes when structural urogenital abnormalities have been ruled out, it has only recently become apparent that many enuretic children are in fact hyperactive [14]. Success in the treatment of a hyperactive child may resolve a problem of enuresis (this is also true in occasional cases of encopresis—poor bowel control.) Now, for reasons quite unconnected with any theorizing about the relationship between hyperactivity and enuresis, it has been customary for many years to give bed-wetting children an evening administration of either an amphetamine or of imipramine, and there are many documented successes with both these methods. The formal proof has not yet been gathered to confirm that it is in the impulsive and distractible enuretic that these agents selectively work. But it is certainly possible that the enuresis is somehow related to the impulsive and distractible cognitive style, and that it is by controlling impulsiveness that these agents remedy enuresis. So cases of children who have problems with bed-wetting or soiling should be carefully documented and examined for the possible occurrence of a more generally impulsive and distractible temperament; if that is found, such children should be offered the possible benefit of a stimulant or imipramine. Conversely, the presence of enuresis in a hyperactive child should be documented, and any effect on that symptom in the course of the treatment by medication should be noted.

Some laboratories have reported rises in the pulse rates and blood pressures of hyperactive children on stimulant therapy. These were incidental findings unassociated with any particular symptoms or known long-term consequences. Our own studies suggest that such effects are of negligible significance and do not contraindicate stimulant therapy.

Physicians often wonder whether the use of stimulant drugs might lower the seizure threshold in children who are epileptic as well as hyperactive. This does not usually occur. Nor do stimulants appear to interact detrimentally with the commonly used seizure medications.

A month or two after a child begins stimulant therapy a mild tolerance often develops, as indicated by a lessening of control over impulsiveness. The parents should be warned that this might happen. If it does, a slight increase in dosage usually reestablishes a beneficial effect which is much longer-lasting. Major or cumulative tolerance reducing a drug's effect on impulsiveness is very rare, in sharp contrast to the rapid tolerance that develops when such drugs are taken in much larger doses by addicts for their euphoric effects. Note that a similar lack of tolerance is found in the stimulant therapy of narcoleptic patients, who suffer from a tendency to fall asleep with pathological ease.

The continued need for stimulant therapy should frequently be reviewed. If the parents are alert, they will be able to observe the variations in the child's level of impulsiveness, particularly on comparing the first half-hour in the morning (before the morning pill has begun to work) with behavior later in the day. If behavior on and off drugs is no longer obviously different, the time is ripe to reassess the need for stimulant therapy. This reassessment should never be based on motor evidence alone. Rather, it should focus on the role that impulsiveness plays in the child's problem-solving and interpersonal relationships. There is no critical age at which stimulant therapy can be expected to become unnecessary. This is because there is no way to tell whether a child's impulsive way of responding will disappear within months or years, or whether it will persist into adulthood. Therefore, no prognosis can be given. All that can be done is to determine whether a child needs stimulant therapy at the time of consultation.

The serious contingency of stimulant addiction is, to say the least, improbable. The reason for this is not definitely known. However, it is probably relevant that hyperactive children take stimulants in doses many orders of magnitude lower than those taken by addicts; and since even a slight increase in these moderate doses induces adverse effects that are quite unpleasant—nervousness, paranoia, and an inert withdrawal—children are unlikely to want to repeat such an experience.

In fact, however, there is no reason to believe that hyperactive children experiment with these drugs. If anything, the danger is greater that they would sell them to schoolmates. Probably the connotation the stimulants have for these children relates to a lack of enthusiasm for the agents. After all, the medication is prescribed as a remedy for what is frequently a humiliating intellectual and interpersonal failure, and the hyperactive child (with a temperamental propensity for denial) will quite likely keep as far away as possible from these reminders of that imperfection. At any rate, it is remarkable how often these children forget to take their pills.

All these factors, however, would probably be of little significance if hyperactive children derived some subjective benefits from the direct action of these drugs, or if they came to associate them with gratifying success. Surprisingly, they cannot even tell a drug effect from a placebo effect. We asked children who were given both an effective dose of methylphenidate and a placebo on the same day to identify the drug and placebo sessions, respectively. The children performed at a chance level on this task. Not only did they fail to discriminate drug from placebo on subjective grounds, but they also seemed not to remember at which session they did better on their tests, and thereby failed to deduce that this must have been the drug session. The finding underlines the dissociation of on-drug and off-drug experience for these children. And certainly, if one cannot tell a drug from a placebo, one lacks the necessary precondition for drug addiction.

Stimulant overdose causes a child to act in a withdrawn, tearful, whining, and suspicious fashion. Such children may abruptly withdraw to their rooms and stay there for hours—behavior out of character for a hyperactive child.

Another indication of stimulant overdose is an unaccustomed flow of speech. The child seems to talk endlessly, in a "stream of consciousness" manner that relates to the child's inner concerns and is often oblivious of other people's concerns and comfort. At a lower dose the symptom disappears.

At even higher doses, some children act as if sedated; at still higher doses, multiple tics appear; and heavy overdoses can precipitate psychotic behavior. All of these symptoms resolve when treatment is discontinued or when the dosage is decreased.

Some children viewed as overactive do not respond favorably to stimulants and even show the "overdose" effects without ever showing the beneficial effects that other children achieve at lower doses. These children differ from the "stimulant-responsive" hyperactives, and stimulant therapy is not appropriate for them. Because such cases are quite common, it is dangerous to prescribe stimulants in a hit-or-miss fashion and then to lose contact with the child for prolonged periods of time. This runs the risk of placing an adverse responder on maintenance stimulant therapy.

The effects of a moderate overdose are to render the child overfocused and withdrawn, suspicious, angry, or whining and miserable. The effects are obvious to parents and teachers, who will spontaneously report them and suggest discontinuing the medication. The correct step to take, however, is instead to reduce the dosage to the optimum level for that child.

The tics and other involuntary movements that can result from an acute overdose are reminiscent of the "tardive dyskinesias" of Parkinsonian patients overdosed with L-dopa. This effect can be countered by use of haloperidol. It is more reasonable, however, to simply reduce the dose.

Longer-acting agents for the control of hyperactivity
As already noted, the typical agent used in the control of hyperactivity has an effective action of no more than about four hours. This imposes serious limitations upon the effectiveness of stimulant regimes for this condition. Admittedly, methamphetamine (Desoxyn) does appear to be usable in a steady-state fashion, but its action on hyperactive children has not been securely documented except in small numbers of cases. Pemoline (Cylert) could be an important exception. It has been claimed that pemoline is cumulative, leading up to a steady-state condition after an initial period of gradually incremental dosage lasting two to three weeks. Our preliminary findings contradict this view. We find it possible to start with an effective dose and to maintain it twice daily without cumulation, but with a longer duration of effect than that obtained with the amphetamines and methylphenidate. If this is confirmed, pemoline might turn out to be the agent of choice in many cases. In sum, there seems no doubt that the future of stimulant therapy is with longer-acting agents; but which is the agent of choice remains to be determined.

BEHAVIORAL METHODS OF MANAGING EXTREME
IMPULSIVENESS [19]
These fall into two categories: methods that purport to implement a cure, and methods that serve a supportive, ancillary function in the context of the total management of the child. In both categories studies are almost all grossly inferior to drug studies in design, manifesting sampling bias and lacking objectivity in the evaluation of outcomes (and even in the statistical treatment of results). Therefore our conclusions, though tentative, will necessarily be bleak.

Behavioral treatments

Hyperactivity is disordered behavior, and it would be both logical and desirable to attempt to correct it by behavioral means. Certainly, any effective behavioral treatment program would be preferable to the use of drugs: Even the most innocuous of drugs causes problems sometimes, and no one would resort to pharmacotherapy if effective behavioral methods were available.

Various attempts have been made to correct behaviors prevalent in hyperactive children by use of reinforcement, modeling, role-playing, videotape replay, biofeedback and other techniques.

A classical approach is to give children praise or material rewards (or tokens that they can cash in for commodities) for desired behavior (or for eliminating undesirable behavior), while ignoring ("extinguishing") undesirable behavior when it occurs. Punishment has been used at times, but more often a "time-out" method is employed—the child is required to leave the situation for a predetermined period of time after each undesired episode. The operant programs are applied by therapists in clinic settings, by parents, or by teachers (or both in conjunction). A more recent vogue has favored "cognitive behavior modification," a method that attempts to impart self-instructional, self-monitoring, and self-reinforcing skills to the child. Other programs focus more on parent training than child training. Finally, relaxation training and biofeedback have been tried.

These various approaches should be regarded as still in the research and development phase. Conclusive evidence of efficacy with respect to hyperactive behavior has not been demonstrated for any of them, and in those few studies in which a particular mode of behavioral therapy has been contrasted with pharmacotherapy, the latter has tended to appear to better advantage. In particular, studies have used few children, have not always targeted relevant behavior, have had outcomes confounded by other concurrent manipulations, and have paid insufficient attention to generalization of any beneficial effects to other aspects of the child's behavior and to settings outside the one in which the therapy was conducted, or to their maintenance in the long term. We can therefore not recommend any particular program, but will confine ourselves to pointing out that for a program to have major impact on the widespread problems of hyperactive behavior, it should be readily available and relatively inexpensive. This means that, almost necessarily, it must be capable of being implemented by teachers or parents. It seems likely, also, that to have any chance of success, it should focus on increasing the frequency of positive behavior, such as effort in school work or consideration of others (rather than merely on eliminating inattentive or disruptive behavior). Finally, it will have to consider the whole social unit (the teacher and other children in the class, the parents, and siblings) because the behavior of hyperactive children is much affected by the reactions (often pathological) that they elicit from others.

Ideally, a behavioral therapy will be found that will eliminate the need for stimulant drugs. Or perhaps, the therapy may be carried out using drugs as a temporary adjunct, later to be discontinued. At any rate, each attempt at behavioral management should be studied in two conditions — when the child is concurrently on drugs and when the child is on placebo, so as to identify important behavioral therapy-drug interactions if they occur.

The evaluation of behavioral management of hyperactivity is complicated because it is difficult to define the particular sample of children studied. Here the classification into favorable or adverse responders is crucial. Information is lacking about whether children who are claimed to have responded to behavioral measures would have responded to stimulant therapy. If they would, then it could be asked which gives better control. If they would not, then this enriches the therapeutic implication of the "response-nonresponse" distinction.

Supportive measures
In contrast to behavioral measures aimed to cure, those playing a supportive role are of essential importance in many if not most cases of hyperactivity. By virtue of their behavior, hyperactive children are prone to generate cumulatively an immense amount of psychological tension between themselves and their parents, siblings, and peers, and to have disruptive effects on the relationships between their parents, each of whom tends to hold the other in some way responsible for a "failure of child-rearing." By the time the child reaches a clinician, a host of explicit and implicit assumptions that are understandable but unjustified have been made by various family members. These must be brought to light and clarified. Even if the impulsive style is successfully corrected by stimulant therapy, the child remains in a psychologically sensitive situation, and supportive psychotherapy can be very useful. Also, such a child is often educationally backward, and the extra work required to overcome this backwardness is a further source of stress. Thus, the question of psychiatric and psychological support for a hyperactive child should always be specifically evaluated in the course of fashioning a program. The best time to do this is as soon as the maximum extent of the benefits to be achieved by stimulant therapy has become clear.

Even after apparently optimal levels of stimulant therapy are achieved, the favorably responsive hyperactive child still tends to be disorganized and emotionally unstable. At least in some cases this is probably due to the imperfect and fluctuating nature of pharmacotherapy with these short-acting agents. However, one suspects that even with optimal management, the disorganized and unstable personality would remain in evidence in a significant number of children. After all, the application of a drug that alters neurotransmitter levels certainly might change the base state of the brain to the individual's general advantage, but it probably cannot replace the fine tuning that is presumably available to children who do not need this chemical assistance.

When children have difficult personalities, as do underfocused (and overfocused) children, they can be substantially helped if they are protected from certain important stresses.

Children who are genetically predisposed to come to harm of some kind or other do not necessarily do so. Rather, the genetic predisposition renders them disproportionately susceptible to environmental adversity [27]; they might succumb to this, while genetically unaffected children could resist the same adversities and emerge unscathed. Furthermore, it has been shown that when there is family discord, it is the temperamentally deviant child who attracts the negative spin-off from the parents' discontents and irritations. Thus while all children deserve protection from adversity, children with deviant cognitive style, being particularly vulnerable, should be protected with exceptional diligence. If they do not experience family discord or separation, overcrowding, poverty, parental criminality, and so forth, their temperamental deviations, though they remain, need not translate into an unhappy or unproductive life.

However adequate an overfocused or underfocused child's management appears to be, that child should always be considered disproportionately "at risk" with respect to severe environmental stress. Sensible management and precautionary measures with respect to family and school attitudes and interactions should be implemented if at all possible.

Further steps frequently taken after the child is stabilized on stimulants are outlined in Chapter 7 (Classroom Structure, p. 178, and Emotional Supports during Remediation, p. 202).

The Dangers of Using Unproven Methods in Hyperactivity

Insidious pitfalls await the parents who are using unvalidated and possibly ineffective methods with their hyperactive child. These are due to the frequency of placebo effects on the people who observe the child, and to the parents not really knowing what end point of improvement to hope for.

Behavior disorders of developmental origin are confusing, in that the parents and others have no standard of comparison, no pattern of previously normal behavior by the child. Nor is it very helpful to compare the child with other children, because individual variation in behavior is so great, and because parents are unsure how much of the child's behavior is due to "disease" and how much to just "the way the child is." They may therefore use some ineffective treatment, perceive some "improvement" (perhaps a placebo effect), and regard the result as the full amount of treatment effect to be expected. If no effective treatment were available, then that would be a realistic appraisal. But as we have seen, stimulant therapy *is* effective for some two-thirds of all hyperactive children. It is thus a serious waste for parents to deny themselves and their child the benefit of effective help by committing themselves to spurious measures.

Once people realize that hyperactivity is a personality trait, and that the treatment goal is to help the child be normally thoughtful, then some of this bewilderment can be overcome. The most effective way of dramatizing what can realistically be hoped for is to let the parents observe the child and interact with the child during an effective single stimulant administration. This can be done without any commitment to stimulant therapy, if the parents are averse to drug treatment. Having observed the child's changed behavior in the short term, the parents then know what to look for with whatever treatment method they prefer.

It follows that studies of nonstimulant approaches to hyperactivity are incomplete and uninterpretable unless they incorporate a stimulant condition as a control (it would also be preferable to include a combined stimulant plus experimental therapy condition). From such comparative studies one can learn not only whether the experimental treatment is at all effective, but also whether it is as effective as stimulants, and whether anything further could be gained by combining the two treatments.

The Hyperactive Child in the Classroom

The goal in managing hyperactivity is to correct it, and in many cases stimulant therapy will achieve that goal. In some cases, however, it is only partially successful or completely unsuccessful, and in other cases parental permission to use this form of treatment cannot be obtained. Finally, when short-acting stimulants are used, as is customary, even the optimally controlled child will go through times during the day when one dose has effectively worn off and the next dose has not yet taken effect. Thus, impulsive behavior will be displayed in the classroom by some hyperactive children all of the time and by all hyperactive children some of the time. How should the teacher respond?

Disruptive and disorganized behavior undergoes spectacular improvement when met with attention on a one-to-one basis. Thus it is very easy for teachers to believe they have tremendous importance for this child's education and general adjustment. They may be tempted to spend much time with this child and necessarily, therefore, to deprive the other children of the attention to which they are entitled. Unfortunately, this attention produces little carry-over effect in a hyperactive child. However much time the teacher spends with such a child, once the teacher's back is turned the disorganization returns. So it is necessary for the teacher to intervene frequently and briefly, watching for lapses of attention and inappropriate conduct. The child does better when sitting alone than when in a position to tantalize neighbors, and is best offered intensely eye-catching and intriguing tasks in rapid succession, so that no single investment of attention is necessary for any long period of time. Firm limit-setting is essential and is best enforced by isolation if the limits are infringed. It is particularly important in these cases for the teacher to communicate specifically in an ongoing fashion with the parents about the nature of and reasons for the policy guiding their child's classroom treatment.

THE HYPERACTIVE CHILD AT HOME

Hyperactives should be treated as normal children when their cognitive style problems are not an issue. For example, when an underfocused child bullies another child or neglects household chores, the bullying or neglect should be stopped. A parent or teacher who would punish that behavior in a normal child should punish it in the underfocused child. Even though the child's aggression and irresponsibility may be secondary to the underfocusing, an adult who shows less disapproval of that behavior than in a normal child will ultimately encourage it. That does the child no favor; it constitutes training the child in antisocial and irresponsible behavior. A similar case can be made for the overfocused child's self-centered or aggressive actions. The situation is different, of course, at those times when the task required of the child primarily involves correct regulation of attention, as with learning in school. Then special environmental modifications and medications are often necessary, and the normative approach does not apply; that is, one cannot treat the child as normal. But even though an underfocused or overfocused child may have trouble *executing* appropriate interpersonal behavior because of the attention disorder, that child will nevertheless absorb an adult's underlying attitude about that behavior. Thus parents and teachers can help underfocused children feel that they have license to behave inappropriately, or they can help such children to feel sorry about that behavior and try to control it. In many cases, appropriate medication gives the children better control over that behavior. But unless a child's behavior disorder is so severe as to call for institutionalization, there is no justification for allowing misbehavior. That only teaches self-centeredness and cruelty.

It can be exceedingly difficult to discipline a hyperactive child. Parents of these children often say they feel as though they are continually running around and setting up structure for the children's lives, trying to minimize their distractions, and trying to teach them that they are responsible for their own actions. Although many of these tasks are easier when the children take stimulant medication, even a medicated hyperactive usually retains some of the basic characteristics of the hyperactive style. So, special problems remain for many parents of hyperactives. In most families the mother spends more time than the father with the children (even in families where both parents are employed outside the home). It is usually the mother who carries out most of the unpleasant interactions — limit-setting, disciplining, enforcing of rules — with the hyperactive child. It is she, therefore, who is likely to feel frustrated when the child seems not to learn the important lessons she tries to teach, fights against her limit-setting, and mistreats siblings. If she offers her hyperactive child warmth and understanding and is met with the typical hyperactive's apparent lack of interest in close, warm relationships combined with a denial of sadness or trouble, she may feel she is in a dilemma. To continue to pour out warmth and understanding is frustrating and depressing; to stop offering warmth and understanding is guilt-producing.

Contrast this with the position most fathers of hyperactive children adopt: they become intensely absorbed in their work. They come home shortly before the child's bedtime (or even afterward) and find work to do at the office on weekends. On the rare occasion that they see the child, they usually arrange to evade the responsibility for discipline. They arrive home, engage in some physical activity with the child, hide behind a newspaper, and send the child to bed. Then, when the mother tells the father how the child frustrated or infuriated her, he does not know what she is talking about. It sounds very different from what he experiences (and indeed, of course, it is). Few people will go out of their way to take on part of the burden for parenting a hyperactive child; and so most fathers generally ignore the mother-child conflicts and frustrations. The worst fathers offer no help but instead criticize the mother's handling of the child. They may be angry that she invests a lot of time and effort in the hyperactive (rather than in her husband), or they may blame her "inadequate" discipline for the child's problem behavior.

One of the tragedies of such a family situation is the way it divides the parents. Another is that it brings further trouble into the hyperactive children's lives, for they invariably sense that they cause conflict between the parents. Yet another sad feature is that the situation deprives the hyperactive (who is usually male) of the companionship of the male parent; and in dealing with a child who has behavior problems, a male with whom the child can identify becomes even more important than usual. In addition, parental conflict over the discipline of one child inevitably hurts the other children in the family, and with a hyperactive child this danger can take at least two forms. One is simply that the parental time and energy absorbed by conflict over the problem child might otherwise have been devoted to the needs of the other children. The second stems from the fact that it is extremely hard for a parent to switch instantly from one type of discipline to another. Therefore, a nonhyperactive child may be subjected to methods of discipline that are necessary for a hyperactive sibling but unnecessarily intense (or even harsh) for a normal child, because of an overflow of parental attempts to discipline the hyperactive.

THE ADVERSE RESPONDER TO STIMULANTS

Whereas a vast literature documents aspects of hyperactive children who respond favorably to stimulant drugs, nothing systematic is known about the one third of children labeled hyperactive who respond adversely. They have not been studied as a group, but instead have been excluded from some studies and left as a minority group in others. We can therefore only give clinical impressions about the group.

Adverse responders are heterogeneous. Many of them are suffering from anxiety, and their nervous fidgeting is mislabeled hyperactivity. The anxiety is often situational; it relates to excessive pressure and work load in the classroom, or to parental friction in the home. In other children the anxiety is of long standing and its origin is obscure. In both cases psychiatric referral is appropriate, but when anxiety is situational, some classroom rearrangements can be tried first, or a family interview conducted (with perhaps family therapy the recommended next step). Some clinicians prescribe tranquilizers, notably Mellaril, for these children, but we prefer to leave this decision to the child psychiatrist to make.

A few adverse responders are normal children who happen to have activity levels high enough to disconcert certain adults: But contrary to some claims, this is quite unusual. If some mothers mistake "boyish" behavior for pathology, they must be rare. Some adverse responders turn out to have psychoses, or borderline psychotic states. Finally, a substantial number of adverse responders fall into the category we have named "overfocused." They are discussed in Chapter 10.

INTERPRETATION

To Parents

However careful the clinician's evaluation and however appropriate the recommendations, they will only be useful if they are interpreted to the parents in a manner that the parents regard as well-informed, that allays their fears, and that enlists their cooperation. This is true in any school problem case, but it is particularly important with hyperactivity and in cases where a drug regime is contemplated. Virtually all of the material in Chapter 4, Personality Testing, applies in these cases, too, but we include here some points that often arise specifically in evaluating impulsive children.

Parents often arrive with preconceptions about the origin of the child's conduct problem and whose "fault" it is. They are likely to have strong feelings and even fears about "drugs," and if they have already had previous assessments that they did not accept, or previous therapies that were not successful, this further complicates the situation. The parents may have formed negative stereotypes about "experts," and an ambivalent alternation of their attitude between hope and hostility may be very obvious.

In the interpretation of a hyperactivity evaluation, the clinician should begin by restating the problem in concrete behavioral terms, in order to establish common ground with the parents about the nature and seriousness of the problem. We focus attention upon what is known for certain about the child and upon the fact that our expertise and judgment are being called upon at this particular session. This will later stand the parents in good stead when it comes to discussing the pros and cons of remediation suggestions. We emphasize that the meeting between parents and clinician has as its primary purpose the specific welfare of the child—that it has not been called either to validate the professional's competence or to allay the parents' anxieties. Whereas information arising from previous evaluations should be diligently sought, the physician should resist the temptation to explain, explain away, or criticize the parents' reports of what experts in the past have said.

Having defined the nature, ramifications, and seriousness of the problem and having taken care to dispel, if possible, any personal guilt feelings the parents might have, it is necessary to clear the ground by dealing with questions of causation and the neurological status of the child. These issues cannot be avoided, especially because it is likely that they will have been raised in the past.

It should be made clear that causation can rarely be established with certainty in the individual case. And although an educated guess might often be possible, any such effort would have purely historical interest, and at the end of the discussion the issue of what course of action to take on the child's behalf would be no nearer to resolution. The presence or absence of neurological signs makes no known difference to the treatment or prognosis of impulsiveness.

Next the results of tests are discussed. This is done fully and frankly, using and explaining the numerical data actually obtained. If facilities permit, parents are encouraged to watch the testing— and particularly to observe comparable testing under drug and placebo conditions. If parents have personally observed a favorable response in the single-dose laboratory procedure, the subsequent discussion of the nature of hyperactive behavior and the type of outcome to be expected from medication is greatly enhanced. Much misconceived debate can be avoided in this way.

Once it has been demonstrated that the child was helped by stimulant administration, the next point to emphasize is the very transient nature of the effect. While this creates problems for smooth coverage in the long term, it has the advantage of making this therapy exceptionally easy to control. Commitment to therapy with short-acting stimulants is never longer than four hours. Thus, the treatment can be monitored on the basis of its moment-to-moment effect, rather than on the basis of future projections.

We emphasize that the goal of stimulant therapy is normalization of behavior. The aim is not to change the child's consciousness or constrain the freedom of expression. Rather, it is to enlarge the range of possible actions from which the child may freely choose. Our laboratory tests demonstrate that treated hyperactives do not merely behave in a way that pleases onlookers. More important, they become better able to accomplish what they themselves set out to do. The treatment is morally neutral and does not force a child to be good. If hyperactive people wished to rob a bank, they would rob it better on drugs than on placebos.

We then discuss the possible hazards of stimulant therapy, as listed earlier in this chapter.

Finally, we stress that a stimulant regime when first prescribed is never long-term. The first few weeks are used as an evaluation period, during which the physician regularly receives the parents' and teachers' observations. Only if all agree that a significant beneficial effect was obtained at a particular dose level is the matter of more long-term stimulant management broached at a separate interview. We can make no commitment as to how long the need for this therapy will continue, because there is no way of knowing that. Instead we assure the parents of regular, thorough review, so that an opportunity to discontinue therapy will not be missed if the child spontaneously outgrows the impulsiveness. Also, we instruct the parents to compare the child's early morning behavior, before the first dose has taken effect, with subsequent behavior. If the two behaviors cease to be clearly different, the stimulant regime should be reviewed.

Once a child is stable on what seems to be an optimal individualized drug regime, it is necessary to review the total situation to see how much of the problem has been resolved and what remains. At this point the question of adopting additional educational and behavioral measures should be considered in detail.

Emotional stress and discipline
Emotional stress aggravates hyperactivity. Some hyperactive children become even more impulsive or distractible than usual at the time of an examination, the birth of a sibling, parental separation or divorce, or other times of stress. The increased impulsiveness occurs both while medication is having its effect and when it has worn off between pills. On or off medication, the impulsiveness can still increase.

Separation and divorce frequently push children into impulsiveness. Before that extreme stress they are considered normal; later they are found to be hyperactive. Naturally, children of divorced parents are likely to receive sudden and intense scrutiny from court inspectors in custody cases or from teachers and parents. So previously existing hyperactivity may only then come to notice. But it seems often to go beyond that. The stress actually makes children more impulsive and distractible. This is not surprising when one considers how often this happens to children and adults who are not hyperactive. These latter people start closer to the reflective end of the scale, but they too, when stressed, often become unable to settle down, focus on their work or studies, relax enough to sleep, or consider alternatives carefully before making a decision.

If the source of stress persists, or if a single event was traumatic, neurotic disorders—notably depression—may result. We then have a child who may behave in antisocial or regressive ways as part of the hyperactivity syndrome, with neurotic symptoms superimposed. This can pose a tricky problem of diagnosis and management, especially because depressed young children commonly act out their feelings aggressively. So a child may display aggressive behavior like this because of the hyperactivity or because of a neurotic depression. Sometimes such behavior will be clearly seen to follow a stressful experience or an upsetting thought (indicating neurotic behavior), and sometimes it will not (indicating hyperactive behavior).

Often the source of stress and depression is the effort of parents or teachers to suppress the hyperactivity without medication. That is not to say that the children involved should be allowed to behave in ways that are upsetting or destructive to others or to themselves; on the contrary, we have discussed the importance of disciplining hyperactive children and the methods for doing so. But it is important to be aware that the behavior acted out by a hyperactive child may have more than one cause, and the limit-setting necessary to control hyperactivity may be one such cause. The realistic choice that parents of such children must make is between teaching their child that any consequence of the hyperactivity is acceptable and teaching their child that hurtful and irresponsible behavior is unacceptable. Taking the first option may make the child happier in the short run, but its long-term consequence may be that the child seriously hurts others, is rejected by peers, or even ends up in reform school. The other option may produce depression in the child, but it meets parents' obligation to teach their children the consequences of their actions. Normal children are not as easily depressed by limit-setting, partly because their need to act upon their impulses is not as great, and partly because they do not seem to experience impulsive needs as often; hence they do not elicit reprimands or limit-setting directives as often. But the realistic approach seems the best for hyperactive children. They do seem to learn gradually that antisocial behavior is unacceptable.

Good parental principles are well-known to include consistent limit-setting and evenhanded treatment of all children in a family. But however hard they try, many parents find it impossible to conform to these principles if the child is severely hyperactive. A constantly recurring difficulty in limit-setting is the tendency of the limit-setting to escalate in significance. The parent may have reprimanded the child with respect to a fairly trivial issue, merely asking that the behavior in question not be repeated. As the child nevertheless continues to repeat the behavior, the parent grows increasingly angry, not so much because of the behavior itself, but because of the child's failure to modify it, which is seen as a direct challenge to parental authority. As this vicious cycle of attempted limit-setting and refusal continues, the severity of the punishment threatened or applied can grow out of all proportion to the nature of the behavior complained about in the first place. This process can lead to an infuriated parent and a battered child. It is important for parents to be alert to the danger, to realize that their feelings of infuriation are understandable, and at the same time that it is necessary to protect the child from the consequences of these feelings by interrupting the vicious cycle before it has gone too far. This is simply accomplished over the short run by sending the child away for a period of time during which both parties can "cool off." Parents may need counseling on these matters in order to deal with their feelings of guilt for not being "good parents." The situation is most explosive when, as is often the case, one of the parents is also hyperactive. Then the confrontations that result between parent and child vary from unproductive to physically damaging.

While impulsive children are difficult to discipline in the sense that they will continue to do that for which they were punished, it is also striking how forgiving they are of the parent who has just punished them. Whereas the overfocused individual will feel very hurt and seem to resent or bear a grudge against the parent for extended periods of time, an impulsive child will be surprisingly forgiving of the parent and will quickly come to act as if nothing had happened.

For the reasons just discussed, it is simply impossible to treat a hyperactive child and a normal sibling in an evenhanded manner, if that is taken to imply equality in the number of privileges and amounts of punishment. The hyperactive child commonly complains of being treated less well than the siblings. The siblings complain that the hyperactive child gets away with misbehavior that would never have been tolerated in them. Both are right. But although it would be ideal to correct this, the situation is such that even the best parents are locked into recurrent conflicts of the kinds described.

In some cases, when stimulant therapy effects a striking improvement in the hyperactive child's behavior, a sibling who was previously normal may suddenly begin behaving in a disturbed fashion. The child is upset because the family pattern has changed. Previously the hyperactive child was the "bad" child. Now the sibling feels "bad." This calls for giving appropriate attention to the sibling, with the help of child guidance if necessary.

INTERPRETATION TO THE CHILD
No consultation of this kind is complete until the results have been clearly explained to the child and care has been taken to discern whether the child understands. Children are as likely as adults to respond to mystery and confusion with fear, self-blame, antisocial behavior, or some combination of these. They are less likely than adults to expect or request explanations for things they do not understand.

The professional should insist on an interpretive interview with the child for three reasons: (1) to allay fear, both by giving clear explanations and by modeling a matter-of-fact, shameless attitude toward the disorder; (2) to identify and, hopefully, dispel related fears and problems (both internal and familial; e.g., does the child feel "Something is weird about my body;" or do the parents treat the child as a problem, an outcast, even when the child is not causing excessive trouble?); and (3) to enlist the child's cooperation for the treatment. If goal number three is achieved, it can be a first step toward knitting together a family that has been divided by the deviance of the child. It can also give the child a sense of worth and power, especially in the sense that the child has partial control over the chances for securing a happier life. Although it is, of course, good for any children to feel that they have some control over their lives and over the way they interact with other people, the need to have such control is an especially hard but important lesson for an extremely impulsive child to learn.

In interpreting to an impulsive child, many of the previously discussed principles involved in interpreting to a child with a cognitive power disorder also apply. But the problem of hyperactivity is more difficult to explain and the interpretation is more extensive in scope. With a hyperactive child you are dealing with the child's inability to pay attention and with other people's dislike of the way the child behaves. So questions of morality and behavior standards arise more quickly and intensely than with a child who has only a learning problem. Even so, there are ways to tell a hyperactive child why there is trouble settling down and paying attention, why it may be necessary to take pills when siblings and classmates do not, and why the pills do not suddenly make them better in every way. It is crucial to explain that the pills will not absolve the child of responsibility for behavior, and that they will not work like magic so that good grades will suddenly result. All of these principles can be explained to the youngest of children, along lines such as the following: "There is a part of your brain that can make it either easy or hard for you to pay attention. There are two things you need in order to pay attention. One is that this part of your brain has to be working very well, and the other is that you have to try very hard." This makes it clear that the child has the responsibility for personal behavior, but also that the tendency to behave wildly is not entirely the child's fault. We say, "If you take your pills as long as the doctor says to, that will make it easier to pay attention *when you try hard.*"

Sometimes a hyperactive child will try to shift the blame for some misdeed onto the medication ("It happened because I took the pill," or "It happened because I did not take the pill"). Any such urge must be hastily countered. "The pills may help you concentrate, but whether you take them or not, you are fully responsible for your actions, like anyone else."

PROGNOSIS FOR HYPERACTIVITY

There is much uncertainty about the long-term consequences of hyperactivity in children. It is clear that as the child grows older, the gross motor aspect of the impulsiveness becomes less conspicuous, so that at some point in adolescence the casual observer might regard the condition as having subsided completely. Yet most reports stress that many hyperactive children become relatively restless adults, though the condition persists in less obtrusive fashion than before. More important, the school failure attributed to inattention is generally just as marked in the adolescent with a history of hyperactivity as it was in childhood when the hyperactivity was first diagnosed [31]. And as a rule those hyperactive children who show aggressive tendencies in childhood continue to show antisocial tendencies in adolescence. Moreover, adult sociopaths almost always revealed antisocial tendencies as children, were often identifiably hyperactive, and as a general rule showed considerable academic underachievement [25]. In addition, family studies have shown an unduly high incidence of alcoholism and psychopathy among the fathers of hyperactive children and of hysteria among their mothers [2]. (Hyperactives themselves tend to become abusers of alcohol, though not of other drugs.) In addition, it appears in retrospect that at least 10 percent of the parents of hyperactives were themselves clearly hyperactive as children.

While alcoholism is by no means limited to impulsive individuals, alcohol does ensnare some such people, and in the process presumably makes them feel good. It seems that what hyperactives enjoy most is being impulsive. Alcohol not only makes them more impulsive, but also gives them license to act accordingly. When people behave in an uncontrolled or idiotic fashion while sober, others are repelled. But when they are drunk, the same behavior is often tolerated or even treated as amusing. Thus a drink permits the impulsive person to act out impulsiveness with impunity.

Among psychopaths there is a large subgroup, sometimes called "primary psychopaths" who tend to commit crimes on impulse, with little prior planning and still less subsequent anxiety, repentance, or guilt. This manifestation of impulsive style may be a continuation into the adolescent and adult years of childhood hyperactivity.

Hysteria often involves behavior intended to attract attention. As has been discussed, hyperactives are often very attention-seeking. Hysterical symptoms attract attention at no cost of deep reflection, soul-searching, or attempting to justify the attention of others by reciprocating concern.

There have been few long-term followup studies of treated and untreated hyperactive children, and those that have been carried out suffer from serious methodological inadequacies. While there is wide variation of opinion, it is generally agreed that a majority of hyperactive children establish themselves adequately in society as adolescents and as adults (admittedly as judged by rather superficial criteria), but that a substantial minority show a variety of social maladaptations ranging from inability to hold a job all the way through to delinquency and habitual criminality [20]. In one study, the individuals studied were more likely to have been in remedial classes, to have repeated one or more grades, to have shown poor socialization, and to have been described as immature, stubborn, inattentive, distractible, sneaky, lazy, easily discouraged, defiant, annoying, and unpredictable. When those individuals whose ultimate outcome was rated favorable were further scrutinized, the impression was gained that even they had not made a full social adaptation, and that they tended to be lonely and unpopular [21].

With regard to educational outcomes, most studies give a rather pessimistic verdict. The children studied are found to be about as far behind on a second set of achievement tests as they previously were on a first set regardless of the drug regime involved (including continuous or intermittent medication with a stimulant, a tranquilizer, other drugs, or a combination of these).

It should be noted, however, that a number of flaws make these conclusions virtually uninterpretable. The problems of personality and social adjustment shown by hyperactive children in later life could indeed represent persistence of their previous personality problems. Alternatively, these problems could be a secondary reaction to these children's educational difficulty, their achievement failures, and their failure to qualify themselves by competitive examination for levels of education that open the door to lucrative and interesting occupations. Thus, these children's failures and their awareness of failure could contribute heavily to the adverse outcomes reported. At present there is no way to distinguish consequences of this kind from the ones that might be associated with the personality problem itself. It would be possible to make the distinction by putting the individuals studied back on stimulant regimes and seeing whether their attitudes and traits remain (because they represent social learning done over long periods of time) or whether they disappear rapidly (because they stem from a correctable impulsiveness). Where children are regarded as having spontaneously recovered from the condition of hyperactivity in adolescence, these assumptions are usually so insecurely based that only a repeated trial on stimulants, with objective double-blind comparison of the patients' behavior on and off medication, could suffice to verify this conclusion; this has not been done in any study.

As for the treatment regimes, those reported seem so varied, intermittent, illogical, and uncontrolled that there is no way to know what one should expect of children managed in this fashion. Finally, the investigators typically take children who are on a stimulant off the stimulant for a period before testing educational and other outcomes. This may reinstate the original hyperactivity, result in performances that underestimate the individuals' actual fund of knowledge, and therefore understate the gains actually made.

At least some cases of hyperactivity persist into adult years. Other cases seem to resolve themselves in adolescence, but we cannot yet be sure of this. For this reason prognostications about recovery are totally unwarranted, and the clinician should be prepared to offer the various modalities of available therapy to impulsive and distractible individuals regardless of age.

This bleak picture counteracts the general impression that the problem diminishes in adolescence (based on a dwindling number of patients with the motoric symptoms classically regarded as hyperactive). There appear to be two reasons for this. At different stages of the human life span the impulsive and distractible temperament expresses itself in different ways; and the relationship existing between adolescent and adult expressions of impulsiveness and childhood expressions of it are not generally well appreciated. Also, the impulsive individuals do not usually come to clinical notice by their own choice, but rather through the prompting of the family, school, and others. As adults, hyperactive individuals may no longer attract their families' concern, and the external pressures to present themselves for treatment may thus be much reduced. Hyperactive adults also are likely to regard their problem as part of their basic makeup, to deny its seriousness, and to continue acting out their difficulties over the long run rather than seeking further help. Of course, some of that tendency could be due to the low self-image and even depression that such people often develop because of years of school and social failure and because numerous attempts at treatment in childhood did not help.

REFERENCES
1. Barlow, A. S.   A Neuropsychological Study of a Symptom of Minimal Brain Dysfunction: Distractibility under Levels of High and Low Stimulation. Ph.D. dissertation, University of Toronto, 1977.
2. Cantwell, D. P.   Psychiatric illness in the families of hyperactive children. *Arch. Gen. Psychiatry* 27:414, 1972.
3. Conners, C. K.   Symptom patterns in hyperkinetic, neurotic and normal children. *Child Dev.* 41: 667, 1970.
4. Conners, C. K.   A teacher rating scale for use in drug studies with children. *Am. J. Psychiatry* 126: 884, 1969.
5. Conners, C. K., Goyette, C. H., Southwick, D. A., Lees, J. M., and Andrulonis, P. A.   Food additives and hyperkinesis: A controlled double-blind experiment. *Pediatrics* 58: 154–166, 1976.

6. Dalby, J. T., Kinsbourne, M., Swanson, J. M., and Sobol, M. P. Hyperactive children's underuse of learning time: Correction by stimulant treatment, *Child Dev.* 4: 1448–1453, 1978.
7. Denson, R., McWatters, M. A., and Nanson, J. L. Hyperkinesis and maternal smoking. *Can. Psychiatr. Assoc. J.* 20: 183–187, 1975.
8. Feingold, B. F. *Why Your Child is Hyperactive.* New York: Random House, 1975.
9. Freeman, R. The Effects of Methylphenidate on Avoidance Learning and Risk-taking by Hyperkinetic Children. Ph.D. dissertation, University of Waterloo, Waterloo, Ontario, 1978.
10. Gittelman-Klein, R., Klein, R., Sbokoff, H., Katz, S., Gloisten, D. C., and Kates, W. Relative efficacy of methylphenidate and behavior modification in hyperkinetic children: An interim report. *J. Abnorm. Psychol.* 4: 361–374, 1976.
11. Hoobler, B. R. Some early symptoms suggesting protein sensitization in infancy. *Am. J. Dis. Child.* 12: 129, 1976.
12. Huestis, R. D., Arnold, L. E., and Smeltzer, D. J. Caffeine versus methylphenidate and d-amphetamine in minimal brain dysfunction: A double-blind comparison. *Am. J. Psychiatry* 132: 868–870, 1975.
13. Humphries, T., Kinsbourne, M., and Swanson, J. M. Stimulant defects on cooperation and social interaction between hyperactive children and their mothers. *J. Child Psychol. Psychiatry* 19: 13–22, 1978.
14. Kaffman, M., and Elizur, E. Infants who become enuretics: A longitudinal study of 161 Kibbutz children. *Monogr. Soc. Child Dev.* 42: 2, 1977.
15. Kapelus, G. Performance Differences on a Pursuit Tracking Task in Two Groups of Hyperactive Children Given a Central Nervous System Stimulant. Unpublished manuscript.
16. Kinsbourne, M. The Mechanism of Hyperactivity. In M. Blau, I. Rapin, and M. Kinsbourne (Eds.), *Topics in Child Neurology.* New York: Spectrum, 1977.
17. Kinsbourne, M. Personality Characteristics of Hyperactive Children and Stimulant Response. Paper presented to the American Psychology Association, Montreal, 1973.
18. Kinsbourne, M., and Swanson, J. M., and Herman, D. Laboratory Measurement of Hyperactive Children's Response to Stimulant Medication. In E. Denhoff and L. Stern (Eds.), *Minimal Brain Dysfunction: A Developmental Approach.* New York: Masson, 1979.
19. Mash, E. J., and Dalby, J. T. Behavioral Interventions and Hyper-Activity. In R. Trites (Ed.), *Hyperactivity in Children: Etiology, Measurement and Treatment Implications.* Baltimore: University Park Press, 1978.
20. Mendelson, W., Johnson, M., and Stewart, M. Hyperactive children as teenagers: A follow-up study. *J.Nerv. Ment. Dis.* 153: 273, 1971.
21. Minde, K., Lewin, D., and Weiss, G. et al. The hyperactive child in elementary school: A five-year controlled follow-up. *Except. Child.* 38: 215, 1971.
22. Mock, K., Swanson, J. M., and Kinsbourne, M. Hyperactive Children's Performance on the MFF on Methylphenidate and on Placebo. Unpublished data, 1978.
23. Omenn, G. S. Genetic issues in the syndrome of minimal brain dysfunction. *Semin. Psychiatry* 5:5, 1973.
24. Pihl, R. O., and Parkes, M. Hair element content in learning disabled children. *Science* 198: 204–206, 1977.

25. Robins, L. N.   Antisocial Behavior Disturbances of Childhood: Prevalence, Prognosis, and Prospects. In E. J. Anthony and C. Koupernik
(Eds.), *Children at Psychiatric Risk. The Child in His Family*, Vol. 3.
New York: Wiley, 1974.
26. Roche, A. F., Lipman, R. S., Overall, J. E., and Hung, W.   The effects
of stimulant medication on the growth of hyperkinetic children. *Pediatrics* In press, 1978.
27. Rutter, M.   Epidemiological Strategies and Psychiatric Concepts in
Research on the Vulnerable Child. In E. J. Anthony and C. Koupernik
(Eds.), *Children at Psychiatric Risk. The Child in His Family*, Vol. 3.
New York: Wiley, 1974.
28. Safer, D. J., and Allen, R. P.   Factors influencing the suppressant effects of two stimulant drugs on the growth of hyperactive children.
Pediatrics 51: 660–667, 1973.
29. Silbergeld, E. K., and Goldberg, A. M.   Hyperactivity: A lead-induced
behavior disorder. *Environ. Health Perspect.* 7: 227–232, 1974.
30. Stewart, M. A., Thach, B. T., and Freidin, M. R.   Accidental poisoning
and the hyperactive child syndrome. *Dis. Nerv. Syst.* 31:403, 1970.
31. Swanson, J. M., and Kinsbourne, M.   Stimulant-related state-dependent learning in hyperactive children. *Science* 192: 1354, 1976.
32. Swanson, J. M., Kinsbourne, M., Roberts, W., and Zucker, K.   A time-
response analysis of the effect of stimulant medication on the learning
ability of children referred for hyperactivity. *Pediatrics* 61: 21–29, 1978.
33. Thurston, C. M., Sobol, M. P., Swanson, J. M., and Kinsbourne,
M.   Effects of methylphenidate (Ritalin) on selective attention in
hyperactive children. Submitted for publication.
34. Weiss, G., Minde, K., Werry, J. S., Douglas, V., and Nemeth, E. Studies
on the hyperactive child. *Arch. Gen. Psychiatry* 24: 409–414, 1971.

SUGGESTED READING
Barkley, R. A.   Predicting the response of hyperactive children to stimu-
lant drugs: A review. *J. Abnorm. Child Psychol.* 4: 327–348, 1976.
Cantwell, D. (Ed.)   *The Hyperactive Child.* New York: Spectrum, 1975.
Wender, P. H.   *Minimal Brain Dysfunction in Children.* New York: Wiley,
1971.

10. The Overfocused Child

As has been explained, the impulsive temperament is one extreme of a continuum that ranges through a normal zone of flexibly adaptive behavior. At one end of the continuum is the extremely impulsive-distractible temperament. At the opposite pole is a decision-making strategy that is so prolonged and deliberate that it hampers the handling of moment-to-moment changes in a situation. Individuals employing that strategy, who can be described as overfocused, compulsive, or sometimes withdrawn, are discussed little in the context of school problems, perhaps because they do ultimately come up with correct answers. But their exceedingly slow, exhaustive, and rigid manner of proceeding detracts from the fluent, flexible, and efficient decision-making that education should seek to inculcate as one of its objectives.

The overfocused child plods from point to point, methodically or even redundantly checking progress, and only reluctantly stopping work when the instruction period ends. Whereas impulsive children are ever eager to adopt a novel task orientation, whether inherent in or extraneous to the classroom situation, overfocused individuals limit themselves to what they feel comfortable undertaking: that which is familiar. Therefore, they are not likely to have trouble in a severely traditional, highly structured classroom. Their primary limitation in such a setting, and the one that may precipitate a referral, is inability to finish their work on time. They hesitate unduly before committing themselves to an answer, and once they record a response they check it and recheck it, even when they see that it is correct. Both in schoolwork and in interpersonal interactions, they do best if given a strict and concrete structure that minimizes the need for them to make decisions. They are amenable to reasonable limits and are not apt to yield to intimidation. Strict discipline is usually overkill for them and typically drives their attention inward, causing them to withdraw. Thus, they are sensitive and responsive to limit-setting; but harshness or intensity of anger and punishment can easily upset them excessively, so that the beneficial effect the over-punisher may have intended is lost in a sea of anxiety, fear, or withdrawal. This, of course, makes sense if one considers that the essence of the overfocusing child's style is the total concentration of all available attention on a single stimulus. Any stimulus would naturally seem more intense to such a child.

For the same reason, such children are likely to withdraw, overwhelmed, from intensely warm approaches. At best, they may feel shy. At worst, they may be unable to make or maintain eye contact. They often limit their own expressions of feeling carefully, since expressiveness tends to elicit expressive responses from others. Thus, they work best and interact best in calm, bland, emotionally rather detached, and matter-of-fact circumstances.

The overfocused child will withdraw from regions of turmoil and high information content, and will restrict personal involvement and the range of personal friendships; in brief, the child will specialize. With respect to this specialty, an overfocused child's knowledge will often grow until it becomes encyclopedic. The child is more often preoccupied with inanimate objects than with people, is apt to be notably studious in habit, and tends toward an isolated way of life.

The depth of these children's problem-solving, and the extent to which they continue to retrieve information about one particular issue while concurrently excluding other challenges, may lead them to attribute undue meaningfulness to a situation; this is a state fertile for paranoid reactions. In sum, the manifestations of overfocused behavior amount to a withdrawn, isolated, persevering concentration invested with an intensity that rejects interference.

Two important points may be made about this behavior pattern. One is that it is closely replicated by dosing normal children and overdosing hyperactive children with stimulant medications. This illustrates the point that the overfocused behavior is at the opposite extreme of a continuum along which appropriate stimulant medication moves impulsive individuals. Moreover, although these children are by no means autistic, it is clear that they share many behavior patterns with frankly autistic individuals, at least in quality if not in degree. They often avoid the gaze of others and avert their gaze from others, restrict dialogue to formalisms, and shun company. When exposed to an information overload they may bite their nails, twitch, or even engage in repetitive activities (head banging, rocking, arm flapping) reminiscent of autistic stereotypies and mannerisms.

The reason such children sometimes display these stereotyped, repetitive gestures and activities is not clear. Classically, such behavior indicates anxiety. Although disturbingly little is known about overfocused people, it is difficult to imagine that they would have other than a high level of anxiety much of the time. The anxiety could perhaps come first and cause the person to focus narrowly and rigidly on one bit of stimulation at a time; essential to this theory is the assumption that the repetitive, automatic nature of the activity acts as a protective shield, to protect the already anxious person from bombardment by too much stimulation. This kind of model could equally well explain the appearance of stereotypies in cases of overfocusing where the overfocusing itself, rather than the anxiety, seems primary. In fact, this explanation has been used to explain such movements in frankly autistic children. There is no obvious reason that it could not apply to any case of overfocusing in a less than autistic child; for, as we have noted, a person who tends to focus all available attention on one stimulus will probably experience that stimulus with greater-than-average intensity. A person who is trying to deal with one intense stimulus is often disoriented, or even made very anxious, if asked to shift to another stimulus or apportion attention between two stimuli. So a protective shield of habitual and repetitive activity would serve a dual function: It would not require much attention, because it is habitual; and it would provide a "noisy" background by means of which potentially intrusive, attention-demanding stimuli would be masked. So whether the overfocusing is primary, or whether it is secondary to high anxiety, the stereotypic movements serve the same function that they serve when they appear (less frequently and rigidly) in normals; that is, they help ward off further anxiety.

These children's use of language is not severely handicapped or deviant in form, as is that of typically autistic children. However, it is likely that a continuum exists between these overfocused children, who still function adaptively enough to be regarded as within the normal range, and children who are frankly disabled by the autistic nature of their behavior.

The overfocused older child or adult seems careful and pedantic, a systematic list-maker who exhausts the potential information content of any topic, and with it the patience of companions. Such people like to do one thing at a time, and they feel disorganized and "jangled" if compelled to attend to several things at once. They are intolerant of distraction, which seems to them to impinge on and contaminate what they are trying to do. This oversensitivity to distraction contrasts with impulsive distractibility, where the individual succumbs to the temptation to discontinue what is being done in order to pursue a novel stimulus. In line with this, overfocusers complain bitterly when they are distracted, while impulsives do not complain about this at all. Overfocused people are not necessarily anxious. But they are easily made anxious by information overload. Under these circumstances they may become incapable of coherent behavior, and they risk losing social approval and even their jobs.

INCIDENCE

Virtually nothing is known about the incidence of overfocusing in children. There are a number of reasons for this. One was mentioned in the previous section: They usually come up with correct answers in school if they are given enough time. Another is that their overly careful, compulsive style does not conflict with typical school standards (except when it is time to switch tasks); rather, it is in many ways an extreme form of what the schools' standards ask of pupils: Work carefully, check your work, stick to the task, don't be distracted by other children's misbehavior, don't disrupt the class with noise and fidgeting. As pointed out in Chapter 2, girls' learning problems tend to escape notice more than those of boys, because girls tend to be better behaved and less disruptive in the classroom. For similar reasons, overfocused children tend to be allowed to continue in their compulsive ways because they are quiet. Sometimes, however, they are branded as slow learners because the teacher does not wait to see if they have really learned the material but merely notes that they answered only half the questions on a timed test, or that they have had trouble finishing all their homework.

The overfocused style has been almost totally ignored as a disorder. In fact, one might take the point of view that it cannot properly be called a disorder, since its manifestations in school only differ in degree, not in kind, from the behavior schools strive for in their children. But this is a rather superficial viewpoint, for two reasons. One is that in some children that difference in degree is so extreme that in fact they become school failures. They may be promoted because of their "good" behavior (often called "mature"), but they may have learned very little in the time allowed. So whether or not one calls this a disorder, it is certainly a poor fit between child and schoolroom, and something has to be done. The second reason for considering extreme overfocusing a disorder is that the style so frequently interferes with the child's interpersonal interactions and happiness, as described in the previous section. People often tend to withdraw from a withdrawn child. Other children make fun of the stereotypic gestures some overfocusers display, and most children find it hard to play with a child whose focus of concentration is excessively slow to shift.

DIFFERENTIAL DIAGNOSIS

There are several conditions which must be distinguished from the overfocused style, and we shall discuss each of these briefly. In addition, we shall note some factors that may be causes or effects of the overfocusing itself.

Overfocusing must be distinguished from *mental retardation*. A child who sits quietly in the classroom, does not volunteer answers, and says nothing when called on to answer questions, may either be a retarded child or an overfocuser. As previously mentioned, the best way to make the distinction is to do one's best to treat the child in a matter-of-fact way that will encourage maximum relaxation and then to wait patiently for the answers. Retarded children will give many more wrong answers, regardless of the time allowed, because of their lacking abilities, their great and general deficiencies in cognitive processes or cognitive power; they simply don't know how to think very well. Overfocusers can think well; they just spend too long in one rut.

Some retarded children are also overfocusers. In some of these cases, both problems seem to be inborn, whereas in others the overfocusing is a style the child acquires to limit the stimulation (and consequent risk of failure) that must be dealt with at any one moment.

Much the same thing can be said for what is usually called the *"slow learner,"* the child whose IQ falls in the low average but not retarded range. Slow learners will come up with more correct answers than will retarded children, but a "pure" overfocuser with normal intelligence will surpass both. We shall have more to say about this in the section on Diagnosis.

Overfocused children are occasionally thought to be *deaf*, because slowness of response is attributed to a failure to hear. When overwhelmed by stimuli they may simply become silent and unresponsive, as though unhearing (see Diagnosis).

In considering other categories included in the differential diagnosis, we encounter the following basic question: Is overfocusing an innate temperament or a learned style? Or is it innate in some cases and learned in others? There appear to be some cases of each. At this very early stage in our attempts to understand and treat the problem, it is most important to identify the overfocusing itself in a given child. The second step, in each individual case, is necessarily to try and determine the extent to which the overfocusing is learned or innate. If it is learned, what was the cause, and how did it happen? Ultimately, of course, we must arrange an optimal learning and interpersonal environment for the child.

Overfocused children can be difficult to distinguish from children with *underfocused attention*. If a teacher or parent asks a child to perform Task A, and the child does not do it, the child may still be concentrating on a previous task or thought; this would be typical of an overfocuser. Or it may be because the child's attention is jumping rapidly from one thing to another, either sometimes or never landing on Task A; this would be typical of an under-focused, impulsive-distractible child. In both cases the children show the same behavior insofar as they are not attending to the task requested by the person in charge. However, the overfocused child complains when distracted by what seem to be excessive demands. The underfocused child does not complain at all. If anything, this child welcomes the distraction.

Some children who are *undermotivated* or frankly *negativistic* may appear superficially to be overfocusers if, when they don't attend to the requested task, one hastily assumes it is because they are simply unable to shift the focus of their attention. Unlike most overfocusers, negativistic children in fact do not wish to do what is asked of them. Finally, whereas underfocused children seem inconstant in their performance on single tasks, the overfocused child can continue for a surprisingly long time without performance decrement. Undermotivated children have no particular trouble in shifting their mental set, if they want to, if they are interested in the subject to which they are supposed to attend. But overfocused children have trouble making that shift, even when they prefer the new task to the one on which they had been working. For the overfocuser, it is a problem of doing the shifting, not of wanting to. Accordingly, whereas overfocusers have trouble switching from any task to any other task, undermotivated children only take unusually long to make such shifts when the new task is distasteful or uninteresting to them.

Overfocusers can occasionally appear to have a *schizophrenic* type of thought disorder. Tending naturally to ruminate, if they are also very anxious or upset about a particular topic, overfocusers may respond to other people's attempts at conversation by persisting in verbalizing only the thoughts about their topic of anxious concern. Thus, one asks them about school and they say their brother hates them; one then asks them about hobbies, and they say their brother hates them, etc. Sometimes attempts to discuss the patient's topic of concern itself can help one to determine whether the thinking is logical and coherent.

Even when overfocusing does not have a clearly innate basis, innate pre-disposition is still likely to play a role. It is hard to imagine that a child innately disposed to impulsiveness and distractibility would become overfocused, except under extreme pressure. But there are at least three kinds of environmental pressure that can push a child along toward the overfocusing end of the cognitive style spectrum. One of these is anxiety. As noted in the previous chapter, some degrees of anxiety have the effect in some people of limiting their ability to focus attention. This may be because they maintain attention on the object of their anxiety. Or it may be that, given a high level of anxiety, a person finds it more than usually difficult to manage more than one task at a time; that is, the anxiety itself is presumably attention-absorbing.

A second external source of pressure that might prepare the way for a child's overfocusing disorder is an overload of demands from the family or school. These demands may take the form of achievement, religious, or other behavior standards or prescriptions. Such demands are in some sense a subset of all the possible producers of the anxiety discussed above. But the anxiety could also come from any other source. One likely source of family standards that encourage overfocusing is, of course, compulsiveness and overfocusing in the parents. The child then may or may not incline naturally in the same direction, but may certainly head that way through modeling the parents' behavior.

Third, an only child who lives in an environment where there is *little interaction with peers or parents* may adopt an overfocused style as a form of escape. Finding little benefit from making active attempts at interaction, such a child sometimes decides to invest all energy in single-minded pursuits (whether automobiles or intellectual activities). This simplifies the need to make choices in an interpersonal environment that has little to offer. It also thereby minimizes interpersonal risk-taking.

DIAGNOSIS

Because nothing has been written about overfocusing disorders in their milder forms (short of autism), there is little that can be said with great confidence about diagnosis. Again, we depend heavily on common sense. Based on the information in the previous sections and on our clinical experience with such children, we now suggest some guidelines for diagnosis through interviewing, behavioral observations, and testing. (Much of the material in Chap. 4 is also relevant.)

INTERVIEWING

When interviewing the parents or teachers of possibly overfocused children, one can ask certain questions aimed at identifying the overfocusing disorder. When interviewing such children themselves, one can sometimes elicit the same information about their own behavior and can sometimes draw conclusions from direct observation of that behavior. One first asks whether the children involved have trouble shifting attention from one thing to the next, even when interested in the next thing. The children themselves will sometimes confirm their parents' or teachers' descriptions of them as having this type of trouble, even when they seem to be well-motivated and well-disposed toward their tasks, parents, and teachers. One also asks about the child's interpersonal style. Does the child appear shy or uninterested in interacting with peers, slow to approach and quick to withdraw from others, and easily overwhelmed by noise or by cognitive or emotional stimulation and richness? Is there any history of stereotypic movements, gestures, or avoidance of gaze? Does the child respond well to detached but well-structured instructions and situations? Does the child do things well, produce correct answers, and keep the room neat if given enough time? When working on such tasks, does the child take a lot of time only because the work is done slowly, rather than because of continually wandering attention?

BEHAVIORAL OBSERVATIONS

Although one can often get accurate descriptions of the child's behavior from parents and teachers, it is important to reinforce information from these sources by making one's own observations. Does the child sit quietly and concentrate well in the doctor's office? Does the child seem confused if there are a number of chairs in the room and quickly relieved if you say "This is your chair and this is my chair," thus giving a structure that makes it unnecessary for the child to make decisions? Does the child withdraw if you become emotionally intense or affectionate, or if you move closer physically and try to make eye contact? (If so, this is very different from the response of the impulsive child, who often reacts to such overtures with wild or silly behavior, taking your interest as permission to behave impulsively rather than as a too-intense approach from which they must withdraw.) Are there stereotypic movements and gestures? Does the child *appear* intense, as though thinking very hard and seriously about something?

TESTING

On intelligence and achievement tests, overfocused children are likely to lose time credits. Given unlimited time, however, they do better. Additional time increases the scores of retarded children relatively little, because they *cannot* perform the cognitive functions in question. If a child is overfocused as well as retarded, as sometimes happens, additional time obviously helps more than with a "pure" retardate but less than with an overfocuser of at least average intelligence. But even with a retarded overfocuser, overlooking time limits can give one a clearer picture of optimal capacities and achievements. Particularly on WISC subtests like Coding, one may observe the overfocuser carefully checking and rechecking each answer before moving to the next. On WISC Similarities and Comprehension questions, they may slowly but compulsively give lengthy detailed responses that go far beyond the information requested.

On any kind of test, overfocusers may have less trouble with questions expressed in multiple choice form. This helps limit the number of possible responses that they must consider and also gives them structure. On essay or short-answer questions they may answer a few interminably and never get to respond to many of the others.

On the WISC Mazes subtest or the Porteus Mazes, overfocusers may be observed to plan their routes in complete detail before ever putting pencil to paper. On self-descriptive questionnaires, overfocusers often portray themselves accurately as loners.

Projective testing has very little built-in structure. On the Thematic Apperception Test, the Rorschach Inkblot Test, or similar instruments, overfocusers may seize on what structure there is and exaggeratedly stay within it. For example, in the TAT the subject is asked to make up a story including the past, present, and future of the situation pictured. Overfocusers may begin each response by saying "Past," then giving the past, "Present," then giving the present, etc. They may restrict themselves to the bare bones of that structure and offer little "unnecessary" elaboration. Or they may compulsively relate uninteresting and insignificant details, as though anxious not to leave anything out. On the Rorschach, subjects are not told whether to turn the cards around and look at them from various angles. If the subject asks whether turning is permitted, the examiner usually says it is up to the subject. Overfocusers may rigidly inspect the cards only from the angle at which they receive them; or they may compulsively inspect every card systematically from many angles; or they may begin in the first way but, once receiving "permission" to turn the cards, may continue in the latter way. In a similar vein, they may give exactly one obvious response to each card, or they may give large numbers of responses as though trying to include every possible detail.

As indicated in the section on Differential Diagnosis, routine testing by an audiologist is sometimes important to rule out severe hearing impairment, and testing by a speech pathologist can help to rule out the possibility of developmental aphasia.

MANAGEMENT

Because overfocusing has been so little recognized and explored, very little is known about forms of treatment. Nevertheless, a few principles can be mentioned.

PSYCHOTHERAPY

For those cases in which anxiety seems to be either the primary cause or an important aggravator of overfocusing, play therapy or other forms of psychotherapy can help. If the parents are a source of that anxiety, counseling for them can be useful in lessening environmental pressures on the child.

BEHAVIORAL METHODS

In some overfocusing cases, regardless of etiology, simply describing the overfocusing style to the children can, by increasing their awareness of their own tendencies and their limitations, give them the power to take an active role in overcoming the problem. For example, such a child might learn to check the clock periodically, so as to be sure not to spend too much time on one bit of homework before moving on to the next. Such a method in some ways amounts to a psychotherapeutic behavioral technique known at its most intense as "implosive therapy" and in its mildest forms as a variety of behavior modification. Implosive therapy involves placing the child in a situation regarded as highly threatening—by saying, for example, "I will not allow you to spend more than 10 seconds on one arithmetic problem, even if you feel that you want to recheck it." Forms of behavior modification might involve gradually decreasing the amount of time one allows the child to spend on each bit of work. But both methods work best if the child thereby learns that failing to constantly recheck work and ruminate does not grossly increase errors. Thus, these behavioral methods would be most likely to achieve success in dealing with milder cases of overfocusing.

In school, special provision might be made for overfocusers to be examined by multiple choice or true-false examinations whenever possible, rather than subjecting them to the less structured essay or short-answer tests. Their anxiety in confronting the enormous number of choices to be made in the latter kinds of tests would be likely to interfere with their attempts to let the teacher know the facts and principles they had learned. For such children a severely traditional classroom is ideal. Open-ended challenges, such as field projects, and open-ended situations, such as the open classroom, leave them perplexed and incapable. For them to make progress, strict and concrete structure is essential. By this we do not mean strict discipline. On the contrary, these children are quite amenable to reasonable limits and are not apt to yield to intimidation. Rather, they wish to know what is the case, and are more likely to comply if told what is theirs, what there is for them to do, where the place is for them to sit, and so forth. All these are statements that designate the state of affairs rather than instruct the child to conform. (See also Chap. 7, Classroom Structure, p. 178, and Emotional Supports during Remediation, p. 202.)

MEDICATION

Because of the apparent positions of hyperactives and overfocusers at opposite ends of a continuum, it might follow that overfocusing children should be treated with the very agents that aggravate hyperactive behavior (for instance, sedatives or minor tranquilizers).

However, the possibility cannot be discounted that, contrary to the discussion so far, some types of hyperactivity and some autistic behaviors are orthogonal and, therefore, could coexist. For instance, it is possible that some children are hyperactive because of relatively deficient action by their norepinephrinergic systems, whereas some autistic individuals show an excess of dopaminergic activity. This would make it possible for a person to be hyperactive and autistic at the same time. In such a case amphetamine would reduce the hyperactivity, but at the cost of aggravating the autism, whereas an agent that opposed catecholamine action might conversely relieve autistic withdrawal but precipitate troublesomely impulsive and distractible behavior. In order to resolve these various possibilities and perhaps finally to develop useful pharmacotherapy for autistic children (which has not so far been achieved), it would be necessary to use agents with validated selectivity for one or another of the catecholamine systems in the systematic fashion suggested by the above considerations.

For present purposes, however, we are only considering the overfocused children whose difficulties fall short of infantile autism. Treatment of such children could involve not only environmental rearrangements in the spirit already outlined but also the use of drugs with anti-dopaminergic activity. The major tranquilizers have this property. In addition, haloperidol is attractive because it selectively blocks dopaminergic transmission in the brain. The best validated area of clinical usefulness is in symptomatic relief of children with Gilles de la Tourette's disease. The more spectacular aspects of this condition are multiple tics (not unlike those that result from an acute stimulant overdose) and use of foul language (coprolalia). But affected children are also notably compulsive and obsessive in their behavior. The obsessive-compulsive behavior is relieved, in parallel with the tics, by haloperidol. It could be that haloperidol would offer the same benefits to compulsive or overfocused children not suffering from Tourette's disease. An attempt at such treatment would require caution, however, as haloperidol has major toxic effects at dose levels not far removed from those which are clinically effective. Probably the use of such agents is most justifiable in children whose quality of life is seriously compromised, not only by overfocusing but also by

the social embarrassment of a compulsion to make repetitive pur-
poseless movement.

A less dramatic approach would be the use of barbiturates—
which are safer, but which, at least on theoretical grounds, are less
likely to be effective.

PROGNOSIS

Little is known about the long-term outlook for overfocused children. If this cognitive style is properly classified as a temperament,
it presumably remains as a component of the individual's personality indefinitely. On the other hand, the severity of its expression
as maladaptive behavior might well diminish, because of the great
range of vocational options available to adults, some of which provide a ready refuge for overfocused people. Also, as adults overfocusers will be relieved of parental scrutiny, and with their relatively solitary and unobtrusive life-style they will not attract the
same degree of adverse attention as do their impulsive opposites.
Extreme cases court social embarrassment through their tendency
toward repetitive mannerisms, a circumstance that tends to make
recluses of overfocused individuals. The prognosis is clearly much
better if affected individuals have made vocational and social
choices consistent with their temperaments than if those choices
place them under constant risk of information overload.

INTERPRETATION

To PARENTS

A compulsive and overfocused temperament must be clearly distinguished from brain damage or emotional disorder. It is important to let the parents know that here one is dealing with an extreme condition *within* limits of normal variation. This relieves
them of the need to search for precipitating events (physical or
psychological) and to attribute guilt to one or both of themselves
for some presumed misdeed. Incidentally, it is often possible to
point to essentially similar behavioral tendencies in some other person who might have made a successful adaptation and who can
serve as an encouraging model. This also may help to demystify
the overfocused trait within the family. If the parents understand
that the behavior complained of is inherent in the child's personality, that the child would have turned out essentially the same regardless of the child-rearing options they adopted, then they may
avoid useless self-criticism regarding child-rearing choices they
made in the past. Instead, the real issues can be faced: how to accommodate to the child's limitations and how to help the child
accommodate to the realities waiting in the outside world.

The basic information is that the overfocused child is not merely overanxious, although information overload may readily induce anxiety as a consequence. Whereas the anxious individual thrives on reassurance, the overfocused individual would prefer to be left alone. Thus, it is as much a mistake to overwhelm the child with praise and warmth as with blame and rejection. The best approach to such a child is a muted one that is unobtrusively supportive and sensitive to the child's natural inclination to safeguard a sense of well-being. Heavy-handed exhortation insisting that the child behave differently is counterproductive.

With respect to repetitive movements in particular, specific guidance only makes things worse. Such movements are best ignored. At the same time, one can note the particular forms of overload that precipitate these movements and can frequently minimize them. This can never be totally successful, because novelty and the child's excitement in reaction to novelty are typical precipitating factors; and novelty cannot and should not be guarded against, as it would be too limiting for the child to have the wealth of experience so radically reduced.

In the long term, the parents should be prepared for a thoughtful and retiring adolescent, who will probably choose a vocation specialized in nature and far from the limelight.

To the Child
The child must be acquainted in general terms with the nature of these concerns and the outcome of the investigations. The emphasis should be on the fact that overfocused behavior is not abnormal, deranged, or different in kind from what other people do. Some people just like to concentrate more than others, and other people may at times become impatient. This is natural, but it does not imply that the child has achieved badly or should be blamed. Rather, these children should explain their preference for working deliberately and with care and should not permit others to push them into uncongenial situations calling for hasty decision-making.

To the Teacher
Explanations to teachers resemble those to parents. The child's plodding and persistent ways do not represent obstinacy or negativism, nor are they abnormal or in need of correction. There should be provision in our heterogeneous society for people like that. Confrontations between teacher and child are absolutely to be avoided, and idiosyncratic behavior by the child which, after all, is quite innocuous as far as others are concerned, is best ignored. Rigid time limits are unjustified, and rapid pacing of schoolwork is to be avoided.

Index

Index